FOCUSED GENOGRAMS

FOCUSED GENOGRAMS

Intergenerational Assessment of Individuals, Couples, and Families

by

Rita DeMaria, Ph.D.
Gerald Weeks, Ph.D.
Larry Hof, M.Div.

Routledge
Taylor & Francis Group
New York   London

Routledge
Taylor & Francis Group
270 Madison Avenue
New York, NY 10016

Routledge
Taylor & Francis Group
2 Park Square
Milton Park, Abingdon
Oxon OX14 4RN

International Standard Book Number-13: 978-0-87630-881-3 (Softcover)

Library of Congress Cataloging-in-Publication Data

DeMaria, Rita
    Focused genograms : intergenerational assessment of individuals, couples, and families / by Rita DeMaria, Gerald Weeks, Larry Hof.
        p. cm.
    Includes bibliographical references and index.
    ISBN 0-87630-881-7 (pbk.:alk. paper) ISBN 0-87630-881-7 (hbk.)
    1. Family psychotherapy. 2. Family psychotherapy—Technique. 3. Behavioral assessment—Charts, diagrams, etc. I. Weeks, Gerald R., 1948-. Hof, Larry. III. Title.
    RC488.5.D39 1999
    616.89'156—dc21   98-51083

Visit the Taylor & Francis Web site at
http://www.taylorandfrancis.com

and the Routledge Web site at
http://www.routledge.com

CONTENTS

List of Figures   vii
Preface   ix
Acknowledgments   xiii
Introduction   xv

PART I
OVERVIEW

1   Introduction to the Multifocused Family Genogram   3

2   Focused Genograms in Practice   25

PART II
BASIC COMPONENTS OF THE MULTIFOCUSED
FAMILY GENOGRAM

3   The Basic Genogram   37

4   Family Maps   57

5   Time Lines   65

PART III
THE FOCUSED GENOGRAMS

6   Attachments Genograms   75

7   **Emotions Genograms**   101

8   **Anger Genograms**   125

9   **Gender, Sexuality, and Romantic Love Genograms**
     Ellen Berman, M.D.   145

10   **Culture Genograms**   177

11   **Conclusion: Using the Multifocused Family Genogram
     in Practice**   197

     Bibliography   201
     Appendix   211
     Index   215

LIST OF FIGURES

Figure 1.1. Elements of the Multifocused Family Genogram (MFG). 11

Figure 1.2. MFG with themes of Focused Genograms identified on left side of page. 13

Figure 1.3. Symbols for developing the Basic Genogram. 14

Figure 1.4. Example of writing in information in the Basic Genogram. 15

Figure 1.5. Illustration of the MFG on one page. 16

Figure 1.6. Outline of a Basic Genogram with limited information. 17

Figure 1.7. Sketch and table methods for Focused Genograms. 18

Figure 1.8. Detail of the table method for the Cultural Genogram. 19

Figure 4.1. Symbols and relationship descriptors. 61

Figure 4.2. Illustration of Internal Models Map. 63

Figure 5.1. Ruth's Time Line. 70

Figure 6.1. Internal Models Mapping symbols. 83

Figure 6.2. Margaret's Internal Models Map. 84

Figure 6.3. Formulation of the family dynamic. 87

Figure 7.1. Pain and pleasure in my family system. 106

Figure 7.2. Illustration of an Emotions Family Map with wife's Internal Models Map. 115

Figure 8.1. This Anger Family Map indicates interpersonal violence between spouses and mild corporal punishment is noted as "C.P." 134

Figure 10.1. Alex Haley Family Genogram. 192

PREFACE

"Children are the living messages we send to a lifetime we will never see."—Unknown

Genograms are a popular and universally applied technique for assessment with individuals, couples, or families. Family therapy theory and practice, in particular Bowen systems theory, have popularized genograms. Over the past three decades, genograms have been used to help understand the dynamics of couple and family systems and the forces that help create intrapsychic dynamics. Despite the popularity of genograms, however, the genogram has received little attention in the way of theoretical and clinical development, refinement, and application. This book grounds the genogram in attachment theory, presents a clinically useful, practical, and comprehensive method for collecting information in key areas of individual and family functioning, and describes a multilevel process for collecting information that we have named the *Multilayered Focused Genogram* (MFG). Comprised primarily of Focused Genograms, the MFG is the document created by developing the Basic Genogram, the Family Map, the Time Line, and Focused Genograms. The MFG is a summarizing tool assembled based on a thorough assessment of the family system.

The art of constructing an MFG, however, goes beyond an academically and theoretically informed process. The genogram process intersects the professional-personal boundary between client and therapist. Effective development of the MFG requires the clinician to address or suspend personal issues in a variety of areas—culture, gender, sexuality, emotions, health, and sibling issues to name a few. On the other side, the client must be prepared, and willing, to address all aspects of personal and family history. The MFG that emerges is both systemically and personally informed by the therapist's self-understanding and clinical knowledge.

Perspective is defined as the *true* relationship of objects or events to one another. Although relationship is the substance of family systems, truth is less easily defined. In order to develop a perspective of family life, relationships between and among family members and the developmental events of childhood, adolescence, adulthood, and family life must be taken into consideration. Because experience is temporal, family life is by its very nature a time-bound interpersonal phenomena. In order to understand family life and individual development, links between the past, the present, and the future must be taken into account.

How do two people form a family and parent their children? Therein lies the challenge of determining how family history becomes intertwined with individual and family development. In some ways, this clinical task is like unraveling a ball of yarn. Compounding this effort to understand the nature and source of symptoms is the notion that a couple is a unique entity, part of, yet separate from, the family system. The dynamics of intimate relationships profoundly influence the evolution of new family units even though the couples must be seen in context, as part of a larger extended family. Although having a child creates a new structure and gives the concept of family its meaning, the marital relationship is being seen by many clinicians as a healing crucible for prior interpersonal deficiencies experienced in the family-of-origin. Consequently, child development and the influence of these processes also must be taken into account.

Attachment theory provides a concrete way to discuss and detail patterns of family behavior and interaction. Consequently, the use of the Attachments Focused Genogram is an important foundation from which to construct the MFG. Although attachment theory links the individual with the family system, the messages handed down from one generation to the next can be examined through many lenses—culture, gender, sexuality, and emotions. The challenge is to identify these messages and decide which ones need to be changed. The end goal is to create new, more loving and constructive messages for our children, grandchildren, and great-grandchildren. In the process of exploring the harms of the past, it is essential to enhance and build self-esteem. Family intervention is both proactive and regressive. The regressive, working-through, grieving process that takes place during treatment can become debilitating without proactive interventions to build self-esteem. A family systems perspective and strategy helps insure that treatment goals are neither incongruent nor destructive to the individual's family and social system.

This book is an effort to help other clinicians who work with individuals, couples, and families examine the legacies from the past with respect and appreciation. The genogram is a powerful tool to explore these patterns. Understanding the emotional forces that influence one's life is an important part of making choices about attitudes and behaviors that need to be changed. Our hope is that clinicians will use the structure provided by the MFG to expand their views of individual, couple, and family dynamics.

On a more personal note, I (Rita DeMaria) began practicing as a family therapist in 1973. It took me years to realize that I was searching for answers to questions I had within myself about why and how I lived my life. Over the years, I have come to realize that being a family therapist was a way of helping myself understand my family-life experiences and legacies. The professional journey that I took overlaps a vital period in the evolution of family therapy and systems theory. My professional training and experience forced me to explore not only family systems dynamics and development but also individual development and ecosystems. Now I am in the fortunate position of having information that not only is helpful to me, my clients, and even my family and friends but can also be shared with colleagues. What helped me most in my journey was maintaining macroscopic and microscopic perspectives.

My experiences with juvenile delinquents and child-protective services gave me another vantage point: the effects of abuse and neglect on children and family life. Abuse and neglect in their various forms seem to have longstanding deleterious effects on interpersonal relationships. The themes and patterns of family violence I saw in severe cases were repeated in my practice and the practices of my students and supervisees, albeit in milder forms. In order to understand the complexity of these effects, family violence, corporal punishment, and anger have been emphasized in this book. Attachment theory has provided me a useful model to assess the impact of these and less-toxic childhood experiences. Disrupting intergenerational patterns of family aggression and violence has become a key focus of my clinical work. I hope that the lenses of the MFG will provide a useful way to examine these issues and, consequently, develop effective interventions.

ACKNOWLEDGMENTS

This book project gave me (Rita DeMaria) the opportunity to organize my years of clinical practice, teaching, and research. Gerald Weeks and Larry Hof have been supportive and gracious mentors throughout the process, and I am grateful that they provided me the opportunity to work on this book. Their constant encouragement and collaboration was crucial in bringing this project to completion.

I was fortunate to have the support of family, friends, and colleagues throughout this process. My husband, Richard, motivated me and kept me balanced. My children, Amanda and Jeffrey, gave me encouragement, as well as time, to keep the writing moving. They also helped me maintain balance in my life. From Grand Master Byung Yul Kwak's lessons, I have learned to hone my spirit, persistence, and self-control to complete this project.

My readers were invaluable to me: Anthony Kelly, Elaine Braff, Jay Cherney, Ron Kissick, and Susan Bernstein. Jean Reeves helped with the task of reviewing and putting together the extensive reference list. Dennis Haggerty worked with me, generously, on the graphics; and Veronica Haggerty was also a source of support. Doris Maguire, my Office Manager and Executive Assistant, helped with many details. My thanks to all of you for your time, support, and encouragement.

Ellen Berman's contributions on the Gender and Sexuality Focused Genogram are an important part of the MFG, and I especially appreciate her work with me on the Cultural Genogram. I would like to thank the students who participated in the Family Evaluation and Interviewing course, which I taught at Allegheny University during Spring 1997 as I developed the thematic concepts of the focused genograms, for their feedback.

Finally, Linda Yoo Kelly has my deepest gratitude and appreciation for her generous support through this project, from beginning to end.

INTRODUCTION

Since their introduction as a clinical tool, genograms have come a long way. However, no one text has consolidated the literature on the use of genograms in clinical practice. *Focused Genograms: Intergenerational Assessment of Individuals, Couples, and Families* updates, expands the use of genograms for clinicians, supervisors, and academicians and describes the practical use of Focused Genograms. Based on extensive clinical practice, teaching, supervising, and research, the authors have developed a method that organizes and structures the pedigree genogram, the "Family Map," and the "Time Line."

In this book the authors provide a practical guide for creating a Multifocused Family Genogram (MFG). Based on the concept of Focused Genograms, the MFG is a combination of graphic tools that helps the clinician visually and conceptually organize and use psychohistorical information gathered during clinical interviews. The purpose of the MFG is to give therapists both a systemic and a comprehensive assessment of a client system and a method to organize the data. Integrative and comprehensive, the MFG goes beyond current genogram technology. If current genograms can be compared to an x-ray of a family system, then the MFG can be considered an MRI, providing a more in-depth examination.

The MFG, with a Basic Genogram as the template, summarizes the themes that result from constructing Focused Genograms. In this text, seven Focused Genograms are presented: Attachments, Emotions, Anger, Gender, Sexuality, Romantic Love, and Culture. In addition to these Focused Genograms, the MFG includes a Family Map and a Time Line. These two features of the MFG broaden the scope generally provided by the traditional genogram. A flexible structure and system for organizing information, the MFG is designed to help clinicians enable their clients to explore their family system in depth. Because the MFG is not a rigid structure, it is quite adaptable and practitioners can develop their own preferred styles.

This book is written in three parts. Part One includes Chapters 1 and 2 and covers the basic elements of the MFG and the Focused Genograms. Chapter 1 reviews the history and uses of the genogram and describes the MFG, its structure, and its components in detail. Figures help the reader visualize a completed MFG. Chapter 2 pays special attention to the use of Focused Genograms in practice.

Describing the key components of the MFG, Part Two is comprised of three chapters. Chapter 3 describes the Basic Genogram (a Focused Genogram in its own right) and establishes a format that is used with all of the chapters on Focused Genograms. The first part of Chapter 3 presents questions, organized by topics, that direct inquiry for the Basic Genogram. The second section of Chapter 3, "Theoretical Underpinnings," highlights the major topics of the Basic Genogram, providing the beginning practitioner an overview of these topical areas. This format—first presenting the themes for a Focused Genogram and then presenting a discussion of these themes—is used for each chapter in Part Three. However, this text is not intended to be a comprehensive overview or in-depth analysis and critique of the literature pertaining to all the themes that have been identified. Consequently, at the end of each on chapter Focused Genograms, readings are recommended.

Chapters 4 and 5 present the Family Map and the Time Line, describing their respective functions and uses. These three components, the Basic Genogram, the Family Map, and the Time Line, are the foundations of the MFG. With the belief that family-of-origin experiences form a template upon which other relationships develop, we demonstrate how these experiences can be diagrammed intrapsychically, interpersonally, and intergenerationally, using the MFG structure and process. With the Attachments Genogram, we present a method for graphing internal working models, a concept first introduced by Bowlby (1977). Despite our emphasis on organization, our goal with this book is to help the practitioner establish clinically useful goals and enhance the therapeutic alliance.

Part Three includes Chapters 6 through 10 and presents essential Focused Genograms: Attachments; Emotions; Anger; Gender, Sexuality, Romantic Love; and Culture. Each Focused Genogram comprises several topics. The Attachments Genogram, for instance, includes attention to the topics of bonding, temperament, and attachment style; the Culture Genogram examines race, ethnicity, religious orientation, and socioeconomic status.

The chapters on Focused Genograms, like the Basic Genogram chapter in Part Two, have two key sections: The first section describes the construction and unique aspects of each of the Focused Genograms; the second section addresses basic theoretical concepts related to the specific Focused Genogram. The reader can use the first part of each chapter as a guide to constructing the Focused Genogram. The second part of each chapter, on theoretical underpinnings, is for the reader who wants to explore the theoretical concepts and research that support the inclusion of the particular topics for each Focused Genogram. For example, for Culture Genograms, themes of race, ethnicity, immigration, religion, and socioeconomic status are discussed. For Gender Genograms, themes of gender identity, gender roles, sexuality, and romantic love are explored. As previously discussed, these parts of each chapter, however, are not intended as a critical literature review or as complete exploration of the topical areas. Rather, these sections are aimed at providing an overview of salient topics and orienting the reader to further literature on the subject. Practitioners are urged to pursue written information, training, and personal experience in these conceptual areas in order to develop and maintain a comprehensive knowledge base and an experiential framework that can be drawn upon in clinical practice. Again, suggested readings are provided at the end of each chapter.

Grounded in affect and attachment theory as well as family systems theory, the MFG is essentially a structured process that allows the clinician to explore psychodynamic, interpersonal, and intergenerational areas of psychosocial experience. With the attachments lens, it functions as a microscope to examine family process and dynamics. Attachment has been described as the psychobiological glue that holds the family together (Stosny, 1995). A variant of object relations theory, attachment theory provides bridges among intrapsychic, relational, and family systems theories and provides theoretical constructs that enrich and expand former uses of the genogram. These concepts are detailed in Chapter 6, which describes how internalized working models influence family relationships. Although the authors introduce the internal models Family Map, a method for depicting internal working models of interpersonal experience, in Chapter 3, in Chapter 6 the method is described in detail.

The emotions and anger lenses of the MFG described in Chapters 7 and 8 examine affect theory, the study of emotions and emotional experience. In Chapters 9 and 10, the MFG provides a macroscopic view of gender, sexuality, romantic love, and culture influences and their effects on the family. Along with the basic family systems genogram (Chapter 3), the template for the Focused Genograms, these chapters provide the practitioner with a model for comprehensive assessment of the client system.

Through a series of suggested questions, each Focused Genogram insures a thorough examination of family structure and process. This kind of examination is essential in order to develop strategic macroscopic and microscopic interventions. The questions included facilitate direct assessment and support brief interventions required by many behavioral-health programs.

In the Conclusion, we summarize the usefulness of the MFG in clinical practice. Although computer technology is not commonly used, the Appendix includes highlights of two available computerized genogram programs.

The genogram has become one of the fundamental tools in the assessment of individual, interactional, and intergenerational patterns within family systems. The genogram and Bowen systems theory have been inextricably linked. Guerin and Pendagast (1976) published one of the first chapters on the genogram. Their chapter provided the basic outline of the genogram and appeared in a text on Bowen systems theory that contained several references to conducting genograms throughout the book. Further details on the use of the Bowen model were described by McGoldrick and Gerson (1985), who published the first "how-to" text on genograms. Emphasizing life cycle events, relational patterns and triangles, and family balance and imbalance, they detailed the construction of the genogram. Although Bowen systems theory provides a coherent model for development of a genogram, it provides only a limited number of lenses to examine family process and dynamics.

The fields of marital and family therapy and family psychology have seen tremendous growth and development since the publication of McGoldrick and Gerson's text. The genogram now is used widely by clinicians of varying theoretical orientation, and Bowen's system theory is no longer the only model that promotes development of genograms in clinical practice to detail family structure, dynamics, and process. Although the MFG uses attachment theory to link the individual with his or her family relationships, it maintains an ecological, systemic view as well. Consequently, the MFG can be expanded, modified, and used based on the practitioner's clinical orientation and needs.

Focused Genograms are a new and important contribution of the MFG for clinical practice. The development of these Focused Genograms began over a decade ago to cover a considerable range of materials relevant to individual, couple, and family practice. Each Focused Genogram allows for the inclusion of focused Family Maps and focused Time Lines or expansion of the basic Family Map and basic Time Line. The Family Maps detail interactional patterns around the particular issues of the Focused Genograms and allow for the inclusion of individuals, organizations, and systems outside the family. The basic Family Map combines Minuchin's "structural Family Maps" (Minuchin, 1974; Stanton, 1992) and Hartman's (1978) ecomaps. Noting individual as well as family events, the Time Line provides a developmental lens to organize information gained during the interviewing process. Developing and maintaining Time Lines throughout the assessment and treatment processes can direct therapists' attention to gaps in information as well as areas of stress.

The Focused Genograms guide the exploration of topics such as culture, gender, emotions, attachments, health, sexuality, love, and marriage. Family Maps help in the understanding of transactional patterns; Time Lines provide a broad temporal context for a specific issue with focused attention to developmental and transitional issues. Depiction of interactional patterns and dynamics typically has been based on Bowen systems theory and often does not go beyond noting cut-offs, enmeshments, or conflict. The unidimensional effect of mapping interactional patterns limits the usefulness of Family Maps. However, Family Maps can be a useful tool to help the clinician assess and track family dynamics and environmental and social influences and forces. With the lenses of the Focused Genograms, the Family Maps become an integral and useful part of the assessment. This structure helps the clinician conduct a step-by-step thematic assessment of the client with specific themes chosen by the practitioner or the client. Clinical need, experience, orientation of the therapist, and client goals determine which themes the practitioner chooses.

The MFG is a method to examine the depth and breadth of each unique family constellation. Each layer of the MFG guides the clinician in establishing clinical goals and intervention strategies. Without this understanding of family dynamics and how patterns and beliefs are internalized, interventions may be shallow or misguided. It is important to examine various levels offered by the MFG because each contributes to family structure and process in unique ways. Intergenerational patterns produce external constraints upon the family system. These patterns influence interpersonal behavior, psychodynamic experience, and often career or vocational success or failure. Attitudes about achievement, about marriage, and about personal options are shaped by the heritage of one's family.

Current interpersonal experiences influence behavior on a daily basis. A satisfying marriage is an important factor in having a positive sense of personal well-being. Couples with constant conflict struggle in their relationships at work and with their children. Children who grow up in homes with ongoing conflict struggle in their peer relationships and in their academic endeavors. The more severe the conflict at home, the greater are children's difficulties at school. The bully is often a child who is growing up in a violent and destructive home. Children who are cruel to other children are often children who are growing up in homes in which they are ridiculed and shamed on a daily basis. These patterns are explored in the various Focused Genograms.

The MFG is a continuous work in progress that the clinician develops throughout the treatment process. As relevant Focused Genograms are completed, patterns and themes that have been identified can be summarized. The Focused Genograms are like drawings or snapshots, revealed by the lenses of the MFG, that layer upon one another to form a pictorial description of the client-family system. The detailed Focused Genograms provide a microscopic and macroscopic examination of specific issues that effect the client and his or her family and social systems.

The MFG is a way to assess and organize information about a client system. Assessment tools often are underutilized by clinicians because they are not interactionally based. The MFG, however, provides questions that can be used flexibly as part of the interviewing process. The structure of the Focused Genogram provides a way for the clinician to record (and organize according to his or her preferred style) the information that is gathered. It is not intended, however, as an end-all, be-all tool.

Working with people systemically is a challenge to a therapist's ability to understand the multifaceted array of human experience. The MFG is one method of expanding the clinician's capacity for empathy and rapport. By providing a broad list of questions, the Focused Genograms guide the clinician's inquiry and usually result in important information about the client's unique life experience, personalizing the therapeutic encounter for therapist and client. As the therapist becomes informed about many areas of the client's life, the MFG aids in constructing hypotheses about the family system's development and functioning. Regardless of the conceptual models that influence one's clinical practice, the MFG is useful. The format of the MFG insures that all relevant dimensions of the client's biological, psychological, and social functioning can be assessed, making the MFG an important new tool for clinicians who use family systems theory to guide their practice.

PART

I

OVERVIEW

CHAPTER 1

Introduction to the Multifocused Family Genogram

In this chapter, we present the Multifocused Family Genogram (MFG) as a tool for conducting a comprehensive and systemic assessment of a client's family system. After a review of limitations of genograms as they currently are used in clinical practice, the components and construction of the MFG are described.

Because assessment in family focused clinical practice requires a comprehensive approach and is a complex process, the genogram provides a systematic method for gathering information about a family system and for identifying themes and patterns that influence personal development and relationships with spouses, children, business associates, friends, and acquaintances. Often perplexing behaviors and attitudes can be better understood, even explained, by developing and examining a genogram. Not only can therapists use genograms to organize information about families or individuals and their unique experiences, but they also can use genograms in developing working hypotheses that guide subsequent clinical interventions.

Intergenerational legacies and family dynamics are multidimensional. Depicting these patterns is generally a difficult process. However, the genogram is one of the primary clinical aids for exploring these patterns and influences on the nuclear family. The MFG broadens the scope of the traditional genogram format used in family practice. Employing it, the clinician can examine thematic issues systemically and individually. The integrative theoretical foundation of the MFG incorporates interpersonal-intrapsychic family systems theories, and advances in understanding individual and family emotional process, by using Focused Genograms.

Because it provides a comprehensive, in-depth method of assessing family structure, history, and process, the MFG is an important clinical tool. The MFG helps the clinician achieve greater perspective about the complexity and detail of the client's life, and it also can foster the development of the therapeutic relationship. For example, a client who has experienced a childhood with serious corporal punishments will be sensitive to confrontational or judgmental interventions by the therapist.

With the MFG, the clinician has multiple perspectives from which to view the family system. Beginning with the Basic Genogram and through the inclusion of Family Maps and Time Lines and the addition of Focused Genograms, the MFG combines a series of composite pictures blended together to form a collage. Each aspect helps the clinician determine appropriate treatment goals and objectives. The MFG identifies key intergenerational themes and patterns, reveals relationship patterns, and highlights developmental issues. The structure of the MFG addresses these issues in detail. Consequently, the MFG expands traditional use of the genogram.

☐ Overview

The genogram has been used primarily with intergenerational models of treatment, the Bowen school of family therapy in particular. Widely used in graduate programs in marriage and family therapy, McGoldrick and Gerson's text, *Genograms in Family Assessment* (1985), popularized Bowen theory and the pedigree genogram method. Other clinical theories use the genogram method in a variety of ways. For example, in structural family therapy it is employed more as a map, graphing the current hierarchical dynamics of relationships within the family. In Boszormenyi-Nagy's contextual theory (1987), the genogram is used to identify the family legacies and loyalties that frequently manifest themselves in "destructive entitlement." In contrast, Satir's experiential theory (1967) emphasizes the family's chronology and historical influences. Hartman (1978) developed the ecomap, which outlines, in a dynamic way, the family's ecological environment and the flow of resources and energy into and out of the family system.

Genograms are used in most American Association for Marriage and Family Therapy clinical training and supervision programs and processes.

Each academic and postgraduate training center in marriage and family therapy uses the genogram to exemplify the clinical theory being taught. For both supervisors and trainees, the genogram is a foundation for discussing family systems and setting treatment goals. At the Penn Council for Relationships (formerly the Marriage Council of Philadelphia), an accredited postgraduate center for marriage and family therapy training, genograms are incorporated into both course work (as cases are presented) and supervision. Trainees use the genogram as a method for detailing intergenerational features of the intersystem model, a comprehensive theory for assessing family dynamics developed by Weeks (Weeks, 1989; Weeks & Hof, 1994).

In academic and training programs in family therapy, genograms are integral assessment tools in courses that emphasize theory and practice (Blossom, 1991). Family-of-origin study, which includes developing a personal genogram, is an aspect of many graduate programs in marriage and family therapy (Halevy, 1998). When the genogram process is used to interview potential family-practice residents, interviewees often express the belief that the process is personal, insightful, and intimate, and that it breaks down the formality of the process (Blossom, 1991). Similarly, Schilson, Braun, and Hudson (1993) found that when genograms are used in medical practice, patients report feeling that physicians are more empathetic and physicians report that referrals for psychological assistance occur more smoothly.

Typically used to summarize current and past patterns of relationships, genograms include at least three generations of family members. Regardless of the particular clinical theory or theories informing their practices, clinicians use genograms to characterize the patterns that develop among and between the generations. The structure that a genogram provides for organizing often vast amounts of information is its strength. We suggest that the genogram can be thought of as a microscope that gives the clinician a concrete method for examining the unique details of each client's family system, and, at the same time, as the therapist gathers information and organizes the details of personal and family history, it permits a macroscopic view of patterns and themes that emerge. However, clinical use of the genogram has been limited.

☐ Limitations of Genograms

Despite the popularity of genograms in clinical and medical training, they are not universally applied in practice. Based on the literature and our clinical experience, we have identified five limitations to genograms as they are currently taught: Genograms tend to be static; the collection of information is often overwhelming and hard to manage; they are biased by clinician-client interaction; the emphasis tends to be placed more on "historical" truth in contrast to "narrative" truth; and there are no standards for mapping family relationships. Before we present the MFG, each of these limitations is reviewed.

Because the genogram often is used as a preliminary information-gathering tool in the beginning phase of treatment, the information collected about the family system during this phase of treatment becomes *the* family genogram. Although computerized genograms have helped, updates and expansions of the initial genogram often are hard to manage, and therefore they are not formalized in any way and do not get integrated into ongoing treatment planning. Consequently, genograms frequently are based on the particular moment in time (a snapshot, so to speak) at which the clinician is gathering information with the client, rather than being created and expanded throughout treatment.

Second, so much information can be collected that the genogram can become overloaded with so many patterns and issues that the clinician struggles to determine what is most relevant to the problem being presented. Despite the development of computerized genograms, many clinicians use paper-and-pencil formats to create genograms as they interact with their clients. This can cause a serious problem with constructing genograms, because so much information can be collected that the genogram becomes completely confusing to read or view. Consequently, the clinician's ability to develop working hypotheses is compromised because too many multiple patterns and themes are identified. The genogram then may cease to be a relevant clinical tool and may be assigned to the depths of the case file.

The third consideration is that the genogram is intimately related to the idiosyncratic characteristics of both the therapist and the family at a given point in time. The clinician's theoretical orientation and the family's or individual's style of interaction usually determine the questions and responses during the information-gathering process. Genograms also are biased both by the clinician's focus and attention and by the perspective of the person presenting the information. This happens because the questions asked by the clinician shape the kind of information that is collected on the genogram, just as the person who provides the answers influences the details that are put onto the genogram. A genogram that is drawn based on information by Mr. Smith may not match the genogram drawn and developed with Mrs. Smith or with their children. Focused Genograms help to standardize the information collected throughout the clinical process.

Predictably, there are family secrets, misinformation, and information gaps that affect the development of a genogram. Consequently, the fourth limitation of the genogram method is that it can tend to focus on "historical" truth than on "narrative" truth. Alex Haley, the author of *Roots* (1976), who fictionalized his family genogram, was criticized for his literary freedom with gaps in information, biasing his family history. "Filling in the blanks" is a common phenomenon, however, and an important part of constructing the narrative. In one clinical interview, Jim was recounting the story of his birth. "My father left when I was five months old for reasons I'll never know," he said. The clinician asked, "What do you suspect?" Jim then went on at length to tell the story he believed about his parent's marriage. The story was as real to Jim as the truth.

Finally, another constraint on using genograms in clinical practice is the lack of one defined system used as a standard for genogram mapping. Although McGoldrick and Gerson (1985) compiled the most commonly used symbols for outlining basic family membership, structure, and interaction, to insure readability they urge keeping details on the genogram to a minimum. In contrast, Minuchin's symbols (1974) focus on mapping family structure, boundaries, and transactional patterns. Hartman and Laird (1983) use symbols to describe connections—strong, tenuous or weak, or stressful—and the flow of energy or resources into and out of the family system. To make the symbolic soup even more confusing, Hardy and Laszloffy (1995) advocate symbolic representation of multiracial marriages on the genogram as well, and Lewis (1989) advocates colorcoding the genogram.

Some studies suggest that there is actually very limited agreement among clinicians on using genogram symbols, and that the symbols used do not describe the diversity of family interaction. The symbols focus primarily on closeness, distance, and conflict patterns in families. Rohrbaugh, Rogers, and McGoldrick (1992) found that the highest reliability coefficients among experts reading genograms were in the areas of emotional cut-off, conflictual relationships, and repeated relationship patterns over generations. Coupland, Serovish, and Glenn (1995) found that doctoral students were highly accurate in recording names, dates, and ages; however, they were moderately accurate in recording unnamed persons, occupations, relationship descriptors, medical issues, personal issues, descriptive phrases, and other significant symbols.

These studies suggest that use of the genogram tends to take on a very broad focus. Therefore, broad categories are not always useful in helping the clinician develop working hypotheses that help establish a focused treatment plan unique to the client's needs. Compounding the problem of lack of agreement about the use of descriptors and symbols, there are no standardized symbols for family violence, corporal punishment, child abuse, or addiction patterns.

☐ Introduction to the MFG

The MFG is a means of exploring the client's family and its intergenerational themes, intrapsychic and interpersonal dynamics, interactional patterns, and developmental adjustments. Coping mechanisms and unresolved issues also can be identified from a variety of perspectives. The completed MFG incorporates the Basic Genogram, Family Maps, Time Lines, and Focused Genograms to provide both breadth and depth of focus. Regardless of theoretical orientation, the clinician is aided by the MFG in problem identification and treatment planning.

When the MFG is fully developed, the clinician possesses a comprehensive picture and story of the client that provides direction for further inquiry and treatment. The unique pictorial story created about the client contributes to the ongoing process of assessment, hypothesis formation, and intervention.

Basic Concepts of the MFG

If the traditional genogram is thought of as a simple microscope, then the MFG is like a multilensed and multipowered microscope *and* macroscope that expands or restricts the clinician's focus as he or she works with the client. The microscopic focus of the MFG is on attachment and emotions—the "heart" of family and personal relationships. The macroscopic focus is on gender and culture—the "isms" of life that put boundaries around interpersonal behavior and one's sense of identity. Whether the client system is an individual, couple, or family, the MFG organizes the patterns and themes of specific areas of life: culture, gender, sexuality, emotions, attachment patterns, work, health, and so forth. Through the Focused Genograms, the MFG provides different lenses of varying powers that can be used to examine different aspects and depths of the family system. Focus is possible because the clinician can zoom in on different dimensions, as they are relevant to the presenting problem and the treatment process. Not only are there different focuses for each of the genograms, but each Focused Genogram also can include a Family Map and Time Line that addresses the highlights for that clinical area.

The MFG as an assessment process has its roots in theories of family process, structure, and development. L'Abate and Bagarozzi (1993) suggest that this kind of approach is essential in assessment across the life cycle. The MFG becomes a useful clinical tool for systemic evaluation and assessment by providing a semistructured format for conducting clinical interviews that details intergenerational, interactional, developmental, and intrapsychic patterns. The MFG also provides a method for clinical assessment and treatment planning without mechanizing the interview or disrupting rapport.

The MFG is a method for assessing the family system in a way that takes into account intrapsychic, developmental, interactional, intergenerational, and cultural patterns. Many family therapists have recommended that the genogram be expanded. Woolf (1983) suggested that the genogram include the entire family network as well as describe intrapsychic and interpersonal relationships. Others have called for the genogram to include sexuality (Hof & Berman, 1986), culture (Halevy, 1998; Hardy & Laszloffy, 1995; Watts-Jones, 1997), social class, career decisions (Moon, Coleman, McCollum, Nelson, & Jensen-Scott, 1993), and academic success (Santa Rita & Adejanju, 1993). Additional suggestions focus on particular types of presenting problems, such as patients with spinal cord injuries (Engelman, 1988), crisis intervention (Sproul & Gallagher, 1982), and loyalty and widowhood (Seaburn, 1990). The diversity of these themes underscores the need for, and the importance of, the MFG. The many ways in which these dimensions can be incorporated and expanded using Focused Genograms are demonstrated throughout this book.

As a microscope, the MFG has multiple lenses of differing powers for focusing on the details of specific areas of the client's life. The Family Map is like a live slide that catches the dynamic forces at work as they are viewed through the lenses of the MFG. The Time Line is like a temporal lens, or a microtome, which dissects the family at selected points in time. The MFG thus helps the clinician develop a comprehensive assessment that includes intrapersonal, interactional, and intergenerational processes, themes, and dynamics. Because the MFG process highlights the individuality and complexity of each client system, the clinician gains deeper understanding and, most importantly, more empathy for the client whether treatment is brief or traditional. The MFG provides a flexible assessment strategy for treatment planning.

Comprehensive and integrative, the MFG is a new method for addressing the problems of collecting and charting the overwhelming amounts of information that are likely to emerge during the genogram information collection process. The MFG is comprised of the following parts:

1. *The Basic Genogram*: The MFG uses the Basic Genogram to include all the aspects of the traditional genogram used in family systems practice. Uniquely identifying the client system by organizing names, dates, and descriptors of family members, marriage and divorce patterns, birth order, occupations, health problems, and other important areas of life, the Basic Genogram is an essential family systems clinical tool that is used to graphically depict the client system intergenerationally. The Basic Genogram is also the template for each of the

Focused Genograms and can be used as an organizing document for summarizing the themes that emerge from the Focused Genograms. In Chapter 4, the questions of and rationale for the Basic Genogram are presented in depth, addressing family functioning; marital patterns, divorce, and extramarital affairs; birth order; adoption; infertility and pregnancy loss; self-esteem; health and illness; and addictions.

2. *Family Maps*: A Family Map graphically depicts the emotional and behavioral patterns within the family system and connections with social, political, and community resources. The Family Map graphically portrays the emotional features of family life. Either a generic Family Map or focused Family Maps can be developed.

3. *Time Lines*: Providing a temporal view of individual and family development, the Time Lines identify normative and paranormative developmental themes.

4. *Focused Genograms*: Focused Genograms provide a format for clinicians to explore important areas of family life in significant detail, including attachment styles, emotions, gender and sexuality, and culture. The specific Focused Genograms presented in this book include five Focused Genograms. Each Focused Genogram is made up of topics. The following list identifies the topics for each of the Focused Genograms presented in this text:

> *Attachment*: bonding, temperament, and attachment
> *Emotions*: sadness, loss, and grief; fear; and pleasure
> *Anger*: anger, family violence, and corporal punishment
> *Gender and sexuality*: gender, sexuality, and romantic love
> *Culture*: race, ethnicity, and immigration; religious orientation; socioeconomic status

The Basic Genogram, the Family Map, and the Time Line are the three organizing documents for the MFG. Family Maps and Time Lines can be expanded in each of the Focused Genograms to handle the simulation of transactional patterns and the identification of developmental and transitional issues within particular Focused Genograms.

☐ Constructing the MFG

The term *MFG* refers to the document created by the four components: the Basic Genogram, the Family Map, the Time Line, and the Focused Genograms. Figure 1.1 illustrates these components.

Following the conventions of genetics and genealogical charts, the clinician develops the initial outline of the family system, often referred to as

Basic Genogram

Themes:
    Attachments
    Emotions
    Anger
    Gender, Sexuality,
      and Romantic Love
    Culture

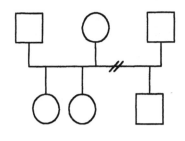

MFG Family Map

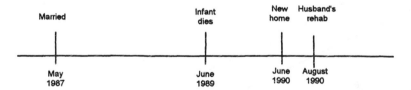

MFG Time Line

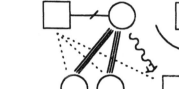

FIGURE 1.1. Elements of the Multifocused Family Genogram (MFG). The Multifocused Family Genogram is comprised of the (1) Basic Genogram with themes summarized on the left side (based on the Focused Genograms), (2) the Family Map and (3) the Time Line.

a *pedigree*, which becomes the Basic Genogram. Maintaining these conventions but expanding the use of the pedigree, Focused Genograms add to the MFG throughout the various phases and stages of interviewing and treatment to shed light on important issues within the family. The Basic Genogram, the Family Map, and the Time Line each usually requires a separate page. In addition, there are two methods for organizing the issues identified in the Focused Genograms—a sketch method and a table method. Later in this chapter, in the section on Focused Genograms, the specifics of each method are described.

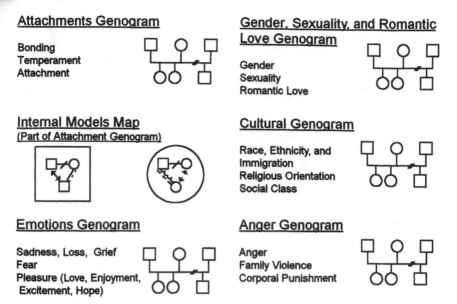

Attachments Genogram

Bonding
Temperament
Attachment

Gender, Sexuality, and Romantic Love Genogram

Gender
Sexuality
Romantic Love

Internal Models Map
(Part of Attachment Genogram)

Cultural Genogram

Race, Ethnicity, and Immigration
Religious Orientation
Social Class

Emotions Genogram

Sadness, Loss, Grief
Fear
Pleasure (Love, Enjoyment, Excitement, Hope)

Anger Genogram

Anger
Family Violence
Corporal Punishment

FIGURE 1.1. (continued) Focused Genograms are comprised of the Basic Genogram and notes of the specific themes. Focused Family Maps and focused Time Lines can be on separate pages or added to the MFG.

The themes of the Focused Genograms can be summarized on the left side of the Basic Genogram as illustrated on Figure 1.2.

These three pages (Basic Genogram, Family Map, and Time Line), with the addition of the Focused Genograms and accompanying maps and Time Lines, can add up to as many as 19 pages. These pages are maintained as part of the clinical record with progress notes, kept by the clinician as part of the file. The MFG format is open to flexible use by the practitioners. The number of pages is completely discretionary. Some therapists prefer to keep significant detail and consistent organization in their MFG notes and records; others prefer to be briefer and less structured. The MFG format provides a structure that can accommodate the needs and styles of different therapists.

The separate pages create the layers of the MFG and provide the therapist a quick view of important issues. Although not transparent like the layering used to create a multidimensional view of the human body in anatomy and science books, the layers of the MFG help the clinician give order to the information collected about the family system. Although the number of pages is not important, it is significant for the therapist to collect information thematically, based on the Focused Genograms. In preparing these layers of the MFG, the clinician focuses on specific issues and explores each topic in depth. The Focused Genogram also struc-

Themes

Attachment
Bonding
Temperament
Attachment

Emotions
Sadness, Loss, Grief
Fear
Pleasure (Love, Enjoyment,
        Excitement, Hope)
Anger
Anger
Family Violence
Corporal Punishment

Gender/Sexuality
Gender
Sexuality
Romantic Love

Culture
Race, Ethnicity & Immigration
Religious Orientation
Social Class

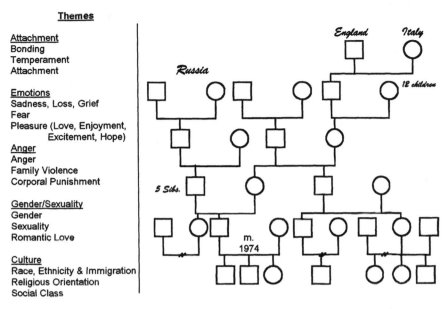

FIGURE 1.2. MFG with themes of Focused Genograms identified on left side of page. Issues related to these are identified and noted.

tures exploration of individual and family development as well as family process and dynamics. Rather than being concerned about a cluttered genogram, the MFG provides a structure that encourages, instead of discouraging, the collection of information.

Drawing the Basic Genogram

As previously described, when the clinician constructs the Basic Genogram pedigree conventions and formats are used. Squares indicate men, circles indicate women, and triangles indicate persons of unknown gender. Horizontal lines indicate marital and parent-child relationships. Dates of marriages, separations, and divorces are written above the horizontal line. Separations are noted with a slash through the marriage line, and divorce is indicated by a double slash. Children are listed in order of birth from left to right. Adopted children are noted with a dotted parent-child line to the child's circle or square. Dotted children lines marked with an "f" indicate foster children. Fraternal twins and identical twins both come down from the same child line. Current pregnancy is indicated by a small triangle. If the sex of the child is known, a circle or square is drawn inside the triangle. Spontaneous abortions or miscarriages are noted by a small dot; induced abortions by an "x" on the child line (with gender noted if

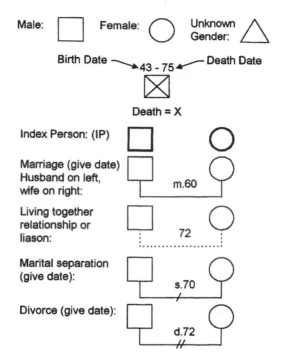

FIGURE 1.3. Symbols for developing the Basic Genogram.

known); and stillbirths by a smaller male or female symbol with an "x" through it (Figure 1.3). These symbols are standard in family-genogram construction (Friedman, Rohrbaugh, & Krakauer, 1988; McGoldrick & Gerson, 1985). (Computer-generated genogram packages are available. Suggestions for computerization of the genogram are included in the Appendix, but otherwise this is not within the scope of this book.)

Many Basic Genograms start out in this format, although many quickly become much more complicated. Sometimes genograms can be quite challenging to draw. As past generations are explored, one should include the names and positions of anyone who was part of the family system. Complications often arise because people are confused about the birth order of their aunts and uncles, grandparents, and great-grandparents, and other kin relationships (often nonbiological). Confusion also surrounds multiple intrafamilial marriages to second cousins, stepparents, and half- or step-siblings. In these situations, one should approximate the person's position on the genogram and use a question mark if the information is uncertain. One can write in "five children?" and make other comments as needed as past generations are explored (Figure 1.4).

Because the MFG is intended to be comprehensive, it is important to include everyone on the genogram who is known, even if there is lit-

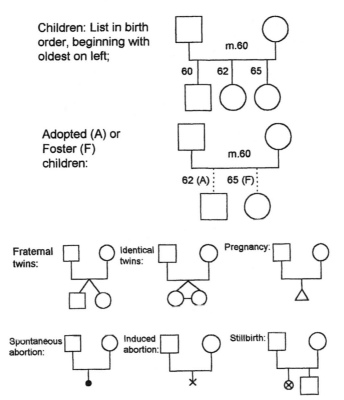

Children: List in birth order, beginning with oldest on left;

Adopted (A) or Foster (F) children:

Fraternal twins:

Identical twins:

Pregnancy:

Spontaneous abortion:

Induced abortion:

Stillbirth:

FIGURE 1.3. (continued) Symbols for developing the Basic Genogram.

tle additional information about them. It is important to avoid excluding members of the system just because they do not fit neatly into the structure. These people often may have a significance that is not discernible at

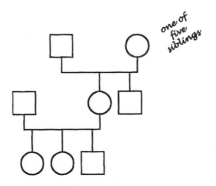

one of five siblings

FIGURE 1.4. Example of writing in information in the Basic Genogram.

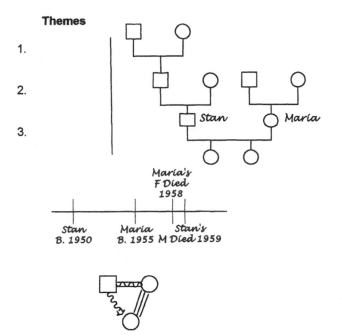

Themes

1.

2.

3.

Stan

Maria

Maria's
F Died
1958

Stan
B. 1950

Maria
B. 1955 M Died 1959

Stan's

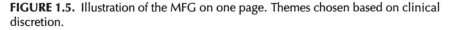

FIGURE 1.5. Illustration of the MFG on one page. Themes chosen based on clinical discretion.

first glance. Through the various lenses of the MFG, the roles and influences of family members become more focused.

The Basic Genogram is used as a template for all the Focused Genograms. It can be drawn on a standard sheet of paper with the long side held at the bottom. The client's name goes at the top of the page. The genogram is drawn to the right side of the page in the usual pedigree format with at least three or four generations. With the sketch method some room is allowed on the left side margin to make note of themes for the specific Focused Genogram being constructed, as illustrated in Figure 1.1.

Some families are complicated and may require taping another sheet along the short side of the paper. Beginning with the Basic Genogram, one adds all known family members and then makes several copies. These can be used for the Focused Genograms. Time Lines can be drawn beneath the pedigree, although a separate page often is preferred. Usually the Family Map and Time Line are drawn on separate pages so that the practitioner has enough room for details.

Figure 1.5 visually illustrates the MFG based on the Basic Genogram, themes from the Focused Genograms, the Family Map, and the Time Line.

A genogram usually includes a diagram of family relationships that displays at least three generations. This may be standard practice, but it

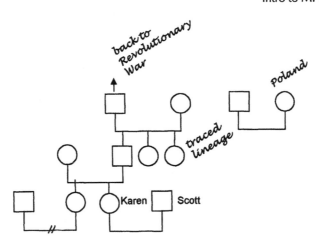

FIGURE 1.6. Outline of a Basic Genogram with limited information.

is important to go back as far as a person's memory will allow. As the clinician guides the client system in identifying members and themes of past generations (three generations and beyond), gaps in information and prevailing family myths become more apparent. These gaps in information and myths become important avenues for further exploration. The stories and myths that people believe about their family members are important in identifying the sources and meanings of legacies for the client.

The more generations that get included in the genogram, the more clear the legacies of the family become. It is important for the clinician to note how far back the client believes he or she can trace the family history, even if there is little or no information known about past generations. Karen knew a great deal of information about her husband's family from talking with his grandmother. The family history stopped and started with the grandmother's immigration from Poland at age 2. Aside from her parents and siblings, little was known of the family in Poland or the circumstances of immigration. On the other hand, Karen knew few details about her own family history except that her aunt had traced the paternal lineage back to the American Revolution. These details can be noted along the top of the page at the level of fourth and fifth generation's back (Figure 1.6).

Focused Genograms

Using the Basic Genogram as a template, the Focused Genograms can be redrawn or copied. There are two ways to write up themes. The tra-

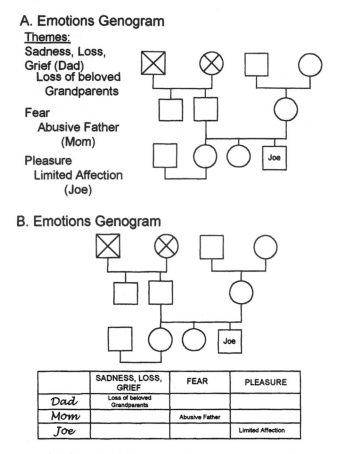

FIGURE 1.7. A. Sketch method for Focused Genograms. B. Table method for Focused Genograms.

ditional method is to write the descriptive data beside the appropriate person. With the addition of themes, using the sketch method, the practitioner adds additional detail. With the table method, the therapist prepares a table that lists each family member's name and the specific topics of the Focused Genogram. Because the table method takes more room on the page, a separate page usually is needed for a Family Map and Time Line. Consequently, each Focused Genogram can be two or three pages, depending on the complexity of the case. Figure 1.7 illustrates the differences in these methods.

The choice of method depends on the practitioner's preference, time constraints, and focus of the interview. If the Focused Genogram is used to help organize information collected during the clinical interview, the therapist may choose to use the sketch method. Therapists sometimes

Person	Race	Religion	Social Class	Ethnicity
Self				
Mother				
Father				
Sibling				
Grandparent				

FIGURE 1.8. Detail of the table method for the Cultural Genogram.

find it useful to draw the genogram and make notes as they gather information. On the other hand, if the practitioner and client have agreed to focus on the genogram during a session and a more structured assessment takes place, the clinician may choose the more structured table method. The table method also can be used later if the clinician chooses to rewrite or more thoroughly organize his or her clinical notes.

A diagram of the areas concentrated on through the Cultural Genogram lens (Figure 1.8) illustrates the table method. The number of people listed in the table is dependent on the number of people in the family of origin, the client's circle of influence, and the specific information the client has about extended family members. Tables are created easily using word-processing programs.

☐ The MFG as a Narrative Process

The topics of the Focused Genogram maintain the therapist's focus, enabling in-depth exploration of areas of personal and family functioning. Using focused, in-depth interviewing, the Focused Genograms provide a structure to identify patterns within the family system. Because the clinician seeks to understand meaning behind these patterns, in-depth interviewing provided by the Focused Genograms explores important areas of personal experience. Initially, patterns often seem indiscernible, insignificant, or incongruent. The clinician must continually, and repeatedly, examine the information collected about the family system in order to develop useful interpretations of legacies and dynamics. Greater clarity usually emerges over time. Thus, the accumulation of Focused Genograms that examine the family system in detail is an important part of an assessment process. Although the patterns are not always repetitive, it is unusual to find one black sheep in a family system, or one gifted child, or one philanderer, or one alcoholic. These findings require further discussion and exploration.

Myths and stories are also an important resource in constructing Focused Genograms and sometimes can be supported with family photographs or heirlooms. Clients can be encouraged to bring in such materials throughout the MFG process, contributing to what Spence (1982) calls narrative truth. "Narrative truth can be defined as the criterion we use to decide when a certain experience has been captured to our satisfaction; it depends on continuity and closure and the extent to which the fit of the pieces takes on an aesthetic finality. Narrative truth is what we have in mind when we say that such and such is a good story, that a given explanation carries conviction, that one solution to a mystery must be true. Once a given construction has acquired narrative truth, it becomes just as real as any other kind of truth; this new reality becomes a significant part of the psychoanalytic cure" (p. 31). For example, Marie believed that men in her family died in their early 50s, despite a family history that revealed erratic ages of death, although there were incidences of early death among men on both maternal and paternal sides of the family. Consequently, she experienced a great deal of anxiety about her husband's health.

Although individuals in a family system are unique, family legacies, the good and the bad, are very powerful and influential upon the whole system. Families usually have some secrets, but they differ in their levels of openness and discussion about these events. Using the MFG, practitioners can help their clients construct unique narratives of their personal and family histories. It is often an important and significant experience for them, touching a variety of feelings.

Making sense of one's family and the many influences that have contributed to its creation is an important part of developing the MFG process. Saari (1991) suggests that the ability to create meaning in one's life is an important feature of psychological health and identity formation and consolidation throughout life. The myths and stories that an individual believes about his or her family are a useful way to explore the themes of the Focused Genograms. The Focused Genogram questions and the semistructured format help in constructing a family systems narrative. The incongruities, gaps, and inconsistencies can be explored continually and reviewed until the client makes sense out of the information for himself or herself.

☐ A Word About False Memory and Secrets

Some might ask, "Doesn't the narrative approach, taking into account family stories, myths, and secrets, lead to false memories?" Our response is that through the lenses of the Focused Genograms, consistent patterns and themes are revealed and can be attended to in the clinical setting. The MFG is not a tool for evaluating specific claims of physical or sexual abuse within a family. However, abuse within a family is rarely an isolated phenomenon. The MFG provides the practitioner with a powerful set of lenses through which family dynamics, behaviors, and attitudes can be assessed. In the discussion of Anger Genograms, more detailed assessment of violence, abuse, and corporal punishment is outlined.

Secrets pose a continuing challenge in constructing the MFG. They are part of many families. The process of putting together the MFG can reveal gaps in information, inconsistencies, and implausible circumstances. As the MFG develops, the therapist must be aware of the possibility of exposing family secrets during the interviewing process and avoid "reckless endangerment" of the family system. Secrets must be approached gently, carefully, and respectfully, acknowledging the power and influence they exert on the family system. However, those secrets often are damaging to members of the family system, and affairs, illegitimate births, addictions, and criminal behavior by members of the extended family are often sources of embarrassment to many people. These secrets often need to be explored directly so that their power to influence the family is mitigated.

The MFG process enables the therapist and the client to explore these issues in a gentle yet straightforward fashion, hopefully contributing to the well-being of the family and to effective family functioning and the development of appropriate treatment strategies. The following questions can help guide exploration of secrets in the family system:

1. What were the taboo subjects in your family of origin?
2. How did you know that such subjects were taboo? Did a family member explicitly tell you or did you simply know implicitly? What happened if anyone tried to raise taboo subjects?
3. What were the "rules" regarding privacy in your family? How have they influenced you and your family?
4. Did a family member ever make a secret with you that excluded other family members? What was this experience like for you?
5. Did you ever make a secret with a family member that excluded other family members? What was this experience like for you?
6. Did your family keep secrets from extended family? How did these affect relationships?

7. Did your family keep secrets from the outside world? What was that experience like for you?
8. How do you think your family's cultural and religious background affected their beliefs regarding secret keeping?
9. Were there secrets that men kept or secrets that women kept?
10. Were there secrets in your family that were eventually disclosed? How did relationships shift? What was the impact on individual functioning and identity?

These kinds of questions are provided for each of the Focused Genograms described in this text. In the next three chapters, the Basic Genogram, the Family Map, and the Time Lines are described.

☐ Summary

The MFG insures that the clinician identifies the critical factors and areas of family functioning. For example, a clinician working with an acting-out adolescent in a step family might begin by looking at interactional patterns that are promoting acting-out behavior. The MFG expands the clinician's attention to the larger picture of this adolescent's life. Using the Cultural Focused Genogram, the adolescent who is the son of a recent immigrant may well have different issues than one who is from a Caucasian, fundamentalist, wealthy family. Culture, ethnicity, faith orientations, social class, gender, sexuality, attachments, and so forth are frameworks included in the MFG that define intergenerational contexts and play a significant role in shaping clinical interventions and treatment outcomes. Thus, each Focused Genogram provides a framework for analyzing and assessing important dimensions of the family.

Each Focused Genogram has a core group of themes that are recorded by either the sketch or table method, and these themes can be summarized on the Basic Genogram or a separate themes page. Each Focused Genogram contributes to the Family Map and the Time Line, or separate focused Family Maps and Time Lines are developed. Practitioners can construct MFGs in a systematic way, based on their own preferred style, to produce a detailed document outlining intergenerational legacies, family dynamics, and developmental themes.

Providing a method for enriching both the clinician's and the client's appreciation for the uniqueness of family patterns and dynamics, the MFG helps the clinician examine crucial features of psychosocial experience. The Focused Genograms included in this book cover a broad range of personal and life experience. Marriage and divorce patterns, race, gender roles, narcissistic vulnerability, and bonding are examples of themes addressed by the various Focused Genograms. Constructing the MFG is a systematic process that helps the therapist maintain a systemic, inter-personal, and individual perspective on the client's problems and needs. This chapter outlines the structure that therapists can use to undertake this comprehensive assessment process.

CHAPTER

2

Focused Genograms in Practice

In this chapter, the clinical usefulness of Focused Genograms is discussed further, along with an overview of the Focused Genograms presented in this text. Projective techniques that can be included in the MFG process also are outlined, as well as the use of the MFG outside behavioral health settings.

A Focused Genogram is a diagnostic and therapeutic process that is structured through a set of questions to explore a particularly salient aspect of the client's family system and process. The genogram is often the first step in a family journey that leads to individuation and possible restructuring of family alliances in the present. When clients explore patterns in their family systems they often gain insights that can lead to changes in attitudes and beliefs. These shifts in awareness often are accompanied by increases in motivations to change contemporary behavior.

Family theorists have written extensively on various ways that individuals can make contact with their families, with and without a therapist present, both for retrieving the past and for reconnecting and redefining family relationships in the here and now (Hof & Berman, 1989). Keeney (1983) stresses the importance of ecological assessment of family systems to distinguish and collect information among three basic levels of the family system: the behavior and characteristics of the individual, social relationships indicated by dyadic interaction, and social-group structures that organize the relations among dyadic interactions. Family Maps and Time Lines aid in assessing individual behavior and development as well as dyadic interaction. Each of the Focused Genograms provides a special lens to examine social relationships and structures within the family system.

The client must be prepared carefully for this process, because each theme may be a serious and important part of the problem the client is experiencing, as well as an opportunity for positive attitudinal, emotional, or behavioral change. First, the therapist and client should collaborate in creating the agenda for the sessions. If the client agrees to address a particular theme, the therapist explains the particular program she or he has in mind. The explanation can be general at the outset, with the therapist providing a rationale for the process and what is to be learned. In Chapters 6 through 10, theoretical background for each Focused Genogram is provided to give the clinician a broader perspective on the use of the Focused Genogram in clinical practice. The therapist should present a rationale that makes sense to the client, connecting his or her current presenting problem to past history. Some clients automatically see the value of talking about family history; others wonder why it is important to talk about something so "irrelevant" that happened "such a long time ago." The therapist should ensure that the client appreciates the value of the MFG before beginning.

It may be that the client's concern about "digging up the past" is an indicator of traumatic experiences or of displaced emotions or needs. The therapist can explain that people develop attitudes and behaviors based on what they experience in their lives. The experiences that are most significant in life are childhood and family relationships, peer and love relationships in adolescence and early adulthood, adult love relationships, and friendships. The client can be asked to think about how these formative experiences and relationships are useful to them and to discuss their clinical importance. A fully informed and educated client, who believes he or she is part of his or her own treatment planning, is a powerful ally.

As the Focused Genograms are completed, the themes and patterns often are noted on the Basic Genogram, or on a separate page, depending on the clinician's preference. Throughout the treatment process, however, the therapist can return to the Focused Genograms if new information is gathered. Time Lines can be updated and Family Maps modified. Therapeutic interventions can be guided by the increasing understanding that the therapist gains about the client and the family system. An understanding of the client rather than the application of a clinical model guide modifications in treatment strategy and approach using the MFG.

When the clinician creates specific Focused Genograms, Family Maps, or Time Lines depends upon the presenting problem, whether crisis intervention is required, the complexity of the family system, and the involvement of other helping professionals. Mary was referred for counseling concerning her son Michael, age 10, who was acting out in school and not doing well academically. There were severe marital issues (including two separations), two deaths, and a recent job change within the immediate family system. In this situation, the clinician chose to begin with a Time Line to identify family events and individual stresses. Then a Family Map exploring the family dynamics in play over Michael's school performance was developed. The Basic Genogram was used to explore academic patterns, birth order, and family rituals. Because the Family Map revealed patterns of intense conflict, the clinician next conducted the Anger Focused Genogram. In this case, the MFG became an organizing structure providing the clinician with a method to include information considered important in developing a treatment strategy.

☐ Focused Genograms

The exploration of family dynamics using the Focused Genogram is a very powerful approach to breaking through defense mechanisms and fostering insight into historically driven patterns of behavior.

Each Focused Genogram consists of a set of questions on a particular theme. However, Focused Genograms are much more than just a simple set of questions. The questions serve only as a starting point for discussion. The clinician should not just read off the questions on the list one by one but should use the topics to facilitate exploration of the client's perspective about himself or herself and his or her life situation. The genogram is not a substitute for establishing clinical rapport and alliance. It is a tool to help both therapist and client appreciate the complexity of the family system. The genogram is not a useful tool if it becomes cluttered and unfocused; the practitioner's attention then will be directed by other variables such as the theoretical model or the client's pressing concerns. The therapist can address specific topics using the Focused Genograms, each of which is written on separate pages, with the main advantage being that of keeping focused on one theme.

The strength of the MFG is that it directs the collection of details and information and insures that important conceptual themes are not overlooked. We have designed and identified five basic Focused Genograms as particularly helpful: the Attachments Genogram, the Emotions Genogram, the Anger Genogram, the Gender and Sexuality Genogram, and the Culture Genogram. Each Focused Genogram examines these areas in depth, based on research and clinical experience. Practitioners, however, are encouraged to create as many Focused Genograms as needed to address the unique needs of each client and to foster a meaningful therapeutic experience. Although there are core Focused Genograms, such as the Culture Genogram and the Gender Genogram, other Focused Genograms may be developed as needed, for example in the cases of spinal-cord injuries and crisis intervention. For clients struggling with issues related to work or career, a specific vocational or academic genogram may provide benefits.

Systems theory suggests that families attempt to balance themselves over time. In cases of severe stresses, families will spiral into more and more destructive patterns. Karen came for consultation because her 15-year-old daughter was depressed. During therapy, Karen learned that her daughter was being sexually harassed at school. Karen became anxious and seriously depressed as she tried to help her daughter cope with the challenges of standing up for herself and making decisions about transferring to a new school. As treatment progressed, Karen became more and more depressed. Exploring sexuality in the Gender Focused Genogram revealed patterns of sexual abuse in Karen's family of origin and extended family. Karen's depression was linked to denial and repression of her childhood and adolescent experiences. These experiences included sexual harassment by neighborhood boys, about which Karen had never told anyone. She reconstructed her own experience and shared it with her husband, Tom. He revealed to her a rape experience of his own that had taken place when he was 15 years old. Tom had never told anyone of his experience, either. The parents shared these experiences with each other for the first time and provided one another with needed support and empathy. Consequently, both parents provided their daughter with greater nurturing and advocacy.

Each Focused Genogram has a set of topics and questions. Each set of topical questions should be explored slowly and thoroughly—ideally after a therapeutic alliance has formed. Empathy is an important part of the interviewing and assessment process that fosters disclosure and comfort for the client. The therapist must rely on the client as a reliable reporter. In order to extract as much information as possible, the therapist must listen with a "third ear." A client may attempt to skim over a point or may say one thing but through facial expression or body posture reveal a hidden or deeper feeling. The therapist then can point out discrepancies in presentation to try to get to the deeper level. Clients can be encouraged to talk to their parents and siblings regarding their perceptions about a specific topic or issue. The therapist may choose to provide the client with lists of questions as the guide to getting this information. Sometimes parents or siblings are reluctant or unwilling to discuss family history or relationships. Clients can be encouraged to observe dynamics during family gatherings, speak with other family members (grandparents, aunts, uncles, and cousins), or present the inquiry as part of a project, similar to a "family tree" assignment often given to children at school.

Sometimes memory distortions occur in reporting historical events. This is due to the way emotional memories of traumatic events are stored in the brain (Goleman, 1995). Emotional relearning can take place only when emotional experiences are expressed and discussed. This concept is described in the discussion of the Emotions Genogram (Chapter 5). One way to stimulate more memories and increase their accuracy is looking at old photographs or videotapes of the family. The therapist asks the client to tell stories about the family at that time, what they were feeling, and what feelings they see expressed in the photographs. Sometimes the spouse or a significant other has long-term first-hand experience with the family, often possessing another view of how the family deals with specific issues.

Each of the Focused Genograms hones in on important aspects of a significant topic. The Basic Genogram examines family functioning based on standards of healthy family systems, sibling relationships, adoption, patterns of marriage and divorce, self-esteem, and health (including examination of alcoholism or other substance abuse). The Attachments Genogram examines touch, bonding, temperament, and attachment styles and scripts. The Emotions Genogram presents affect theory and assesses emotional patterns of fear, loss, and pleasure as well as a model for addressing emotions. The Anger Genogram examines patterns of anger expression, narcissistic vulnerability and rage, corporal punishment, and intimate violence. The Gender Genogram examines sexual identification and roles, sexuality, and romantic and love life patterns. The Cultural Genogram examines race, ethnicity, socioeconomic status, and religion.

Each Focused Genogram is part of, and contributes to, the MFG, giving the clinician and the client a larger systemic perspective. For example, the influences of culture and gender are explored and guide the clinician's attention to setting treatment goals. A first-generation American woman who grew up in an Italian family environment might be encouraged by her family to prioritize family life, while a women from an Irish family environment might be encouraged by her family to pursue independence to compensate for the predetermined failure of men. As these diverse people and circumstances are explored, the number of possible Focused Genograms is limited only by the creativity of the client and the therapist.

Frank was a successful businessman who had serious difficulty maintaining a commitment to his marriage. In detailing his family history in terms of culture, gender, love, sexuality, attachments, and emotional expression, his struggles, successes, and challenges in life became part of a much larger picture. Frank's response to having this larger perspective on his life was, "No wonder I have struggled with these issues. Look at where I come from! Now, how can I make some changes for myself and my family?" As Frank examined the recurring themes and patterns within his family system, he began to realize that his confusion about his relationship with his wife, his difficulty in enjoying his business success, and his periodic bouts of depression were not just a function of his personality. Frank could see how the patterns of marital dysfunction, ambivalence toward achievement, emotional cut-offs and incongruence, and historic family violence influenced his attitudes, feelings, and behaviors in his current life, especially as they related to commitment.

Frank also learned that there was a connection between his many spinster aunts and an abusive, volatile grandfather. Each aunt had been the recipient, as well as an observer, of serious physical abuse. In turn, Frank began to understand the hostility his mother had toward him and his father. He realized that his father's abusive behavior was a continuation of his mother's childhood trauma and that her hostility toward men had a base in the reality of her life. He also began to understand that he was not the source of his mother's disappointment and frustration and that he needed to explore the affect of domestic violence on himself and his wife and children. Further work with the emotions and Anger Genograms helped to develop therapeutic interventions.

☐ MFGs as a Projective Process

In addition to the semistructured format of the MFG and the Focused Genograms, a more projective and creative process of genogram construction is possible depending upon the practitioner's model and comfort with these techniques. In a projective genogram, the energy and creativity of the process is client-directed. During this projective process the client and therapist engage in a more open-ended exploration of the genogram, with more freedom of expression. Projective techniques add a perspective that is not addressed by observational or direct self-report techniques (L'Abate & Bagarozzi, 1993).

The clinician's rationale for using projective genogram methods is important, and projective genograms should only be conducted purposefully when therapeutically indicated. Projective genogram techniques provide clients a medium for exploration of thoughts, feelings, and behaviors within their family system. Significant issues and themes of abandonment, divorce, anger, loneliness, and abuse can be explored with this method. However, some clients find this medium more useful than others, depending on their learning styles.

In the projective genogram process, the client is encouraged to create the genogram on his or her own, with limited guidance. There is less structure and opportunity for more creativity. Large pieces of newsprint, color, paste, magazine pictures, and so forth can be used to provide an unlimited potential for a client to express thoughts and feelings about his or her family relationships and family history. The same basic symbols can be used, but there is no prescribed manner, spacing, coloring, size, or emphasis. The themes of the genogram are not predetermined, although the therapist generally must provide some basic guidance.

Kaslow (1995) has developed the projective genogram as a clinical technique. After the genogram is completed by the client, Kaslow suggests that the clinician asks a series of questions based on these general questions: (1) With whom did you begin? Why? (2) Whom did you omit or exclude? Why? (3) Whom would you like to eliminate? Why? (4) Whom would you like to add? Why? These questions provide the practitioner with opportunity to assess the family system from a unique vantage point.

Use of Color

Lewis (1989) encourages enhancement of the genogram through color coding. Colors are randomly assigned by clients and used to express a range of issues. Pink might represent a dependent personality, red could represent violent expression of anger, and orange could represent substance abuse. Colorless family members can help evoke meaningful clinical information. Assigning colors to family members is no simple exercise and can evolve into a therapeutic challenge for the client. The discussion of the rationale for choosing a particular color for a particular person can be a revealing and rewarding aspect of the therapeutic process.

Art Techniques

Art techniques in genogram construction can be very useful and enhance the clinician's assessment of the client system. A few techniques are listed here as suggestions, based on L'Abate and Bagarozzi's (1993) review of the most frequently used techniques.

Family Art Therapy

Art therapists have introduced a variety of techniques into family treatment. Kwiatkowska (1978) developed a comprehensive and empirically based art evaluation procedures that includes six drawings: a freestyle picture, a picture of the family, an abstract portrait of the family, a picture developed from a scribble, a joint family mural, and a freestyle scribble. Art techniques generally encourage drawing the family-of-origin using whatever symbolic imagery comes to mind. Some art techniques include asking clients to use their nondominant hands for the drawings.

Family Sculpting

Satir (1967) is best known for the use of experiential techniques, and she developed the family sculpting method. This method has participants act out in role playing the various roles of the family members in a physical way. In addition to family sculpting, Satir developed the "parts party," an experiential technique to foster self-exploration. In the parts party, the client identifies six to eight famous people that represent different aspects of his or her personality. These parts are role-played in a group format by other people. The purpose of the parts party and sculpting is to use physical movement and space to portray personal and family dynamics and roles. The family sculpture test is a variation of sculpting and was developed by Kvebaek (1974). It is a projective assessment instrument, which Bagarozzi and L'Abate (1993) suggest is effective with very young children.

Kuethe Felt-Figure Technique

This technique, developed in the 1960s (Kuethe, 1964), involves the use of a felt board and figures that represent a man, woman, child, dog, cat, rectangle, triangle, and circle. The client arranges the various pieces and the placement is then assessed for themes and patterns. Similar to the family sculpture test, the felt-figure technique is a projective test with guidelines for interpretation provided by the author.

Use of Photographs and Videos

Family therapists have adopted the technique of using photographs to reveal family members' feelings about past experiences (Kaslow & Friedman, 1977). Photographs foster reminiscence of personal and family experiences, and video recordings of family events are also useful in reviewing past relationship patterns. Videos can be especially helpful with clients who do not recall past experience. Both photographs and videos provide the clinician with factual and historical data, as well as subjective data. When exploring such visual material with the client, questions such as the following may be helpful.

1. When was the photograph taken?
2. What do you remember from that time?

3. What do you think of the expressions on the faces of the various family members?
4. Tell a story about the photograph.
5. What were you feeling in the photo? Is your feeling congruent with the situation?
6. What does the photo tell you about the family relationships?
7. What is the same or different now in these relationships?

☐ Use of the MFG Outside of Psychotherapy

The genogram not only is useful in clinical practice but also can be used in medical practice and business and organizational settings. Time constraints in medical practice often preclude the extensive exploration that the MFG provides. However, briefer exploration of a specific Focused Genogram can help the medical practitioner identify psychosocial aspects of medical illness. Although physicians often explore family history of illness during the diagnostic process, this is often where the use of the genogram ends. Genetic counselors have extensively used the genogram in assessing genetic patterns and preventive counseling.

In business settings, a modified MFG is a useful tool to examine historical organizational patterns, developmental themes and stresses, and interpersonal dynamics between individuals or departments. The systematic thematic approach of the Focused Genograms can be used to explore organizational dynamics. Family-owned businesses, in particular, can benefit from the comprehensiveness of the MFG to identify sources of strength, conflict, and strain.

☐ Summary

Providing a method to zoom in on significant topics of interest to the client and clinician, Focused Genograms are lenses that amplify the detail and richness of a client system. The semistructured interview questions help the practitioner clarify strengths, deficiencies, and delays that require therapeutic intervention, depending upon his or her theoretical framework. Based on either clinical judgment or experience or supervisory guidance, the therapist can choose which Focused Genogram to use as a starting point. As Focused Genograms are explored, the clinician creates an MFG, which can be used as a guide for treatment planning or as an integral part of treatment with the client.

The construction of Focused Genograms and the MFG is not a rigid, predetermined process. Not only have genograms been used in a variety of settings, such as family business development, but many projective methods have been developed that can be used during the Focused Genogram process as well. The clinician's comfort and familiarity determine the specific techniques. Clinicians, therefore, are encouraged to add the MFG to their clinical toolbox because it adds to their current interviewing process and style. The goal of creating an MFG is to broaden the systemic assessment and to improve therapeutic interventions.

II

BASIC COMPONENTS OF THE MULTIFOCUSED FAMILY GENOGRAM

CHAPTER 3

The Basic Genogram

As presented in Chapter 1, the Basic Genogram is the organizing genogram for the MFG and the template for the Focused Genograms. Keeping in mind that the MFG allows for a comprehensive individual and family assessment, the Basic Genogram begins the process by providing the clinician an overview of the level of functioning for the family system. The specific topics that are explored in the Basic Genogram include overall assessment of functioning, marriage and divorce patterns, affairs, birth order, adoption, infertility and pregnancy loss, self-esteem, health and illness, and addictions.

This chapter uses a structure that is used in the chapters on Focused Genograms. The first part of the chapter briefly describes each theme, and then a series of questions is provided that serves as a guide for the practitioner. Thus, each theme for each Focused Genogram has been deconstructed to help the therapist explore these topics. Then, to aid clinicians' formulation of hypotheses, we present a selected overview of pertinent theory related to the foci of the particular Focused Genogram. In this chapter, we begin with the themes of the Basic Genogram, as commonly described in the literature.

☐ Overall Assessment of Family Functioning

The Basic Genogram helps the clinician identify the family's level of functioning on a continuum from dysfunctional to healthy. This is a useful step in establishing treatment goals. Drawn from a variety of models, clinical experience, and collaboration with colleagues and students over the years, the following list of questions is a compilation of the factors to be considered in assessing basic family functioning. These features can be assessed regardless of the family style (intact family, single parent household, blended family, etc.). These questions may be asked at various phases during the treatment process, but they are important in establishing a basic understanding of the client system, and practitioners are encouraged to make them part of the basic interview process for a systemic assessment of the client's psychosocial network. This set of questions examines family structure and process, providing a perspective on the family's functioning.

Questions About Level of Family Functioning

1. What are the patterns of expressing appreciation?
2. What are the patterns of time together, and how is family life structured to insure that time is spent together?
3. Is communication direct, open, and congruent?
4. Do family members express concern for each other's happiness and well being?
5. Is there a commitment to a spiritual lifestyle?
6. What ability do family members exhibit to cope with crisis?
7. Is good self-esteem promoted, and how?
8. Are family rules and expectations clear and expressed?
9. What are the individual family member's links to the wider community? How effective are they in these roles?
10. Are there firm parental coalitions?
11. Are there high levels of initiation for contact and activity within the family system?
12. Does the family encourage individual uniqueness as well as understanding for individual needs and motives?
13. Are there strong kinship bonds?
14. Is there a clear work and achievement orientation?
15. Are the family system and its members adaptable and flexible?
16. Is there physical and emotional closeness and attunement between and among family members?

17. Do family members provide support, security, and encouragement to one another?

Responses to these questions can be placed on a continuum from extremely dysfunctional to extremely functional to aid the clinician in developing a global impression of family functioning.

☐ Marital Patterns, Divorce, and Extramarital Affairs

The legal, spiritual, or common-law marriage of two individuals forms the core of the family structure. Patterns of marriage, divorce, and affairs are important and form the basis of family stability. In this section we provide an overview of marriage patterns. Sexuality and romantic love patterns are presented in greater detail in Chapter 9.

Questions for Marital Patterns, Divorce, and Extramarital Affairs

1. What are the patterns of marriage and divorce in the family system? If there are divorces, what are the known circumstances about the divorces?
2. What types of marriages are there in the family system? Have family members participated in premarital counseling or marital therapy?
3. What are the patterns of sexual infidelity in the family system? Are there reconciliations? Were any children born of these liaisons? Are there secrets about infidelity?
4. What kinds of stresses have resulted for the family if there has been a divorce?
5. How have parents worked out custody and visitation?

Affairs often are implicated in marital problems. Westfall (1989) delineated eleven factors to differentiate affairs, and questions can be asked on these topics to assess extramarital affairs in more depth:

Type (heterosexual/homosexual) and level of sexual activity (flirting, petting, intercourse)

Frequency and duration, as well as location of extramarital sex (EMS) activities

Number of EMS partners (past and present)

Unilateral or bilateral nature of EMS

Degree of secrecy surrounding EMS

Degree of acceptance of and consent for EMS behavior in the marriage by both spouses

Degree of emotional involvement with and commitment to the EMS partner

Relationship of the nonparticipating spouse to the EMS partner

Degree of spouses' emotional involvement with and commitment to each other

Tolerance of EMS behavior within the couple's ethnic community or social group

Timing of and special circumstances surrounding the revelation of the EMS

☐ Birth Order

Sibling position and role, often referred to as *birth order*, affects individual development and personality in a number of ways. These questions focus attention on this area of family life:

Questions About Birth Order

1. What is the birth order in your family-of-origin?
2. What is the spacing between siblings? Was spacing planned? Are there half-siblings, stepsiblings?
3. What is the gender of the siblings? Was there an expressed preference for males or females?
4. What are the temperaments of the siblings?
5. Which siblings are most similar to one another and which siblings were most different from one another?
6. Who is like mother, father, grandparent, aunt, uncle, or other relative?

☐ Adoption, Infertility, and Pregnancy Loss

Adoption is another facet of birth order. Following are issues and themes to be taken into consideration when examining the affects of adoption.

Questions About Adoption

1. Who were the birth parents? What beliefs exist about young unwed parents, abusive or neglectful parents, or biological parents in general?

2. How was infertility addressed? What methods were attempted to achieve pregnancy, if any? What was the decision-making process? Were family reactions explored?
3. Regarding the adoption were there difficulties with other children in the family (if there were any), school problems, secrecy, inheritance issues, behavior problems, parent-child "mismatch," older children?

Questions About Infertility, Pregnancy, and Pregnancy Loss

Eunpu (1995), a genetics counselor, developed questions that further explore these issues. She suggests that infertility is a significant developmental crisis for couples often omitted from family therapy texts. The following questions help address this important issue in family life.

1. What is the family's expectation regarding childbearing (i.e., number, timing of first child, spacing between, timing of last child)?
2. What messages did you receive from family members about the importance or role of children?
3. What messages did you receive from family members about abortion and contraception?
4. Were there conflicts between family attitudes or beliefs and those of your community, cultural, or religious group?
5. What messages, myths, or beliefs did you receive about pregnancy loss?
6. What were your family's experiences of pregnancy loss or of childhood death?
7. What does it mean not to meet your family's expectations for childbearing?

Combined, the exploration of birth order, adoption, fertility, and fetal loss provide a broad scope of the potential affects of siblings on clients and their sense of self.

☐ Self-esteem

Self-esteem, also referred to as *self-concept* and *self-identity*, shapes and is shaped by family relationships. Satir (1967) believed self-esteem to be the foundation of family life, with level of self-esteem having widespread effects throughout the family system. The following questions help determine whether family members have secure high self-esteem or if self-esteem is low.

Questions About Self-esteem

1. What are the patterns of uniqueness, belonging, power, and role models within the family?
2. Who are the heroes and heroines in the family? Who are the "scapegoats" and "black sheep" in the family?
3. What are the patterns of employment, career, and academic performance within the family?
4. Who is and is not financially successful in the family? How is financial success defined?
5. What are the patterns of community and social involvement?
6. What are the patterns for leisure and hobbies?
7. Is there a balance in the family system between work and enjoyment?
8. What are the patterns of spiritual affiliation and expression?

☐ Health and Illness

Assessing patterns of illness and death due to illness is common in medical practice and useful in family therapy. Assigning death dates and causes of deaths often can reveal important family history. Eunpu (1997) developed questions appropriate in cases of genetic illnesses and diseases that are useful regardless of the specific health problem:

Questions About Patterns of Health and Illness

1. What are the patterns of illness in the family?
2. What are the known causes of death? Are there mysteries about how family members died?
3. Are there genetic illnesses within the family?

Questions About Health Illness Beliefs and Attitudes

These are especially appropriate if there is a genetically affected family member (Eunpu, 1997).

1. Who was regarded as affected (sick or ill) in your family?
2. Who believed himself or herself affected?
3. What messages did you receive from family members about the diagnosis?

4. What were the attitudes of family members to those who were or are affected?
5. What obligations or loyalties were created by the presence of an affected family member?
6. What is the meaning of doing something different regarding the genetic risk in your family (e.g., having or not having testing, terminating a pregnancy)?

☐ Addictions

Patterns of illness and death, however, are too narrow of a lens. Addictions, which affect individual health as well as family functioning, may pervade and demolish family life. Milkman and Sunderworth (1987) identified four styles of addiction: arousal seekers (gambling, sex, work, shoplifting, cocaine); satiation addicts (sedatives, food, alcohol, opiates, shopping, TV, computers); addicts (rock climbing, skydiving, airplanes); and fantasy addicts (sex, relationship). The consequences of addictions include lowered self-esteem, promiscuous sexual behavior resulting in sexually transmitted diseases and AIDS, and financial disaster for gamblers and telephone sex addicts, as well as family turmoil and dissolution, career and work difficulties, loss of friends, and loneliness. Genograms are very useful in detailing intergenerational patterns of addiction and identifying vulnerabilities. Behind an addiction a clinician will often find depression, bipolar disorder, post-traumatic stress disorder, or adult attention-deficit hyperactivity disorder. Many practitioners believe that active addictions must be treated before other family and personal issues can be addressed.

Questions About Addictions

These also can be translated to drugs, gambling, sex, and so forth.

1. Is alcohol a problem in the family system? How widespread is the problem? What types of alcoholism exist—alpha, beta, gamma, delta, epsilon—or what are the characteristics of the alcoholic behavior (see description elsewhere in this chapter)? If yes, how has the problem been addressed? Have family members participated in Alcoholics Anonymous? Have there been hospitalizations for detoxification?
2. Is drug use—illicit as well as prescription drugs—a problem in the family? By whom? To what extent? Has there been treatment intervention?

3. What kinds of addictions exist in the family: arousal, satiation, super-reality, fantasy?
4. What are the patterns of psychiatric disorders: depression, bipolar disorder, post-traumatic stress disorder, adult attention-deficit hyperactivity disorder? Do individuals seek treatment? How does the family handle this?
5. What other addictions exist in the family: gambling, shopping, food, or so forth?

☐ Other Issues in the Basic Genogram

Many health-related disorders and difficulties are found in families. These disorders are examined using the Basic Genogram. Eating disorders are one example of how the Basic Genogram is adapted. First, the clinician needs to obtain background information about the difficulty under consideration. It is useful to review the literature about a problem. In the case of eating disorders, there are no universal features; however, Giat-Roberto (1986) identified the following frequently occurring features: lack of sustained conflict and conflict resolution; disqualification of messages using rejection, confusion, or denial (producing poor conflict resolution); coopting of the symptomatic daughter into parental distress; enmeshment with adulation from the outside world; overprotection; detouring of family conflict into psychosomatic symptoms; importance of appearance consciousness; and symbolic meanings of food and eating. In families with an identified bulimic legacy revolve around weight, attractiveness, fitness and success, and eating of food. Often food is prepared by the mother and her culinary skill (and knowledge of nutrition) is seen as her major achievement and value—vomiting up the food right after mealtime becomes viewed as an act of rejecting her. The father's emphasis is on achievement and a secure and successful home. Genograms of the extended family often show traumatic loss in the third and fourth generations, often involving financial ruin, expatriation, separation from the nuclear family, chronic (treated or neglected) illness, and death. Surviving grandparents and the second generation show a determination to make up for, cover over, and overcome these losses at all costs, although discussion of these may be forbidden. Attractiveness, physical fitness, and general appearance-consciousness become enmeshed with the familial mandate to get ahead, do the family proud, and be a model wife, daughter, or mother. Based on identifying these patterns and characteristics, the clinician can develop his or her own list of questions to explore with the client.

Questions About Eating Disorders

1. What is the family's communication style?
2. What are the issues around weight, achievement, and success?
3. Are there traumatic losses in past generations?

☐ The "Basics" of the Basic Genogram: Theoretical Underpinnings

The questions of the Basic Genogram yield a tremendous amount of data for the practitioner to consider as the treatment process proceeds. Each of the themes of the Basic Genogram also can be explored in greater depth. In this section, we provide a selected review of pertinent issues that are addressed by the Basic Genogram. Reflecting the biases of the authors, salient aspects of theory have been selected that may be helpful to both beginning and experienced clinicians.

Family Functioning

As Fleck, Quinlan, Jalali, and Rosenheck (1988) note, family assessment is a stepchild in the fields of psychiatry and family therapy. They identify five parameters that describe family dynamics: leadership, boundaries, affect, communication, and task and goal performance. In contrast, the McMaster model of family functioning, a clinically oriented model, identifies six dimensions of family functioning: problem solving, communication, roles, affective responsiveness, affective involvement, behavior control, and general functioning (Epstein, Baldwin, & Bishop, 1983). A third model, the circumplex model of family functioning (Olson, Russell, & Sprenkle, 1983), a research-based model, identifies family cohesion, adaptability, and communication as the essential aspects of family functioning. Family cohesion is defined as the emotional bonding that family members have toward one another. Family adaptability is the ability of a marital or family system to change its power structure, role relationship, and relationship rules in response to situational and developmental stress (Olson et al., 1983). Consolidating the findings of earlier work on indicators of successful family functioning, these models are useful in determining a family system's overall level of functioning.

Marital Patterns, Divorce, and Extramarital Affairs

Patterns of marriage and divorce form the essential rubric for the Basic Genogram. In many families, multiple marriages and divorces create a confusing pedigree. At the same time, it is not uncommon to work with clients whose grandparents or parents had arranged marriages and whose social networks were an integral part of the family system. Immigrants from some countries are still influenced by arranged marriage customs. Genograms can become especially complicated if brothers marry sisters or a man marries his stepmother's sister, for example. The marriage lens provides another way to examine these patterns.

Along with marriage patterns within the family, divorce patterns are important to explore. Until the divorce reform movement of the 1970s, divorce doctrine could only be understood by examining the long history of English divorce law, which was dominated by concepts of canon law, the influence of the Roman Catholic origins of English domestic-relations law. Traditionally, divorce was fault-based—an innocent, injured spouse was able to end a marriage typically on the grounds of adultery, desertion, habitual drunkenness, criminal behavior, impotence, or cruel treatment. By the mid-20th century, many state legislatures recognized some no-fault grounds for divorce. During the 1970s, divorce reform focused on granting divorce when marriages were "irretrievably broken." No-fault divorce is currently the standard in all states; however, child custody and property distribution still create significant stress for families. When divorce is a theme in a particular family, understanding the time period in which the divorce took place and how decisions were made is important.

Many families experience separation and divorce. The divorce process and the dissolution of a marriage often create havoc within a family. Erosion of the marriage, which usually takes place over a period of years, is replaced by ambivalence toward the marriage and emotional turmoil. With the marital breakup, there is often a tremendous amount of anger as each partner strengthens his or her commitment to divorce. As the divorce proceeds, sadness, loss, and grief mix with the anger as the reality of the family break-up takes hold. Children usually struggle with intense loyalty conflicts that can be exacerbated if parents want a child to "take sides." Divorce is never a complete emotional break, and families often contend with the dynamics of previous marriages.

Single-parent families often suffer most from economic deprivation due to the need for two incomes to support a family. However, the most commonly stated negative aspect of single parent homes is the consequence of parental absence for socialization and supervision of children. For sons, the absence of the father undermines sex-role identity. Mother's absence creates a range of emotional difficulties including depression.

Birth Order

Many clinicians believe that identifying and exploring birth order and sibling roles is an essential part of family systems intervention. Toman (1988), who conducted research on family constellation patterns and their effects, emphasizes the importance of family dynamics on personality dynamics. Perlmutter (1988) encourages clinicians to explore sibling bonds and roles rather than assume that the ecology of the sibling subsystem is simply a reflection of parental functioning. Believing that these sibling effects have a profound consequence on society as a whole, as well, Sulloway (1996) suggests that family patterns have affects on personality due to the consequences of sibling competition on individual development.

Hoopes and Harper (1987) identified more than 20 assumptions about the sibling system and birth order. Many of these assumptions are useful to keep in mind when developing the Basic Genogram. They suggest that multigenerational family structure, process, and development significantly influence sibling positions and experiences and that siblings are influenced by the unresolved emotional issues of their parents; the uniqueness of the family environment at the time of each child's birth shapes the characteristic response patterns for each sibling position; siblings are assigned separate, unique, permanent, functional family system roles when they are born into the family; every sibling position has an identity and a sense of well-being characteristic of that position; after the fourth sibling, the position patterns begin to repeat, with the responses taking into consideration the increased complexity of the family; twins and other multiple-birth siblings may receive role assignments characteristic of the order in which they are born, or they may receive blurred role assignments; spacing of siblings has an unspecifiable affect on the characteristic response patterns for the basic sibling positions; the gender of the sibling affects the way in which a role is performed rather than what the role is; deletions or additions of siblings may alter or blur the role assignments of sibling positions (likewise, deletions or additions of parents affect the way in which siblings assume their roles); and, sometimes characteristic response patterns for two or more sibling positions appear to be similar, but the motivational factors are different.

Sibling positions are functional and only become dysfunctional if exaggerated, blocked, or distorted by family life events. Although his model was neither systematic nor comprehensive, Adler was the first to recognize the psychological affects of birth order (Toman, 1992). Stewart and Steward (1995) examined trends in birth-order research and found that through the 1970s to the mid-1980s topics such as achievement, intelligence, personality, and psychopathology received attention. They found that birth-order research evolved toward increased emphasis on cross-cultural factors, parent-child interactions, development, and family relations. Romeo (1994) suggests that birth order is a useful frame of reference for teachers to assist them in understanding children in the classroom. Dolega (1981) also found differences in school adaptation of first graders between firstborn, secondborn, and thirdborn children.

Studying political attitudes, Eisenman and Sirgo (1991) found that all the firstborn females in their study identified themselves as liberals. Their study suggested that liberals favored nonrestrictive controls both on self and on children, while conservatives tended to favor the opposite. Nelson and Harris (1995) tested the hypotheses that firstborn children have a higher need affiliation, higher group orientation, and membership in more organizations and a higher grade-point average than later-born children. They did not find significance on affiliation needs or group orientation; however, they found that firstborn children did hold more membership and demonstrated higher grade-point averages than those born later. Similarly, Dhillon (1989) found that leadership style seems to be determined by ordinal position and sex. Sulloway (1996) reaffirms that eldest children identify with parents and authority and support the status quo, whereas young children rebel against it.

Birth-order effects are summarized as follows (Ansbacher & Ansbacher, 1956; Hoopes & Harper, 1987):

Firstborn children tend to be overachievers and underachievers, function within the rules, are good with adults, tend to be more analytic and rational, do well in the eyes of others, and are linked to continuous productivity.

Secondborn children, being aware of underlying structure, need to have well-defined boundaries in unique places, and they pay attention to the emotions and needs of others.

Thirdborn children pay attention to the marital relationship and maintain dyadic rules, in and out of relationships.

Fourthborn children are responsible for family unity, harmony, purpose, and goals; connect with everyone; and are impulsive and highly demonstrative, with warmth and closeness expressed openly.

Youngest children are generally the most pampered and subject to spoiling, but due to stimulation and many chances for cooperation youngest children can become quite successful.

Only children grow up as the center of attention and often in a family environment that is anxious; only children tend to be pampered by their mothers and have difficulties when they are not the center of attention.

As this overview suggests, sibling issues are an important aspect of assessment.

Adoption

Adoption is another aspect of family structure and process that is examined by the Basic Genogram. The historical and sociolegal context of secrecy in adoption has affected the ways in which these issues are addressed within the family. Because adoption has a lifetime impact on all the members of the family, it is important to assess the ways in which adoption shapes family development. Decisions regarding search and reunion with biological parents are an important part of consolidating the adoptee's identity. Divorce, single-parenthood, remarriage, and various forms of dual parenting also impact adoptive families. Identifying the effects of age at adoption is part of the assessment process.

Stresses for adoptive families involve revocation of consent; knowledge of adoption; questions of the rights of the adoptee, the biological parents, the adoptive parents, and the grandparents; pressures to open sealed adoption records; and the innovative practice of surrogate motherhood (Hartman & Laird, 1990; Hartman, 1993). Families also can struggle with powerlessness and empowerment, the salience of adoption, the "bad seed" myth, the adoption story, kidnapping guilt, the "perfect parent" requirement, cut-offs and connections, and leaving home (Sonne, 1980). These are important issues for the therapist to review with the client.

Infertility and Pregnancy Loss

The inability to conceive, miscarriage, or stillbirth creates stress for a couple who desires to have children. Eunpu (1995) encourages professional attention to these issues because of their effect on individual, interactional, and intergenerational functioning. Her treatment recommendations include treating the couple as a unit, educational services to make important decisions about treatment and family-building alternatives, improving assertiveness skill for dealing with medical specialists throughout infertility evaluation and treatment, supportive counseling, stress-reduction techniques, bibliotherapy, and identifying support systems within the family and community.

Self-esteem

Mental health is a state characterized by psychological well-being and self-acceptance. Human well-being and the sense of having worth or value are intimately connected. Usually included in the definition of self-esteem is the capacity to love and relate to others, the ability to work productively, and the willingness to behave in a way that brings personal satisfaction without encroaching upon the rights of others. The developmental processes of self-esteem are not well understood, although the psychological structures that regulate self-esteem are believed to emerge out of the early positive affective expressions and states of well-being in childhood. The Attachments Genogram provides a special focus on these areas of life. However, mastery in life, which can be defined as the subjective satisfaction that accompanies the achievement of a task a person considers worth doing (Mack & Ablon, 1983), and the development of self-confidence build on small accomplishments.

At every stage of life, self-esteem determines action, learning, relationship, feelings, and productivity. Self-esteem is both a conscious experience, accessible to introspection and description, and an unconscious process, reflecting a person's inner psychic structure (Cotton, 1983). Many studies have shown the correlation between self-esteem and achievement in school. Six developmental trends characterize the growth of self-esteem in general: self-esteem lowers as a person moves from one developmental stage to another; self-esteem is enhanced as each developmental period is successfully negotiated; the period of formation of the self is a sensitive period for positive self-esteem; during the course of development, the individual shifts from relying exclusively on external sources of self-esteem to greater dependence on internal structures; self-esteem will always depend to some extent on recognition, validation, and praise from external sources; and during periods of "new learning" there is a return to external sources of self-esteem with a telescoped recapitulation of the shift from external to internal sources of self-esteem (Cotton, 1983). These transitions trigger demons of childhood consciousness (Gould, 1978), which can result in limiting love relationships and not realizing one's talents.

Self-esteem is the feeling of satisfaction with oneself that arises when a person's needs are satisfied. Needs are met in two ways: by using personal capabilities and resources to influence an event, and by the environment providing the necessary conditions to enable personal accomplishments. Family-of-origin influences are expressed not only in personal relationships but also in work, civic, and community groups. Weinberg and Mauksch (1991) use the genogram technique in a workshop format to help people identify and assess family-of-origin influences as they relate to work stress.

Mastery in life is essential for correcting weaknesses in self-representations, self-esteem, and character. Mastery fosters emotional maturity, which raises self-esteem and further promotes motivations to work, love, play, and create. Motivation is accomplished in three ways: by fear, by incentive, by positive mental attitude. The work of Hill, Stone, Ziglar, and Covey addresses the importance of positive mental attitude in life. Covey (1989) specifies the character ethic as a basic principle of effective living: True success and enduring happiness come only if proactive principals are integrated into one's life emphasizing the importance of cooperation, living by conscience, competence, and love.

Health and Illness

The use of the genogram to explore illnesses, diseases, and genetic disorders, beyond that described previously, is beyond the scope of this text. However, patterns of health and illness are an important part of the Basic Genogram and often are included in medical family histories. Unfortunately, health is a factor that often is overlooked unless there is a serious or terminal illness that affects family functioning. Both psychiatric and physical illnesses are important components of the health-and-illness focus of the Basic Genogram.

Addictions

One of the first stages in treatment that the therapist must address is the presence of addictions within the client system. Addictions can control and destroy the individual as well as the family. Alcoholism treatment, strongly influenced by Alcoholics Anonymous, has become the standard for treating the wide variety of addictions. Therapists need to have a basic understanding of these concepts when they use a family systems perspective, in order to assess the degree of addictive patterns in the family system.

Alcoholism can be defined as a chronic disease that carries with it a universally recognizable set of symptoms, including impaired control over drinking, preoccupation with the drug alcohol, use of alcohol despite adverse consequences, and distortions of thinking, most notably denial. Symptoms can be continuous or periodic, and although it is often progressive and at times fatal, alcoholism is treatable (West, 1997). Alcoholism is considered a progressive illness with early and late stages; it takes many forms and crosses age, gender, social, educational, and cultural boundaries. There is evidence that alcoholism is genetically predetermined, with males more predisposed to become alcoholic. According to West (1997), hospitalized patients were most likely to be between the ages of 45 and 64 years. One of the most persistent symptoms of alcoholism is the blackout. Those who have developed a high physical tolerance to alcohol, which develops over a period of years, usually experience blackouts.

The extent and predictors of alcoholism are unknown. Most professionals in the alcohol treatment field believe that environment acts as a trigger to the onset of alcoholism in an already genetically predisposed person. Jellinek (1960) developed a taxonomy of alcoholism that has been useful in clinical practice. He denoted his categories as alpha, beta, gamma, delta, and epsilon alcoholism. These categories can help the clinician sort out the extent of addictions within the family.

Alpha alcoholism is characterized by the presence of symptoms such as hangovers or blackouts and by psychological, but not physical, dependence. Beta alcoholism is characterized by physical symptoms, such as ulcers or liver disease, but not by physical dependence. In beta alcoholism drinking remains stable in terms of quantity consumed and the relative absence of psychological and social problems. Gamma alcoholism includes both symptoms and physical dependence (in late stages). Gamma alcoholics develop tolerance to alcohol and experience withdrawal symptoms if they stop drinking; they are alcohol-dependent. They suffer emotional and psychological impairment; their social and economic functioning is compromised. Gamma alcoholism is a chronic, progressive disease and creates the prototypical alcoholic. Delta alcoholism is characterized by physical dependence. Delta alcoholism is typical of heavy wine or beer drinkers who do not lose control nor do they get drunk or pass out. They cannot stop without withdrawal symptoms, however, and consequently there is a physical addiction. Epsilon alcoholism is also called *binge* or *periodic drinking*. The binge alcoholic goes on binges that end in collapse, and then he or she does not drink until the next binge. These intervals vary; they may be constant or erratic. These types are not completely discreet; however, they provide a framework for assessing the type of alcoholism that an individual may have.

Differentiating alcohol abuse, alcohol dependence, and social drinking is important in family assessment. Because of the pervasive use, and misuse, of alcohol, therapists often are asked about the addiction status of a spouse or child. If alcoholism, or drug addiction, is present and active within the family, the therapist must attend to these issues.

West (1997) defines *alcohol abuse* as a pattern of drinking that leads to the failure to fulfill responsibilities at work, home, or school, or repeated drinking in situations in which it is physically hazardous, such as driving a car or flying a plane. Alcohol dependence, on the other hand, may include abuse, but it is a pattern of alcohol use that can be characterized by a drinker's increase in tolerance and signaled by the withdrawal syndrome, which is a cluster of physical and psychological symptoms following the reduction or cessation of drinking, or by persistent but unsuccessful attempts to cut down, or even quit drinking altogether. The cardinal features of alcohol dependence are compulsion (inability to refrain from taking that drink), loss of control over alcohol (inability to quit), and continued drinking no matter what the consequences (West, 1997).

The *Diagnostic and Statistical Manual of Mental Disorders* (fourth edition), published by the American Psychiatric Association (1994) to guide psychiatrists and others in diagnosing mental and emotional problems, offers a questionnaire to assess the behavioral danger signs of substance abuse.

Fanning and O'Neill (1996) have identified seven forms of denial of addictions that are commonly seen and heard in clinical practice:

1. Stonewalling: "I don't have a problem, I can handle it, I'm not hooked—I can quit any time I want. Leave me alone—it's my business. I'm not hurting anyone but myself. So what?"
2. Minimizing: "Sure I drink [smoke, snort, etc.], but it's not a problem. It was just a little dent in the car. At least I didn't hit anyone. It's no big deal. At least I didn't behave as badly as [someone else]. I made it home all right. Everything must have been okay. It will be all right if I just apologize and cool it for a while."
3. Blaming: "It's not the booze, coke, pills, etc., it's the stress, coffee, cigarettes, allergies, medication, etc. It wasn't my fault—it was someone else's fault for getting me drunk. I need it because of my bad back (nerves, rotten childhood, etc.). My wife, husband, mom, kid, etc. drive me to it. I would have been all right if I hadn't mixed drinks, drank on an empty stomach, been sold coke cut with speed, etc."
4. Excusing: "I'm self-medicating. It helps me relax, cope with pain, digest, etc. It's been a day that would drive anyone to drink. I got carried away because I was so happy, sad, mad, upset, nervous, etc. Everybody makes mistakes once in a while. I'll have just one drink, hit, etc., to steady my nerves. I must be doing okay—I always get to work on time, manage to cook dinner, finish assignments, pick up the kids, etc. I'm not hung over. I have a touch of flu, food poisoning, etc. My mom and dad and all my aunts and uncles and cousins drink. It's practically a family tradition. I'm under an incredible amount of stress right now. We're Irish—what do you expect?"
5. Rationalizing: "A nightcap will help me sleep and if I get a good night's sleep, I won't feel such a strong need to drink tomorrow. I need the hair of the dog that bit me. It's hot, cold, rainy, nice, etc., let's have

one. I'm already loaded. One more won't make any difference. I'll quit tomorrow. I deserve a reward. I need one for the road."

6. Distracting: "Alcohol and drugs aren't the cause of my problems, they're just a symptom of my crazy life. I don't know why I have this strange pain [when one knows it is probably an ulcer or liver damage caused by alcohol]. We need more fiber in our diet [when one knows drinking causes diarrhea or constipation]. My allergies are awful today [when one has the coke sniffles]. You'd drink too if you had my life. Let me tell you about. . ."

7. Attacking: "You've got a lot of nerve talking about my drinking! Get off my back! As soon as I unwind a little, you're breathing down my neck. You're just like my mother—nag, nag, nag. I'll stop doping, drinking, smoking, etc., when you stop throwing money away, get a job, stop crying all the time, stop cheating on me, etc. Why don't you clean up this dump instead of counting my drinks? And who wrecked the car, ran over his own dog, set the mattress on fire, etc.?"

These are important signals that clinicians can attend to during treatment. If addictions are present, all other interventions are compromised. Ignoring, or disregarding, warning signs of addictions in the client's family system can lead to a breakdown in the treatment process as well as significant lost time.

☐ Summary

The Basic Genogram focuses on overall family functioning and is the template for each of the Focused Genograms. Patterns of marriage and divorce, sibling order, adoption, and mental and physical well-being of family members are assessed. Beginning the genogram process with this lens provides the clinician with a method to explore family cohesion and family adaptability. Both are crucial to understanding the particular idiosyncrasies of the client's intergenerational, interpersonal, and individual life experience.

Because family-of-origin influences also are expressed in work, civic, and community affiliations, the Basic Genogram incorporates these areas as well. Addictions are a specific focus because of their often insidious and pernicious impact upon the family system. With the information gleaned from this part of the MFG, the clinician can choose to examine the fundamental basis of interpersonal relationships by looking at attachment theory (presented in the next chapter) or at broader issues of gender, sexuality, and culture (presented in Chapters 9 and 10).

☐ Recommended Readings

Ahrons (1994), *The Good Divorce: Keeping Your Family Together when Your Marriage Comes Apart*

Becvar & Becvar, *Family Therapy: A Systemic Integration*

Carter & McGoldrick (1980), *The Family Life Cycle*

Kahn & Lewis (1988), *Siblings in Therapy*

Karen (1994), *Becoming Attached*

Nichols & Schwartz (1997), *Family Therapy Concepts and Methods*

Satir (1967), *Conjoint Family Therapy*

Walsh (1982), *Normal Family Processes*

CHAPTER

Family Maps

Although practitioners often identify cut-offs, enmeshments, and conflictual relationships when they create genograms, these become global assessments that do not always address the complexity of relationship patterns and intergenerational legacies. Charting interpersonal dynamics within the family system, the Family Map separates relational patterns from intergenerational legacies (via the Basic and Focused Genograms) and developmental issues (via the Time Line, discussed in Chapter 5). Through the use of the Family Map, the clinician can explore kinship and community affiliations and also tailor the therapeutic posture toward the client's unique needs. The Family Map is a flexible tool. Practitioners can choose to have one basic Family Map, or they can create a series of Family Maps based on each of the Focused Genograms. Consequently, the Family Map is an integral, essential part of the MFG. In this chapter, we discuss the practical use of the Family Map in clinical practice, give a brief review of mapping within family therapy, and discuss the role of the Family Map in clarifying and refining the therapeutic alliance.

☐ The Function and Use of a Family Map

While the Focused Genograms emphasize the pedigree structure and intergenerational themes of the family system, and the Time Lines focus on individual and family development, the Family Map illustrates relationship patterns, both dysfunctional as well as nurturing and supportive. A unique advantage of the Family Map is that it provides a structure for depicting the functional role of kinship patterns and remedies the biological biases of the genogram. Watts-Jones (1997) emphasizes the "inadequacy of the standard genogram because of its underlying assumption that 'family' is strictly a biological entity" (p. 375) and points out the need for alternative methods to depict kin relationships.

As presented in Chapter 3, the Basic Genogram outlines hierarchical, biological, and legal relationships of at least three generations, with accompanying details, such as name; dates of birth, death, and marriage; occupation; manner of death; and descriptive terms. In contrast, Family Maps do not use the pedigree format for drawing family and kin relationships; they specifically address contemporary interactions. In the Family Map, grandparents or great-grandparents are included only if there are current relationships. Aunts, uncles, cousins, nannies, and even pets can be included in a Family Map.

Significant interactions with social, political or community systems also can be depicted. Based on Hartman's and Laird's conception of family needs and resources (1983), the following questions are a guide for the practitioner's assessment of the family in its environment.

Questions for Assessing the Family's Resources and Social Supports

1. Are basic needs for shelter, nutrition, protection and health being met? If not, what resources are being provided, by whom, and since when?
2. Are basic needs for education being fulfilled? If not, what resources are being provided, by whom, and since when?
3. Are basic needs for productivity being met? If not, what resources are being provided, by whom, and since when?
4. What other community, human-service, social, and political organizations are involved with this family system? For how long and why?
5. Are there other significant professional or helping relationships?
6. What is the relationship with the referral source?

These questions guide the clinician's exploration of resources being used by the family system and insure the therapist's attention to the effects of these individuals and systems. Borrowing from Hartman's use of ecomaps (1978), the Family Map includes significant people, organizations, or services that are important in the client's contemporary functioning. These people may be significant in positive ways, such as a Big

Brother, in the case of a fatherless boy, or a spouse's involvement in Al-Anon. The map can also include probation officers, psychiatrists, physicians, or others who are part of the family's world. The Family Map of a family who has struggled with alcoholism and child abuse might include many service providers. Family systems therapists usually are interested in working with these representatives of the various human service delivery networks.

☐ Background on Family Maps

Both Minuchin (1974) and Hartman and Laird (1983) used mapping to detail boundaries and transactional process. Emphasizing behavioral patterns among the parental and sibling subsystems, Minuchin (1974) was the first to distinguish mapping as a separate process. From a social work framework, Hartman (1978) developed the ecomap as a method to represent information about the family system and its relationship to outside resources, organizations, and agencies. Stanton (1992) went on to differentiate the Structural genogram, which accents behavioral relationships, from the Bowen genogram, which incorporates biological and legal relationships across generations. However, these methods are not widely used or documented in the family therapy literature.

Creating Family Maps gives the clinician a way to examine transactional patterns to determine which patterns need to be modified, and to establish treatment goals. If a relationship is conflictual, communication skills and anger-management or anger-regulation skills must be taught. If a relationship is distant and disengaged, the clinician must bring the parties together in nonthreatening ways. If there is violence, or serious corporal punishment or abuse, immediate protective interventions are needed. If there are estrangements, the reasons for these cut-offs must be explored to assess the likelihood of reconciliation.

As discussed, mapping the family has been one of the least-developed parts of family assessment. Most clinical interventions are guided by a theoretical model that the therapist has adopted or developed. Consequently, the model often determines overall clinical strategy. Structurally, mapping usually is done to help formulate intervention strategies. In brief treatment, the focus is on solving the presenting problem. In family therapy, the focus is on understanding and working with family legacies and relational patterns. In play therapy, the emphasis is on a reconstructive process that allows a child to express underlying needs and fears. In sex therapy, focus is on improved sexual functioning. There are many, many other approaches to psychotherapy, and research suggests that most approaches are effective. The overarching factor, however, that determines clinical effectiveness is the therapeutic alliance (Horvath & Luborksky, 1993). In the next section, we discuss the therapeutic alliance in more detail and discuss a role for the Family Map in promoting the therapeutic alliance.

☐ The Therapeutic Alliance

Mapping is a tool that helps the clinician identify and develop the therapeutic interpersonal style needed for each family system. Patterns of disengagement in a Family Map suggest the need for slower, less-threatening therapeutic approaches. Because of its emotional estrangement, a disengaged family tends to experience resistance to interventions that foster communication. Working on the genogram is one type of therapeutic activity that engages family members with one another and fosters conversation and even camaraderie.

Creating a Family Map gives the clinician important clues about the emotional climate of the family. Is the family conflictual or disengaged? Is there emotional volatility or emotional constraint? Knowing the emotional climate helps the clinician foster an emotionally corrective therapeutic alliance. The term *therapeutic alliance* was first used by Zetzel (1956), a psychoanalyst, to describe the treatment relationship. Bordin (1979) identified three aspects of that alliance: mutual goals of treatment, agreement on tasks to achieve success, and the interpersonal bond. Reviewing psychotherapy research, Horvath and Luborsky (1993) examined the concept of therapeutic alliance and emphasized the importance of the quality of the therapeutic alliance in successful treatment.

Family Maps foster the therapist's ability to accommodate the family's relational style from the beginning of treatment. This kind of *affective attunement*, a term developed by Stern (1985) to describe a shared emotional experience, helps the clinician create an atmosphere comfortable for the family system. For example, an enmeshed and conflictual family with high levels of emotional intensity requires more emotional intensity from the therapist in order to develop the therapeutic alliance. Family Maps are especially useful in determining and developing a therapeutic alliance. Because a Family Map focuses and clarifies the therapist's attention on the client's specific interpersonal needs, the therapeutic alliance can be strengthened by using information gleaned during the construction of the Basic and Focused Genograms.

Based on the client's unique psychosocial and familial history, a Family Map details the relationship patterns: enmeshed, conflicted, distant, or abusive. Family Maps can be focused uniquely on each of the Focused Genogram themes. Unfortunately, mapping can lose its usefulness if the symbols used do not describe relationship patterns that are found

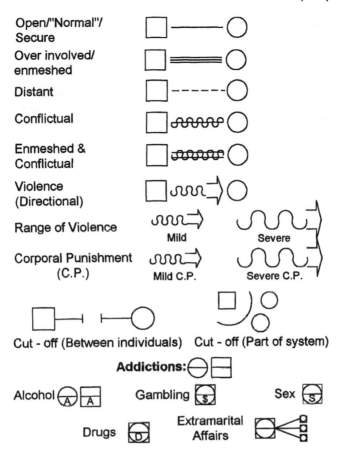

FIGURE 4.1. Symbols and relationship descriptors.

in family systems. We have developed a set of suggested symbols for the MFG that addresses the complexity of relationship dynamics. These relationship-interaction patterns are graphically depicted using the symbols in Figure 4.1.

Treatment models vary in their approach to therapeutic posture. Some models are directive (e.g., structural and strategic therapies); others are nondirective (e.g., Rogerian models); and others are confrontative (e.g., addictions treatment). Differential therapeutic alliances are more characteristic of integrative models or eclectic models of intervention. Luborsky (1976) identified two types of helping alliance: type 1, a supportive therapeutic relationship, and type 2, a therapeutic alliance based on a sense of working together. Although broader definitions of therapeutic alliance have been described, DeMaria (1987) has identified four therapeutic styles, borrowing from parenting styles identified by Clarke (1978): confronting, authoritative, reflective, and nurturing. The authoritative and the confronting styles are appropriate in cases of family violence, child abuse, suicidal gestures, substance abuse, or serious acting out by family members. The choice of confronting or authoritative styles depends primarily on the immediacy of the violence and the danger involved. Use of the nurturing and reflective styles also depends on the presenting problem as well as the client's attachment and relationship experiences. The nurturing style includes validation, guidance, coaching, and supportive behaviors. Based on mirroring and empathic listening, the reflective style is useful when a client is working through attitudes, beliefs, or emotions. Elaboration of these styles and their use in clinical practice is beyond the scope of this text; however, many practitioners use differential therapeutic styles in their clinical work. Family Maps are a tool to help therapists become clear and specific about the client's relational strengths and deficits.

Because no one therapeutic posture or style is effective with all clients all the time, the clinician can use this information to determine which therapeutic approach is appropriate to the client system and can vary this approach depending on the issues being addressed. The therapist can tailor his or her approach based on the family's style of relating with one another, along with the presenting problem and the stage of treatment. In addition to the family's style, individuals within the family need to establish relationships with the clinician as well. Boszormenyi-Nagy (1987) termed this therapeutic stance *multidirected partiality*, with the therapist maintaining relational connectedness with each member of the family system. In many cases individuals within the family require variations in therapeutic posture based on their previous relationship experiences.

☐ The Internal Models Family Map

Mapping is also a useful method for describing past interpersonal relationship dynamics. The MFG introduces the internal models map (Figure 4.2) as a method to depict childhood relationship experience and attachment style. Identifying attachment style helps the clinician moderate therapeutic postures used in the therapeutic alliance as well as develop a treatment strategy. Attachment styles are discussed in detail in Chapter 6. However, a brief overview is presented here.

Attachment theory's concept of *internal working models* (Bowlby, 1958; Main, Kaplan, & Cassidy, 1985) is the foundation for the Internal Models Map (IMM) that is part of the Attachments Genogram. Internal working models describe the mental representations that each

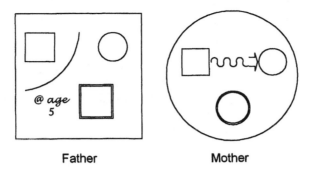

Father   Mother

FIGURE 4.2. Illustration of Internal Models Map. This illustration depicts the abandonment experienced by the father at age 5 and the physical abuse experienced by the mother. Detail for constructing Internal Models Maps is presented in Chapter 6.

family member carries of his or her relationship experiences. Understanding the dynamics of these internal working models is crucial to the development of a systemically focused treatment plan. For example, the Internal Models Map provides a method for depicting a father whose own father abandoned him at age 5 years. The deficiency in his internal working model regarding fathering of children 5 years old and older is illustrated in the Family Map as a cut-off between father and son at age 5. However, this map will be inside the father's symbol (see Figure 4.2). Similarly, a woman whose mother was physically abused by her father will have an internal working model in which the husband is abusive to the wife (see Figure 4.2). These concepts are further detailed in the chapter on the Attachments Genogram.

In contrast to other Family Maps that may be created by the clinician, the internal models Family Map expands the usefulness of mapping by depicting earlier relationship experience. An example is the case of Michael. Michael's father was a binge alcoholic who was also violent. When he was not binging, the father was supportive and encouraging of Michael's academic performance throughout elementary and high school. While Michael was in college his father stopped drinking completely. Family Maps, which are connected with each of the Focused Genograms (Basic, Emotions, Anger, Gender, etc.), help the therapist identify these varying levels of relational dynamics and the intricacy of the client system. Consequently, the various focused Family Maps, developed as part of the Focused Genograms, illustrate the complexity of Michael's relationship with his father. Emphasizing the early effects of the father's violence and alcoholism, the Internal Models Map separate past experiences from contemporary experiences.

☐ Summary

Clarifying and expanding the role of a Family Map, this chapter describes the specific roles of the Family Map as part of the MFG. The Family Map provides a method to graphically illustrate both contemporary and historic relationship patterns. The practitioner can choose to create a master Family Map or a series of focused Family Maps. In sum, Family Maps are an integral and useful aspect of the MFG.

The MFG contributes to the therapeutic alliance by providing the therapist with a useful tool to examine the individual client's needs within the complex scope of the family system. A positive therapeutic alliance is key to successful treatment outcome. The Basic Genogram, Family Maps, and Time Lines, along with Focused Genograms, provide a way to explore important areas of life that sometimes might be overlooked. Often, this process results in the sharing of information that is clinically relevant, and clients experience the attention to detail in a positive way. Mapping family relationships is a way for practitioners to understand the emotional and behavioral strengths and deficits a client brings into the treatment setting. The therapist can then focus himself or herself in ways that enhance the therapeutic alliance. If the client comes from a distant, generally uncaring family, a nurturing therapeutic posture is unfamiliar and sometimes uncomfortable. On the other hand, a client who comes from an involved, albeit highly enmeshed family can be equally confused and sometimes suspicious of a distant therapeutic posture.

☐ Recommended Readings

Hartman & Laird (1983), *Family Centered Social Work Practice*
Minuchin (1974), *Families and Family Therapy*

CHAPTER

Time Lines

Although the MFG's strength is in identifying historical themes, individual development cannot be overlooked. Noting deviations from normative family development, the third component of the MFG is a Time Line. Developmental, environmental, interpersonal, and life cycle transitions can be visually portrayed and identified on a Time Line. The Time Line provides a simple method for examining developmental and transitional issues, both individual and family, that often are left out of the genogram. As in the case of the Family Map, clinicians can choose to create a series of Time Lines as they construct the Focused Genograms, or they can choose to maintain one master Time Line. In this chapter we discuss the use and function of the Time Line and the application of the Time Line to exploring multiple lines of development.

☐ The Use and Function of a Time Line

Among family systems therapists, Satir (1967), in particular, encouraged close attention to the historical events taking place during pivotal life transitions. Through use of the family life chronology, she focused on the circumstances surrounding an individual's birth, his or her marriage and the birth of his or her children. Unfortunately, developmental issues often are overlooked in family systems assessments. By graphing the timing of each child's birth, coincidences of life events and anniversaries (both normative and traumatic), timing of major moves or migrations, and social, economic, and political events, the clinician obtains important developmental information about an individual or family system and gains a historical perspective not easily discerned on the traditional genogram.

Compiled based on information gathered during exploration of the basic and Focused Genograms, the Time Line marks normative and situational transitions for both individuals and family members that the clinician and clients identify as important events (e.g., Carter & McGoldrick, 1980; Duvall, 1977; Erikson, 1963; Walsh, 1982). Normative transitions are those that evolve during the natural phases of life—marriages, births, deaths. Situational, or paranormative, transitions, on the other hand, occur if there are crises or developmental disruptions such as suicide, divorce, illness, miscarriages, accidental death and injuries, and unanticipated retirements or job loss.

The Time Line specifically notes important events and transitions and attends to developmental information. It allows the clinician to see what normative life cycle milestones and transitions are achieved, delayed, or extended. Developmental and temporal information is often critical in developing and generating hypotheses regarding the presenting problems and complaints. There have been several attempts to integrate and develop Time Line genograms (Friedman et al., 1988; Stanton, 1992) to facilitate the incorporation of temporal aspects into systemic assessment. Chiefly because they become unwieldy, these methods have not received widespread clinical support. Stanton (1992) suggests that the Time Line is a useful tool for answering the "why now?" question in assessing the presenting problem, as well as for discovery and hypothesis generating.

☐ A Brief Review of the Family Life Cycle

The family life cycle has been explored by a number of theorists and is an important way to identify problems (and strengths) for a family system. Duvall (1977) was one of the first to identify the major stages of the family life cycle: marriage, birth of a child, child rearing, adolescence, leaving the nest, the empty nest, and aging. Similarly, Carter and McGoldrick (1980) identified these stages as

1. Between families: the unattached young adult;
2. The joining of families through marriage: the new couple;
3. The family with young children;
4. The family with adolescents;
5. Launching children and moving on;
6. The family in later life

The Group for the Advancement of Psychiatry (Fleck, 1989) refined these stages more discretely to include the following: marriage, reproduction, pregnancy, neonation, family formation, nurturance, toddler family, grade school, adolescence, emancipation, midlife stages, aging, and dying. From generic as well as male and female perspectives, Sheehy (1984, 1995, 1996, 1998) has examined the adult life cycle in depth. These stages are useful markers for developing the Time Line, because each stage has unique challenges and stresses. Assessing and clarifying the impact of deviations and traumatic experiences is an important part of the assessment process.

Family life, however, is not so continuous. Often child bearing and child rearing extend over many years, with overlapping cycles of toddlers, grade school-aged children, adolescents, and emancipated children. Divorce, retirements, teenage pregnancies, and geographic moves also affect family life and family functioning. Individuals within the family also can be circulating through developmental events in discontinuous patterns as well. Consequently, developmental and transitional events have different effects upon different individuals within the family and often, create anniversary reactions on the part of clients. Multiproblem, poor families do not fit the life cycle models well at all. However, the importance of understanding the family life cycle is in knowing which life events bring the family stability and cohesion and which ones disrupt family functioning. Traumatic losses can have particularly devastating effects on the family system.

Anniversaries of significant events also can be charted on the Time Line. Often unpleasant anniversaries center on family trauma. *Anniversary reactions* refer to the reliving or reenacting of some stressful life event without the awareness of the initial event. Often, anniversary reactions center on deaths in the family, although they can be quite complex. The Time Line is an essential tool for noting a sequence of stressful events, often revealing anniversary reactions.

The delay of achievement of family as well as individual developmental tasks can have significant affects on family and personal functioning. This is most obvious in cases of serious developmental delay in children but also can be seen in families in which grown children do not "leave the nest" and become a source of anxiety and stress for parents who expected to have greater freedom in their lives. Teenaged motherhood is an example of conflict between development status (adolescence) and role (parenthood). The Time Line allows the clinician to duly note such life cycle issues for further consideration in the therapeutic process.

Not only can clinicians explore past developmental issues and family transitions, but the Time Line also provides a method for examining future transitions as well. Knowledge about future events and transitions, such as retirement or succession in a family business, is often important information that the clinician can use during treatment.

☐ The Family-Individual Interface

Interpersonal problems within the family system too often are separated from individual developmental problems or needs. Individual development of family members—physical, cognitive, moral, emotional, and social—must be taken into consideration when conducting a family assessment. An adolescent struggling with a learning disability or attention-deficit disorder not only is affected individually, but there often are effects on siblings and parents. A mother suffering from severe depression after the death of her mother will affect family stability and functioning. Because the Time Line generally notes deviations from normal development, knowledge and understanding of individual development is essential in constructing the MFG. For example, Time Lines are an effective way to record if a child has developmental delays, if someone marries for the first time at age 35 years, or if a mother died of breast cancer at age 35 when the client was 12 years old. When these events are noted, the therapist can determine whether it is clinically appropriate to explore the event further or to gain a more systemic assessment.

The purpose of the MFG is to provide a method that helps the practitioner collect, organize, and review information that is gathered about a client and his or her family system. Basic knowledge of child and adolescent development—physical, cognitive, emotional, and social—is crucial in developing Time Lines. The details of developmental stages are found in basic texts and courses on child and adolescent development. Special attention to the impact of events during the first 3 years of a child's life is important in examining the quality of parent-child bonds. These factors are examined in detail in discussion of the Attachments Genogram.

Multiple lines of development and multiple determinants of behavior affect children. Assessing a child's development and behavior is an important part of the MFG process. Greenspan (1981) formulated the developmental structuralist approach to assess how a person organizes experience at each stage of development. He suggests that systematic observation of children should include attention to physical and neurological development, mood, human-relationship capacity, affects and anxiety, use of the environment, thematic development, and subjective reactions.

Greenspan's model for developmental assessment of children is a useful one. In this model, three areas are explored: the level of basic ego functions, including organic functioning (physical and neurological development) and psychological functioning (capacity for relatedness, organizing mood, affects and anxiety, organizing themes, and subjective reaction of the interviewer); the degree of personality rigidity (styles and range of relatedness, stereotypical mood, range of affect, richness and depth of themes, and subjective reaction of the interviewer); and the child's concerns and conflicts (content and style of relatedness, content of mood, content and sequence of specific affects, sequence of themes). As the clinician develops Time Lines, these areas can be considered throughout the assessment process.

Because children's issues and needs easily can be overlooked in the complicated process of systemic practice, assessing children's physical problems that masquerade as emotional ones also is part of developmental assessment. Examples of symptoms to watch for are clumsiness and staring, ignoring questions and requests, sleep disorders and insomnia, headaches, laziness, fatigue, lethargy, sudden behavior and personality changes, inappropriate body movement, and uncontrollable grunting and swearing. These behaviors can provide important clues about a child and the parental level of functioning. A 1988 report from the Academy of Pediatrics suggested that many children are under stress because of two parents working (insufficient quality and quantity of time spent with children yields less guidance), parental separation and divorce, superachieving parents, an increasingly sexualized and drug-oriented culture (pressures children to make decisions at a very early age), and conflicting messages in the media regarding sex, drugs, and violence. These are important areas to explore with the Time Line, because the child's level of development is important in determining the potential and real effects of these influences. The reader is encouraged to become knowledgeable about basic child development, childcare, and parenting. Often a pediatric consultant can be extremely useful as well.

Similarly, adult development is a continuation of age-related stages that are captured on the Time Line. Each stage is marked by periods of transition, and these periods of transition often are accompanied by feelings of restlessness and the need for reevaluation of life structure. These stages are dated and noted on the Time Line. Erikson's stages of adulthood (1963) serve as a solid (and well-known) framework for examining adult development and have been enhanced by the work of Gould (1978), Levinson (1978), and others.

These stages provide markers for the Time Line. For example, Mary, aged 45 years, a private-school administrator, had not married and had devoted her entire adult life to her school. She contacted her physician because of chronic fatigue that was determined to have no physical origin. However, her Time Line revealed that she had not created an adult life for herself and still was quite active with her parents and siblings.

☐ Using the Time Line in Clinical Practice

Developmental milestones and deviations are noted on Time Lines for each member of the nuclear family. In complicated clinical situations, more than one Time Line may be needed. The MFG incorporates Time Lines, but not at the expense of the structure and familiarity of the genogram format. Each Focused Genogram can include a Time Line, drawn underneath the Focused Genogram or on a separate piece of paper.

The Time Line is simple to construct. The clinician draws a horizontal line, sets an arbitrary beginning point, and notes the pivotal events and dates related to the particular lens of the MFG that is used. The Culture Time Line, for example, focuses on dates and timing of racial, ethnic, socioeconomic status, and religious changes and events. The Gender Time Line notes developmental issues related to gender role, gender identity, romance, and sexuality. Each focused Time Line helps the clinician concentrate his or her attention on developmental issues. If the clinician believes events or developmental issues are crucial they are noted on the master Time Line that is part of the MFG. Dates are very useful in determining the overlapping of various individual and family stresses. For example, the Time Line for Ruth's family (Figure 5.1) included Ruth's husband's entrance into a 3-month addictions treatment program 1 month after a move to a new home, which coincided with the 1-year anniversary of her infant son's death. In this Time Line, her marriage (normative event), her infant's death (situational event), her husband's entrance into rehabilitation (situational event), the move into a new home (normative event) all are noted. The therapist was able to focus the family's attention on the grieving for the infant and discuss the implications it had on the husband's addiction. Moving also had triggered Ruth's depression because she had finally cleaned out the baby's room.

The decision to use more than one Time Line is a matter of clinical choice. These notations help the clinician quickly assess excessive or paranormative stresses. Although we encourage placing the Time Line underneath the pedigree chart or on a separate page, Satir (1967) and

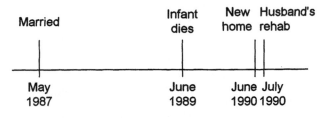

FIGURE 5.1. Ruth's Time Line.

Duhl (1981) developed chronologies that were drawn top to bottom. In the MFG the horizontal method is preferred because historical Time Lines usually are written in this manner. The horizontal method also allows for numerous horizontal lines on a page in those cases in which a great deal of family history is known. Ultimately, this is a matter of preference for the clinician using the MFG.

Summary

Because family life usually does not follow a smooth developmental path, Time Lines provide a useful method to graph developmental and transitional events. By providing a temporal lens, Time Lines enrich hypotheses formed about individual and family functioning. This chapter provides a basic overview of family, adult, and child development. The reader is encouraged to expand his or her knowledge base and incorporate these features of family systems and individuals into the Time Line. A method of exploring the historical context of presenting problems and overlapping stresses, the Time Life is a simple, yet useful, aspect of the MFG.

Recommended Readings

Carter & McGoldrick (1980), *The Family Life Cycle*
Erikson (1963), *Childhood and Society*
Gould (1978), *Transformations*
Leach (1977), *Your Baby and Child*
Sheehy (1984), *Passages*
Sheehy (1995), *The Silent Passage: Menopause*
Sheehy (1996), *New Passages: Mapping Your Life Across Time*
Sheehy (1998), *Understanding Men's Passages: Discovering the New Map of Men's Lives*
Walsh (1982), *Normal Family Processes*

III

THE FOCUSED
GENOGRAMS

6

CHAPTER

Attachments Genograms

With the structure of the family outlined by the Basic Genogram, the Attachments Genogram examines the psychological bonds within the family system. The Attachments Genogram links family-of-origin experience, marital dynamics, and interactional patterns within the family. Attachment theory, a psychobiological model proposed by Bowlby, provides a model that addresses the intricacies of intrapsychic-interpersonal process and suggests that bonding is essential for psychological comfort and security.

Patterns of touch, holding and bonding, emotional resonance and empathy, attachment patterns, temperament, and the effects of abuse and neglect on attachment scripts are explored in this chapter. The Internal Models Map (IMM) is presented in this chapter, a method to chart attachment relationships with primary care givers. The Time Line is presented from a developmental perspective that uses attachment theory as an underlying construct. Consequently, this lens of the MFG—the Attachments Genogram—reveals and clarifies the affective and emotional quality of interpersonal relationships within the family and the effects of these relationships on the psychological development of the individual.

☐ Bonding, Touch, and Holding: From Psychobiology to Object Relations and Back Again

Who raised you? How were you raised? These essential questions effect emotional health and overall relationship satisfaction. Biological, sociological, and psychological theories of human relationship strongly suggest that people tend to recreate their interpersonal wounds by recreating patterns of interaction established by early caretakers and maintained in family-of-origin systems. Attachments Genograms add a unique dimension to family assessment because many models of psychotherapy and family intervention are based on the assumption that the quality of interpersonal relationships influences self-esteem and stability within the family system.

This chapter also introduces a method for mapping internal models. These internal models are a way of identifying intrapsychic patterns and internal working models (based on attachment theory) and linking them to interpersonal dynamics using the genogram. This approach is a unique application of mapping relationship dynamics.

☐ Constructing Attachments Genograms

Current research in human development, psychology, and sociology documents the importance of the quality of parent-child relationships in the first few years of life (Goleman, 1995). This period of life is a time during which the brain, the emotional system, and sociability develop. Secure attachment appears to be an essential ingredient in establishing effective social relationships fostering optimal psychological development (Karen, 1994). Fortunately, the research is showing that although some childhood experiences have significant negative effects, other important relationships in life, such as marriage and mentors, can ameliorate some of the negative aspects of these early experiences. Generally, genograms have not been used to assess these early relationship experiences. The Attachments Genogram provides a framework to examine these patterns.

Preparing for Attachment Genograms

Attachments Genograms often are conducted as the therapist explores the client's relationship history. The timing of Attachments Genograms depends on the nature of the presenting problem and the client's comfort with discussing early family experiences. Information for Attachments Genograms is obtained throughout the interviewing process, and the practitioner can keep track of these issues even when the Attachments Genogram is not formally being conducted.

Attachments Genograms are quite useful for the clinician who practices a humanistic or experiential approach to treatment. Tuning into the client's history of closeness with others will help the therapist gauge his or her own therapeutic approach to the client. Clients with preoccupied attachment styles need a great deal of consistency during treatment. Clients with dismissive styles may require the therapist to reach out more than usual and to confront issues around vulnerability and dependency. These patterns are applicable to marital relationships as well (Hindy & Schwartz, 1994; Jackson, 1991b; Johnson & Greenberg, 1995).

Touch and Bonding, Temperament, and Attachment

Patterns of touch and bonding, emotional attunement, and temperament shape attachment behaviors in the family to create a unique relational experience for each individual. Based on attachment research, these experiences can be classified as specific types of attachment patterns. In the Attachments Genogram, bonding and attachment are explored as separate processes. Bonding occurs between individuals who are in both physical and emotional contact with one another (Casriel, 1972). Attachments form between people who bond with one another on an ongoing basis. Emotional attunement and empathy foster both bonding and attachment. Temperament may make any of these processes more or less comfortable for an individual. If physical or emotional abuse and neglect complicate relationship experiences, exploring attachment patterns is an important part of treatment planning. Child abuse and family violence are considered in more detail in the chapter on Anger Genograms.

Questions About Touch and Bonding

Because tactile communication is an important form of nonverbal communication in family systems as well as important in bonding and holding, these patterns are closely examined in the Attachments Genogram.

1. How were you comforted as a child? How were others comforted? Were there similarities or differences in the way you were comforted compared with your cousins or other family relatives?

2. Were you rejected, were there separations or losses? Were there rejections, separations, or losses for others in the family? What were the circumstances?
3. Is your family physically affectionate? In what ways? Are you affectionate with other relatives? Describe any differences among members.
4. Is touch comfortable in your family? Are some individuals in the family more comfortable with touch than others?
5. Are there inconsistencies in the kinds of holding and touch that goes on in family relationships?
6. Were there occasional or frequent negative or inappropriate touches?
7. Rate your family's touch comfort level in these areas:

> Positive affect touches (including support, appreciation, sex, and affection)
> Playful touches (playful affection and playful aggression)
> Control touches (compliance, attention getting, announcing a response)
> Ritualistic touches (greeting and departure)
> Hybrid touches (greeting-affection and departure-affection)
> Task-related touches (i.e., reference to appearance)
> Accidental touches

8. What kinds of hugs (if any) are the norm in your family?
9. Are you or others in your family sensitive to certain kinds of clothing or touch, such as seams inside the toe of the sock or clothing tags at the neckline? Do these family members like to be "rough and tumble?"

Questions About Temperament

The Attachments Genogram would be incomplete without an assessment of temperament. Individual differences in behavioral style affect the way bonding and attachment takes place. Temperament also can affect the way secure or anxious attachment is expressed (Belsky & Isabella, 1988).

1. Would you describe yourself as easygoing, slow to warm, cautious, or difficult? How would you describe other members of the family?
2. Rate yourself and your family members in these areas on a scale of 1 to 10 (10 being the greatest): activity level, intensity, distractibility, moodiness/sulkiness, irregularity, smiling and laughter, fear, soothability, comfort with extended interpersonal contact. What are the patterns of temperament for you and your family members?

Questions About Attachment

Attachment behaviors and styles are an integral part of human relationships. Attachment theory was developed by Bowlby (1977) to describe the propensity of human beings to make strong affectional bonds to particular others and to explain the many forms of emotional distress and personality disturbance, including anxiety, anger, depression, and emotional detachment, to which unwilling separation and loss give rise. He differentiated attachment and dependence. Dependence does not involve a biological function nor an enduring bond. Attachment, on the other hand, is a specific connection with one or a few individuals. Attachments endure over the life cycle, even if attachment figures are punishing. These relationships involve intense emotions and have an essential biological survival value for infants. In adults there are behavioral manifestations of the consolidation of these relational experiences that Byng-Hall (1995) calls *attachment scripts*. Byng-Hall prepared a table that describes features associated with attachment relationships. This is a useful chart that describes parent, child, and relationship factors (Table 6.1).

1. Do you find it easy to get close to others or difficult to get close to others? How is this pattern for other members of the family?
2. Do you worry that others do not really care about you? Do other members of your family have these worries or fears?
3. Would you describe your mother and father (or other caregiver) as warm and consistent, as unavailable and rejecting, or as attentive but out-of-sync with you? Were they different with you at different times in your life? Describe these different times.
4. Do people in your family respond quickly to one another? How? Who reaches out? Does anyone hold back?
5. Is independence applauded and encouraged within your family? By whom? How?
6. Does your family tend to be compliant, unresponsive, or demanding with each other? Are there differences between the generations?
7. Were you described by your parents or caregivers as easily comforted, difficult to soothe, or angry and demanding?
8. When you communicate with others do you ever act sarcastically, with hostility, affectedly cute, or ingratiating?
9. Do you tend to maintain stable friendships, tend to be on your own, or have lots of ups and downs with your friends?
10. When you think about your parents and your childhood, what is your perspective? Is there a balanced view of parent, have you worked through hurt; are the parents dismissing of love and connection; is the parent idealized; or is there poor self-reflection, still

TABLE 6.1. Features associated with attachment relationships

	Secure	Insecure/Avoidant	Insecure/Ambivalent	Disorganized/Unresolved
Child strange situation category	B	A	C	D (or A+C)
Child's style	Autonomous; explores readily	Pseudoindependent; avoids closeness; attachment behavior deactivated	Demanding and/or caregiving to parent; attachment behavior overactivated	Disorganized; becomes controlling or caregiving later
Parent adult interactive interview category	Autonomous/free (F)	Dismissive (D)	Preoccupied/entangled (E)	Unresolved mourning (U)
Narrative	Coherent	Incoherent; denial of past pain	Incoherent; preoccupied with past	Incoherent about unresolved losses
Parental style	Sensitive and caring; good care planning	Rejecting	Intermittently available	Maltreatment (by some)
Relationship				
Distance	Free to come and go	Distant	Over-close	Approach/avoidance conflict (some)
Transactional style	Adaptable	Disengaged	Enmeshed	?Chaotic
Shared strategy	Maintains contact; responds to child when child wants it	Avoids emotional or physical closeness	Mutual monitoring; blurred boundaries; role reversal common	No common strategy; idiosyncratic reunions; ?Dissociation when frightened/frightening

Reprinted with permission. (Byng-Hall, 1995)

embroiled with anger and hurt and a limited sense of seeing your own responsibility in relationship?

☐ The Internal Models Map

After completing the assessment of these varied components of the Attachments Genogram, the practitioner can move to determine the internal models through the Internal Models Map. The purpose of the Internal Models Family Map is to examine the complexity of attachment patterns within the family system, especially in the differences between mothers' and fathers' styles of relating. In contrast to the multigenerational genogram, the Internal Models Family Map focuses on the individual attachment histories of each family member. The Internal Models Map is a mechanism for identifying secure and insecure relationship attachments by examining patterns of availability and responsiveness by caregivers, especially during the first 10 years of life. Providing a model for assessing the intrapsychic Family Map, the Internal Models Map is a diagram of the individual's internal working models based on parental attachment relationships. Based on Bowlby's concept of internal working models, the Internal Models Map enables the client and therapist to develop a map of relationships that are usually unconscious or unspoken.

Research by Ainsworth, Blehar, Waters, and Wall (1978) on children's response to a strange situation—or the effect of separation on children—resulted in the classification of three types of attachment: secure attachment, anxious-ambivalent attachment, and anxious-avoidant attachment. Their primary caretakers provide securely attached children with warmth and reliable availability. The other two types of insecure attachment (or anxious attachments) are created by inconsistent availability and warmth, leading to ambivalent attachment, or by nonresponsive availability and warmth, leading to avoidant attachment. A fourth style, disorganized attachment, was identified in children with abusive parents (Main & Weston, 1982). One of the most common sources of insecure attachment is what child psychiatrist Selma Fraiberg called "the ghost in the nursery," a parent's unresolved mourning for a loved one (Fraiberg, Adelson, & Shapiro, 1975). Unresolved mourning is also a factor in the disorganized attachment style. Replication of Ainsworth et al.'s research with German families who are characteristically dismissive suggests that the mere fact that parents are behaving in accordance with a cultural norm does not necessarily spare the children any harm (Grossman & Grossman, 1991).

Avoidant children have caretakers who do not provide a high level of physical contact and who are low in expressiveness. The children tend to be aggressive at home and passive outside the home. Anxious-ambivalent children, on the other hand, have caretakers who are inconsistent. These children tend to have temper tantrums and can be inappropriately demanding. Irritability in a child, however, does not necessarily mean anxious attachment is a cause; the quality of interaction is important and must be explored. Temperament can be a factor, as previously discussed.

Main et al. (1985), who explored what Bowlby (1973) called *internal* working models, followed Ainsworth's research. Main et al.'s research studied the ways in which attachment styles are transmitted intergenerationally. Internal working models of attachment figures and the self are constructed by the child to help appraise and guide behavior in new situations. Working models conveys an interactive development process; research suggests that working models are amenable to modification during life (Jackson, 1991).

George, Kaplan, and Main (1985), to assess the internal working models of parents and their 6-year-olds devised the Berkeley Adult Attachment Interview. Their research resulted in three classifications: secure-autonomous, dismissive, and preoccupied. Secure adults have characteristics that include the following: showing little evidence of self-deception, seeming willing to depend on others, having a balanced view about their own roles in their relationships, recognizing that they were similar to their parents in various ways (not all of them positive), and generally seeming to accept the importance of relationships in their lives. The majority of their children turn out to be securely attached.

An inability or unwillingness to take attachment issues seriously characterizes dismissive adult attachment. Adults answer questions in a guarded way, without much elaboration, and often have trouble remembering their childhood; some exhibit an underlying animosity and speak vaguely about their parents, frequently describing them in idealized terms. However, when pressed for incidents that might illustrate such descriptions, their memories contradict their assessments, as negative facts leak into their narratives. These adults play down the effect of early hurts or embrace them as having built their character. Seventy-five percent of the children of these dismissing adults are avoidantly attached.

Preoccupied adult attachment styles seem like the ambivalent child grown up. Feelings of hurt and anger are evident, and these childhood experiences are often characterized by intense efforts to please the parents, considerable rage and disappointment, and role reversals in which the child tries to parent the adult. Memories are expressed in a confused and incoherent manner, as if the adults have never been able to get a grip on what happened to them and integrate it into a comprehensible picture. These preoccupied parents seem to have no sense of their own roles in any of their relationship difficulties and often are flooded with infantile feelings. The majority of their children are ambivalently attached to them.

In a subsequent study, Fonagy, Steele, and Steele (1991) were able to correctly predict infant strange-situation classification in 75% of cases based on interviews with expectant mothers. Furthermore, the most important qualities distinguishing secure adults from anxious adults are their capacity to understand themselves and others, their ability to recognize their own inner conflicts, and their sense of why their parents behaved as they did. The key to secure autonomous adults is not that they had secure attachments, but rather that they had an open and coherent way of reflecting on their attachments. There are inherent limitations to the classification system. Although the original Ainsworth categories labeled specific relationships (i.e., secure relationship with mother, avoidant relationship with father), Main's classification system identifies each adult with a single attachment style. A single relationship style, however, is not sufficient to capture the variety of adult relationship experiences.

Drawing the Internal Models Map

In contrast to the mapping presented in Chapter 2, the internal map is drawn inside the client's representative square or circle. Because space

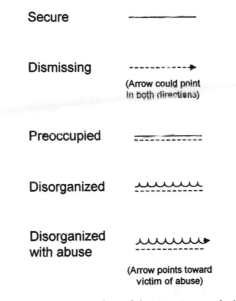

FIGURE 6.1. Internal Models Mapping symbols.

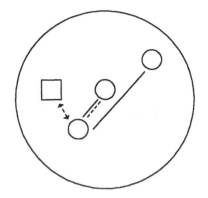

FIGURE 6.2. Margaret's Internal Models Map. Illustration shows dismissing relationship with father; preoccupied relationship with mother, and secure relationship with grandmother.

is limited on the Family Map, a separate sheet of paper often is used. The Internal Models Map can reflect whatever time period the clinician chooses to focus on with the client. The symbols in Figure 6.1 are used to depict secure, dismissing, preoccupied, disorganized, and disorganized-with-abuse attachment styles.

Margaret, abandoned by her father at age 5 years, did not see him again until she was 23 years old. Despite a few memories of closeness and connection, her overall sense of her father was one of loss and abandonment. When her father left, her mother went to work full-time and her grandmother, whom she perceived as extremely loving and kind, took care of Margaret. With further exploration of these relationships, it was determined that Margaret's attachment with her grandmother was secure, her attachment with her mother was mildly preoccupied, and her attachment with her father was dismissive (Figure 6.2). In her day-to-day life, Margaret experienced great comfort with older female colleagues, was more tentative with her peers, and found her relationship with her husband to be distant.

☐ The Attachments Time Line

The Attachments Time Line is another way of looking at family patterns and is a method for organizing often-vast amounts of developmental information. Focusing on both individuals and family developmental processes, the Time Line notes normative transitions (like births and deaths) as well as traumas and developmental delays. An attachment theory based model is presented here to guide exploration of developmental attachments issues between parents and children.

The propensity for exploration and creativity in life is fostered by secure attachment. Fear and stress activate the biologically based attachment system as the infant or young child begins the journey of exploring the world. Attachment behaviors include signals (crying, smiling, clinging), locomotions (looking, following, approaching), and contacts (embracing, clinging). During the first year of life both stranger anxiety and separation anxiety emerge. The quality of parenting during this period lays the foundation for attachment style.

As the child progresses through childhood, it is important that each parent continue to be intimately involved with the child's growth and development. Reliability and continuity in the parental relationships are significant in the formation of the child's character and contribute to secure attachment. It is well documented that mothers influence their daughters' feelings about themselves as women and that men influence their sons' feelings about themselves as men. Through their individual relationships with one another, mothers also influence their sons' perceptions of women and fathers also influence their daughters' perceptions of men (discussed in more depth in the Gender, Sexuality, and Romantic Love Genogram). The parent's relationship as a couple significantly influences child's perception of how a couple relates to one another, unless the child is exposed to other marital role models. Birth order dynamics also are influential, as previously discussed for the Basic Genogram.

Because of the importance of same-sex parent role modeling, one approach to parenting encourages the same-sex parent to serve as the primary standard setter and disciplinarian, with the opposite-sex parent as the facilitator, or ally, who provides understanding and nurturing (Kirschner & Kirschner, 1983). The opposite-sex parent also has an important role in promoting and encouraging the relationship between the child and the same-sex parent. Although the differentiation of these sex-linked roles provides a framework for examining differential attachment patterns, the model is not a rigid one.

Although same-sex/opposite-sex attachment patterns are an undeveloped area of attachment theory (and family theory, as well), these concepts are useful clinically in mapping attachment scripts and internal working models. Based on the work of Benjamin (1989), Browning, Miller-McLemore, Couture, Lyon, and Franklin (1997) provide a critique of the family that suggests that exploration of these divergent parenting experiences is essential to address gender polarity in this culture. Further discussion of gender influences is provided in Chapter 9.

While the parents are negotiating their roles, the infant brings a range of competencies, behavior patterns, and temperaments to the relationship. Sleeping and feeding along with emotional needs are primary in the early stages of development. As the infant matures and becomes a toddler, attachment needs are more visible, in the forms of stranger and separation anxiety, rapprochement, and the development of object constancy (Mahler et al., 1975). Somewhere between 3 and 9 months old, babies recognize the difference between father and mother. The preschool child is negotiating the emergence of self and the separation of fantasy and reality, underscoring the need for secure parental relationships during the first 3 years of life. The need for a secure family base continues with school-aged children. These children need constructive and effective discipline and structure both at home and school in order to foster productivity, self-esteem, and moral development. During these years the parental team consolidates and differentiates further in preparation for adolescence, which often reactivates separation anxiety.

The adjustments that parents and child make throughout the early years of their relationship help them negotiate and contend with the expanding roles that are required of them. As discussed earlier in this chapter, the first step in the process is called *bonding*. Bonding begins with normal mother-child symbiosis that is physical during pregnancy but physical and emotional during early infancy. Bonding between father and child is essential and often is facilitated by the mother. During the first 2 years of life bonding is critical in family life. During this time period mothers, fathers, and infants get to know each other in special ways. As the bond and attachment strengthen, parents begin to foster their child's self-esteem by providing guidance and opportunities for learning and play and setting goals that are set consistent with the child's talents. During the later part of the second year of life the child begins to explore the world around him or her more and more. In ways that are unique to their roles, the mother and father encourage the development of the child's autonomy, socialization, and personal development. A process of differentiation of self begins, balanced by needs for affiliation and autonomy.

Figure 6.3 illustrates the structural evolution of the attachment process through infancy, childhood, and adolescence (DeMaria, 1992).

As the figure illustrates, childbirth, an intimate experience, disrupts the marital bond, which later reconsolidates. The period from the time of the birth a child until he or she is about 18 months old is a very stressful transition period for a marriage. This period often coincides with changes in the emotional and biochemical experience of falling in love. Research on the chemistry of lust and infatuation suggests that these biochemicals last around 2 to 4 years (Crenshaw, 1996). Considering that many couples marry by the time they have known each other 2 to 2½ years and then in many instances have a child right away, the biochemistry of falling in love coupled with the biochemistry of childbirth can wreak

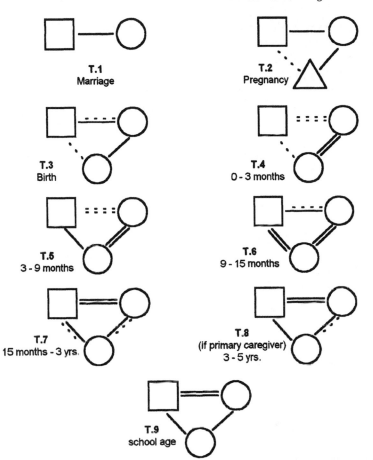

FIGURE 6.3. Formation of the family dynamic (assuming female is primary caregiver). T.1 = the husband and wife are united by their marital relationship; T.2 = the "embryonic" family; T.3 = the "family" is born: husband and wife add a parental relationship between them and share a unique bond; T.4 = the marital relationship weakens as mother-infant symbiosis intensifies; T.5 = with mother's support and encouragement, father's relationship strengthens with the infant; T.6 = as father's bond strengthens with the child, the marital relationship refortifies and the parental bonds are strengthening; T.7 = the advent of the child's independent movement puts increasing demands on the parental system; the importance of discipline and safety create tension in the parent-child bond and solidifies the parental bond; T.8 = as the child begins to explore the world around it, the parents are not the sole source of stimulation and the child's ties with the parents normalize; T.9 = by school age the family unit is balanced by secure relationships and a balanced and secure marital/parental team. (The months/years are approximations of normal child development based on consolidation of work by Greenspan [1981]; Mahler, Pine, and Berger [1975] and others.)

havoc on a young marriage. In assessing early family development, factors such as short courtships and pregnancy at the time of marriage (especially when the partner is known for less than 2 years) are important. Assessing the developmental process of attachment focuses the clinician's attention on normative and paranormative disruptions and enriches the clinician's perspective on the dynamics of the family system.

☐ Making Sense of Attachments Genograms: Theoretical Underpinnings

Bonding: A Basic Need

The 20th century has been one of dramatic change in terms of how children are viewed. Scientific and medical accomplishments have advanced to such a degree that it is sometimes hard to put the lives of parents, grandparents, and great-grandparents in perspective. The parents of a 40-year-old today, who were 25 years old at his or her birth, were born in the 1930s. The grandparents were likely to have been born in the 1900s or 1910s. The great-grandparents were likely to have been born in the late 1800s. The attitudes toward the care of children at the turn of the century were dramatically different from attitudes today.

The quality of parent-child relations for the parents, grandparents, and great-grandparents are very different. Until the latter part of this century, childhood was, at best, a struggle. Even today significant numbers of children still are being raised in poverty. However, an historical view of childhood shows that in past centuries conditions were considerably worse. The medieval period was especially unpleasant for children because of harsh and inhumane treatment (Schorsch, 1985). Although new concern and care for children emerged in the 17th century, these shifts in attitude were not seen in the United States until the late 1930s and after World War II (Montague, 1986). *The Care and Feeding of Children*, first published in 1894 with a 15th printing in 1935, advocated abolition of the cradle, not picking a baby up when he or she cried, feeding by the clock, and avoidance of handling. These attitudes still pervade in some parenting practices today. Families can be found in which new mothers, whose grandmothers were raised under these influences, are cautioned "not to pick up the baby too much or he or she will be spoiled."

The importance of holding began to be realized early in the 20th century. In 1915, the death rate for infants under 1 year age in various foundling institutions throughout the United States was nearly 100% (Montague, 1986). In the early 1900s, as physicians at Bellevue Hospital in New York sought answers for infant death, they found that "mothering" (caressing, cuddling, and cooing) lowered the mortality rate. As they instituted "mothering," the mortality rate fell from 100% to 50%, then to 35%, and down to 10% by 1938 (Montague, 1986). While in England in 1945, Spitz (1945) made observations on the problems of depression, malnutrition, and failure to thrive in infants. He believed that the main reason for growth failure and depression in infants was their lack of emotional stimulation. Bowlby's research and work on attachment furthered these early explorations. Today, touching and holding of infants and children is considered essential.

Harlow's research (1958) demonstrated that physical contact between mother and infant was crucial for the infant's psychological and physical development. Klaus and Kennell (1976) reinforced the importance of bonding for infants. They identified the importance of close contact with a newborn during the sensitive period of the first minutes and hours of life. Their work led to open nurseries and rooming-in for new parents. Restak (1979) found that snuggling and sucking create biochemical reactions in the brain that affect functioning and development.

Neuroscience is reinforcing these early studies (Pert, 1997). The brain's natural opiates, the endorphin peptides, provide the chemical foundation attachment. These endorphins give a sense of security peace and calm. Without bonding, brain development in children can be profoundly affected. *Newsweek* (Spring-Summer, 1997) printed a copy of a brain scan of a Romanian orphan who was institutionalized shortly after birth. The scan shows the effect of extreme deprivation in infancy. The temporal lobes, which regulate emotions and receive input from the senses, are nearly quiescent. Infants and young children who do not receive necessary bonding often suffer serious emotional and cognitive problems.

The brain is also acutely vulnerable to stress. Trauma and stress elevate stress hormones, such as cortisol, that wash over the developing brain like acid. As a result regions in the cortex and the limbic system (responsible for emotions, including attachment) are 20% to 30% smaller in abused children. In adults who were abused as children the memory-making hippocampus is smaller than in nonabused adults. The toxic effects of cortisol also creates hyperreactivity. An inability to self-soothe and, consequently, to calm oneself is one of the most devastating effects. The inability to self-soothe does not simply interfere with interpersonal relationships but also interferes with learning, creativity, and productivity.

Winnicott (1985), a pediatrician and psychoanalyst, was concerned with the quality of relations between mother and infant, and the subsequent effect on psychological development. His attention focused on the nature of the holding environment created by the mother (parental caretaker), which allows the infant's capacity for concern and empathy to unfold. Winnicott emphasized the importance of the parent-child bond in promoting healthy ego development. His concept of *primary maternal pre-occupation* attended to the significance of the mother's physical and emotional connection to the infant. The concept of the *good-enough mother* expressed the idea that no mother can or needs to be perfect. Indeed, she must not be perfect if the child is to abandon grandiosity, not be a life-long nuisance, and become his or her own person. Winnicott suggested that the mother gives the child a sense of achieving what he or she is incapable achieving on his own. By reading the signals and responding to them, the child eventually knows what he or she wants and learns to signal with intent. Kohut (1971) similarly argues that the child experiences the mother as an extension of himself or herself.

In Kohut's view, a mother's sense of emotional grounding contributes to her sense of competence. Through the mother-child mirroring experience, the mother helps keep the child's still fragile self from being overwhelmed by the stresses and tensions that constantly impinge on him or her. Through his research on mother-infant attunement, Stern (1985) reinforces the conclusion that the primary caregiver's emotional attunement and responsiveness is critically important in the development of a positive sense of self.

Casriel (1972), on the other hand, defined bonding as an essential, biologically based need for connectedness with others that includes both physical closeness and emotional openness. The bonding experience is an important means through which human beings give and receive physical and emotional pleasure to and from each other. Although the sexual experience is a form of bonding for adults, sexuality meets only a small portion of the need for bonding. The sexual aspects of bonding receive more attention than its natural place in human experience deserves because of the widescale deprivation of bonding. Prescott's research (1975) supports Casriel's model, linking the deprivation of body contact and touch (which he termed *somatosensory affective deprivation* [SAD] syndrome) and a variety of emotional disturbances. The ongoing attempt to meet the chronically unmet need for bonding is sexualized in a culture in which sexual touch is one of the few socially sanctioned ways of meeting the bonding need. Montague (1986) suggests that the ability of an individual to derive enjoyment from giving and receiving physical nurturing is a measure of his or her personal development. Contemporary research (Durana 1994, 1996) proposes that bonding produces a climate of caring, trust, and safety and provides symbolic parenting, facilitates attachment behaviors, and makes way for love and commitment. Montague, like Casriel, emphasized the importance of bonding for adults.

Object relations theory, and attachment theory in particular, links the physical to the psychological. Winnicott (1964) defined holding as protection from physiological insult, taking account of the infant's skin sensitivity to touch and temperature, auditory sensitivity, visual sensitivity, and sensitivity to falling. Holding includes the whole routine of care throughout the day and night and is not the same with any two infants, because it is part of the infant and no two infants are alike. Holding also follows the minute day-to-day changes of the infant's physical and psychological growth and development. Attachment theory incorporates not only physical holding but emotional attunement. The concept of internal working models provides a bridge between the physical and psychological. A working model implies an open, flexible process whereby new information and experience is assimilated.

Research suggests that the chain of intergenerational continuity of attachment styles can be broken (George et al., 1985; Jackson, 1991b). Hazan and Shaver (1987) contrast the concept of internal working models described in attachment theory with the notion of scripts and schemas in cognitive psychology. They suggest that social development involves the continual construction, revision, integration, and abstraction of mental models. Further, attachment theory proposes that contemporary mental models bear resemblance to earlier mental models; however, few of the earliest models exist unaltered by social experience or exist in mental isolation as suggested by psychodynamic theory.

Touch

Touch is the physical medium that fosters bonding and attachment. The importance of hugging, holding, and touch for psychological and physical well-being cannot be overestimated. Often, the adult who does not like to be touched, which tends to affect marital and parenting relationships in significant ways, may not have received much bonding and touch as a child. The University of Miami's Touch Research Institute reports study after study demonstrating that touch is an important stimulus to the central nervous system. Special nerve pathways send pleasure signals to the brain when the skin is stroked gently. There are separate nerve networks for detecting pain, temperature, and touch. Infants need a lot of touching. Children can be calmed and soothed if holding and touch is incorporated with parenting around temper tantrums. Infants and children must be touched in order for them to thrive psychologically and physically, and the need for touch does not go away.

Touch taboos are determined culturally. Generally, these taboos arise out of a failure to discriminate sexual from nurturing touch (Edwards,

1981). These taboos, however, often insure that adults do not experience purely nurturing touch in adulthood outside the context of a sexual relationship. Prescott (1975) developed the concept of somatosensory affective deprivation syndrome (SAD syndrome) to describe the effect of maternal-social deprivation. His research on links between violence and touch deprivation led him to conclude that deprivation of sensory pleasure is the principal root cause of violence.

Cross-cultural studies lend some support to his hypothesis. In an analysis of 49 societies, Prescott found that in 80% (39 out of the 49), the absence of physically affectionate nurturing is associated with violence. Societies that provide tender loving care to their children tend to be peaceful societies. In 4 out of the remaining 10, adults are nurturing but children grow up to be violent. In those societies, there are strong taboos against premarital sexual relations. In the other six societies, adults are nonnurturing, yet the cultures are nonviolent. Prescott found that these societies tolerated and accepted premarital sex and he concluded that the beneficial effects of physical affection for the infant can be negated by repression of physical pleasure later in life, and the detrimental effect of deprivation of physical affection for the infant seems to be compensated for later in life by sexual body-pleasure experiences during adolescence (Prescott, 1989). Prescott (1975) writes, "The deprivation of physical pleasure is a major ingredient in the expression of physical violence. The common association of sex with violence provides a clue to understanding physical violence in terms of deprivation of physical pleasure."

Highlights of the literature that suggest that human beings need to touch and be touched throughout their adult years include the following: Communication improves when health care providers incorporate touch into their treatment (Aguilera, 1967); people with high self-esteem use touch to communicate loving feelings more than people with low self-esteem (Silverman, Pressman, & Bartel, 1973); there is a positive correlation between touch avoidance and communication apprehension, and males engage in less same-sex touching than females (Andersen & Leibowitz,1978); people perceive that they touch more than they actually do and that self-image is enhanced by comfort with touching others (Mosby, 1978); there is evidence that touching occurs most often among opposite-sex friends and that fathers touch fewer areas of their children's bodies than do mothers (Jourard, 1966); and research on tactile deprivation demonstrates links to excessive masturbation, violence, and poor adult sexual relationships (Montague, 1986).

After reviewing the body of research on touch, Jones and Yarbrough (1985) developed a study to examine the meanings of touch in adult life. Their results found there are several types of touch: positive affect touches (including support, appreciation, inclusion, sexual, and affection), playful touches (playful affection and playful aggression), control touches (compliance, attention-getting, announcing a response), ritualistic touches (greeting and departure), hybrid touches (greeting-affection and departure-affection), task-related touches (i.e., reference to appearance), and accidental touches. This was the first study to examine patterns and styles of touch communication. Their findings suggest that interpersonal touch is significant not only intrinsically but symbolically; interpersonal touch codes include a wider range of meanings and degrees ambiguity than previous research would suggest; and contextual factors are critical to the meanings of touch.

Tactile Defensiveness

Touch is not simply a function of a nurturing environment. There are individual differences in tactile sensitivity. Two specific individual differences that affect bonding are tactile defensiveness and temperament. *Tactile defensiveness*, a term used by occupational therapists, refers to hypersensitivity to touch, movement, sound, taste, and smell. The responses can be difficult to interpret in infants and children; however, there is a distinct pattern. The child may startle easily and cry or he or she may "tune out" or "shut down." Consoling is difficult. In older children, adolescents, and adults there is sensitivity to being barefoot or wearing shoes. There is a preference for long-sleeved blouses or shirts, and pants instead of shorts. Other patterns suggesting tactile defensiveness include the following: New clothes are annoying and must be washed first; socks get pulled up after they slip down and sock lines across the tips of the toes are annoying; and fuzzy shirts, wool, turtlenecks, tags, kisses, barefoot games, being hugged or held, touching the face, and surprise touches are disliked. Tactilely defensive people actually need more touch to help with the defensiveness. However, the type of touch required tends to be deep-tissue touch and full-body contact.

Tactilely defensive infants often are considered temperamentally fussy and seem to dislike being held. Specific tactics for helping a tactically defensive infant were presented by Kinnealy (1990) in a parenting newsletter. She suggested that these infants require firm gentle pressure and warm hands and offered tips for soothing these infants. They do best on their stomachs. A parent can gently hold the child in a flexed position lying over the parent's knees, infant's head down and gentle patting by the parents. In addition, gentle pressure by the parent with their fingers around and in the mouth can help with feeding, which can be affected by oral tactile defensiveness. Swaddling, side-lying, and light touch are intolerable to a tactilely defensive infant. Kinnealy urged parents not to let the baby train them not to touch him or her.

The long-term effects of tactile defensiveness remain to be researched, but this phenomenon is often present in families that are not physically affectionate. Tactile defensiveness also can be extremely distressing to parents if they are comfortable with touch but their child is not. Differences in comfort with touch also can create issues between spouses, such as how they sleep together and sexual activity. In the marital relationship, tactile defensiveness also can be implicated in sexual differences and difficulties between couples. Robert was tactilely defensive and had to sleep in specific pajamas and a specific position on the bed. If his wife touched him during the evening, he was unable to get back to sleep. The sexual relationship also was affected because of his intense aversion to light stroking. Although Robert's behavior had been attributed to obsessive-compulsive disorder, his touch history revealed a pattern of serious tactile defensiveness from early childhood through adulthood.

Temperament

There are several basic temperaments that have been identified by researchers. These temperament constellations can be placed along a continuum. The temperament styles: easy, slow to warm, cautious, and difficult, with some mixtures (Brazelton, 1984; Kagen, Snidman, Arcus, & Reznick, 1997). The difficult child (Turecki, 1985) is characterized by an extremely high activity level, distractibility, high intensity, irregularity, negative persistence, low sensory threshold, impulsiveness, and stubbornness. The difficult child can put stress on a family, particularly on the father. Fathers feel shut out and question what the mother is doing, while the mother has no energy for the father and is jealous of the father's conflict-free relationship with the child's siblings. Temperament styles are based on a number of factors identified by Thomas and Chess (1977), including activity level, rhythms of hunger, elimination, sleep-wake cycle, approach or withdrawal style, adaptability to an altered environment, intensity of any given reaction, threshold of responsiveness, quantity and quality of moods, degree of distractibility, and persistence in the face of obstacles.

Suomi and Harlow (1978) found that heredity seems to determine whether a rhesus monkey is socially forward or retiring, and that monkeys with excessive timidity—similar to the fearful profile observed in some human children—tend to have problems later in relationships. In humans, these tendencies are influenced by the level of nurturing a child receives. If an exceptionally nurturing mother takes the time to teach her fretful child coping styles, the result is that the fretful baby later in life becomes a very effective and high-ranking member of its social group.

However, critic's of attachment theory suggest that too much time has been wasted studying the effects of early environments. They maintain that environmental influences come and go, but heredity lasts. Further research will determine the outcome of this debate, but at this point it is held that the quality of parent-child interaction affects and is affected by temperament. Consequently, temperament is an important factor in constructing the Attachments Genogram.

The Neonatal Behavioral Assessment Scale (NBAS; Brazelton, 1984) is another tool to assess infant behavior and styles. Although the NBAS does not classify infant temperaments, Brazelton suggests that there are important reasons for evaluating newborn infant behavior. The NBAS examines the fluidity and ease of state changes in newborns. Do they move from sleep to wakefulness in an easygoing manner or is the change jerky or dramatic? Observations of the newborn and the reactions he or she engenders in parents in the early weeks are important to understand the way in which the mother-father-infant relationship develops. Secondly, early identification contributes to greater understanding of the relative contributions of the infant and the caregiver in assessing future patterns. Parents often make judgments about an infant's appearance and temperament based on their own identifications. "He's just like my brother" or "she's just like my mother" are usual statements. The assessments do not always coincide with the infant's temperament. The NBAS assesses the infant during the interaction process. It is a test of the infant's capacities to engage his or her physiological system in response to external manipulation (Brazelton, 1984). This translates into assessing the infant's ability to respond to the environment in calm or distressed style. Because parental response to the child's behavior is influenced largely by their own parenting experiences, the NBAS can help the parents experience the child for his or her unique behavioral responsiveness.

Attachment

Interpersonal relationships evolve over time within a particular physical and emotional atmosphere. This atmosphere determines the emotional quality of interactions. The process of emotional growth occurs over a lifetime, interacting with physical, cognitive, and spiritual maturation. These interactions are influenced not only by the need for physical closeness but by the need for emotional and affectional attunement as well. Attachment is experienced as a psychological bond and becomes organized in the second half of the first year of life. Attachment theory describes the expectations that develop with respect to the expectations that people have about how relationships will be supportive under stress. Attachment is about the quality of bonding that is experienced in life: to whom we are bonded, and *how* we are bonded to them. This section explores how empathy and scripts play a part in attachment behavior and style.

Empathic Resonance

Empathy is to attachment as touch is to bonding. Empathic resonance, combined with bonding, forges secure attachments and secure internal working models. Initially, psychologist E. B. Titchener to describe motor mimicry first used the term *empathy* in 1920. Titchener suggested that empathy stemmed from a sort of physical imitation of the distress another that then evokes the same feelings in oneself. Empathy, therefore, is defined as the ability to perceive the subjective experience of another person, and empathic resonance is a crucial part of the parent-child bond. Stern (1985) studied these processes and called them *attunement*. Attunement has several components: mirroring (appropriate responsivity and regulation during core relatedness); attunement (during intersubjective relatedness and reinforcement), and shaping and consensual validation (during verbal relatedness). Stern believes attunement is the foundation for a sense of emotional connectedness. His research suggested that infants begin to differentiate themselves at birth and progress through increasingly complicated modes of relatedness. The stages include the emergent self (birth to 2 months), the core self (2–6 months), the subjective self (7–15 months), and the verbal self. Selective attunement is one of the most potent ways in which a parent can shape the development of a child's subjective and interpersonal life and accounts for "the infant becoming the child of his or her particular mother" (Stern, 1985). Selective attunement is quite powerful, and misattunements are emotionally incongruent responses that result in disconnection between parent and child.

Attunement and empathy are crucial in interpersonal relationships. Empathy requires calm and receptivity, a harmonizing of the head and the heart. Attunement is important throughout the life cycle. In adulthood, making love is considered similar to the intimate attunement between infant and child. In psychotherapy, the term *mirroring* is used to describe the attunement process in couples and in therapy. Empathy, empathic responsiveness, and empathic relationships have been essential in Guerney's conceptualization (1977) of effective interpersonal relationships. He suggests that empathic relationships are characterized by honesty and compassion; reduced anxiety or fear of loss of love; and a sense of general well-being, happiness, and confidence. The ability to be empathic raises self-esteem, ego strength and confidence in the ability to earn the trust and respect of another. Empathic relationships, according to Guerney, are likely to lead to equalitarian, or peer, relationships.

Attachment Scripts

Wachtel (1982) and Woolf (1983) have emphasized the importance of transmission of unconscious family process. Attachment scripts are one way to examine this transmission process. They evolve based on inter-generational and interpersonal internalized models that guide behavior, influence attitudes, and affect emotions. These scripts are a set of conscious or unconscious rules that organize experience, feelings, and beliefs about attachment experience. Relationships with attachment figures affect self-esteem in significant ways, especially in areas of family functioning. Frank's script was to be untrusting and protective of himself emotionally. When Mary, his wife, attempted to show him affection, his early experiences with abusive physical contact caused him to pull away most of the time. Erratic and unpredictable affection and rejection characterized Mary's early experience. The attachment scripts each brought to the relationship interfered with forming a secure adult attachment in their relationship.

The avoidant and ambivalent attachment styles also are similar to Lerner's pursuers and distancers (1985). Pursuers react to anxiety by seeking greater togetherness in a relationship. They place a high value on talking things out and expressing feelings and believe others should do the same. They feel rejected and take it personally if someone close to them wants more time and space alone or away from the relationship. They also tend to pursue harder, and then coldly withdraw, if an important person seeks distance. Their tendency is to negatively label themselves as "too dependent" or "too demanding" in a relationship, and they are critical of their partner as someone who cannot handle feelings or tolerate closeness. Distancers, on the other hand, seek emotional distance or physical space if stress is high, and they consider themselves to be self-reliant and private persons, more "do-it-yourselfers" than help seekers. They have difficulty showing their needy, vulnerable, and dependent sides and consequently receive such labels as "emotionally unavailable." Distancers manage anxiety in personal relations by intensifying work-related projects and may cut off a relationship entirely if things get intense, rather than persevering and working it out.

Casriels' acceptors and rejectors schema (1972) is another way of examining the avoidant and ambivalent attachment styles. Rejecters, according to Casriel, are those who feel that pain exceeds pleasure in relationships, so they repress the need for love and remain aloof from emotional relationships. The lack of emotional connection creates pain, which is defended by withdrawal into a facade of pride and self-sufficiency (Komatinsky, 1997). Acceptors, on the other hand, unconsciously feel that whatever pleasure is received in a relationship is worth any price. To the acceptor, a relationship is necessary for survival, even at the expense of his or her own identity and self-respect.

Object relations theorists have emphasized the importance of the psychological bond between parent and child. In defining primary love Balint (1979) said, "The aim of all human striving is to establish—or, probably, re-establish—an all-embracing harmony with one's environment, to be able to love in peace" (p. 65). Balint's model links psychodynamically oriented family systems theories with object relations and attachment theory through his emphasis on the importance of early relationship experiences. Balint's intrapsychic model, like those of Lerner and Casriel, identifies relationship styles that parallel the behaviorally observable insecure attachment types. He categorized three types of object relationships: the most primitive, experienced as a "harmonious interpenetrating mix-up," the "ocnophilic" clinging to object; and the "philobatic" preference for objectless expanses. These three styles are comparable to Main's secure, ambivalent, and avoidant attachment styles.

In contrast to other object relations theories, Balint (1979) proposes that narcissism and other interpersonal disturbances are secondary to the "harmonious interpenetrating mix-up" (secure attachment). He suggests that narcissism is caused by a disturbance between the individual and her or his caregiving environment, due to lack of emotional resonance. Consequently, the individual differentiates himself or herself from what was until then the "harmonious fusion" of self and environment. Rather than maintain an emotional connectedness with caregivers, the individual withdraws part of his of her emotional energy from the environment and invests it into his or her developing ego. This results in a self-centeredness that is furthered strengthened, or weakened, by additional emotional experiences. This model of narcissism bridges object relations, attachment theory, and family systems concepts. Narcissistic vulnerability (Feldman, 1982) is discussed in the chapter on Anger Genograms and further links these models.

Attachment theory provides a model that extends psychological development into adulthood. As ties to parents gradually weaken as the child gets older, the secure base function slowly shifts to other figures, eventually resting on one's mate. Hazan and Shaver (1987) have explored the relationship between attachment and romantic love. They found that secure relationships are happier, and those in secure relationships see their partner as a good, trusted friend and are able to accept flaws in one another. Relationships last longer and have fewer divorces. Dismissive (avoidant) relationships reveal fears of intimacy. Those in dismissive relationships often are doubtful that romantic love exists at all and find their relationships to be full of emotional highs and lows and jealousy. Preoccupied (ambivalent) relationships are characterized by more intense roller-coaster romance, and partners tend to fall in love easily and become obsessively involved with their lover.

Jackson's (1991b) exploration of marriage and attachment suggests that attachment behavior is subject to modification throughout the life cycle and is not rigidly fixed in childhood. Insight, changes in the parent-subject relationship, and the marital relationship were some of the primary factors that she found that could account for the changes in attachment behavior. Jackson's work supports conclusions made by Main et al. (1985) and Egeland, Jacobvitz, and Sroufe (1988) that relationships with others, specifically marital and psychotherapeutic relationships, modify to some extent the deleterious effect of unfortunate childhood experiences, including abuse.

☐ Summary

The Attachments Genogram provides a new method for assessing the quality of interpersonal relationships within the family and is a significant part of the MFG. By addressing attachment styles identified by research on young children, the Attachments Genogram gives the clinician a "secure base" from which to assess the family system. Emotional attachments with family members determine the kinds of relationships established with others including spouses and children. The lens of the Attachments Genogram permits examination of the place of touch, bonding, empathy, temperament, and attachment scripts in creating foundations for interpersonal effectiveness and security.

Attachment theory is especially useful to family systems practitioners who struggle to integrate often divergent concepts. It describes the importance of a secure base for family functioning and provides a reference point for theories that seek to integrate a variety of theoretical concepts that bridge psychodynamic principles and general systems theories, including biological concepts and principles.

The Internal Models Map is a unique method offered to help clinicians separate family-of-origin experience from contemporary functioning. With the Internal Models Map, the clinician can depict current and contemporary relational experience. The Time Line, another integral component of the Attachments Genogram, presents a developmental framework for examining the attachment process during the first few years of life. This crucial and primary time period often is overlooked, but the impact of early relationship experiences can never be underestimated. Current research suggests that a child's brain is forming associational pathways until the age of 10 years. The experiences and stresses of the first 10 years of life, consequently, form the template for future relationships. The successful construction of the internal models map establishes a base from which the clinician can determine secure and insecure attachment styles and characteristics for both the individuals in the family and the family system itself.

Family systems theory consistently has examined patterns of closeness and distance within the family. The Attachments Genogram provides a method to examine these patterns based on touch, holding, empathy, temperament, and attachment scripts, giving these patterns greater depth of understanding. As with the entire MFG process, the focus of the Attachments Genogram increases the practitioner's ability to empathize with the client and his or her family system, as well as to refine intervention goals.

☐ Recommended Readings

Kagen et al. (1997), *Galen's Prophecy: Temperament in Human Nature*
Karen (1994), *Becoming Attached*
Montague (1986), *Touching*
Stosny (1995), *Treating Attachment Abuse*

Emotions Genograms

Emotion—its expression, repression, and displacement within the family and among the generations—is another important theme in the MFG. The Emotions Genogram is another powerful microscopic lens that illuminates the emotional tone of family process, structure, and dynamics. The purpose of Emotions Genograms is to trace the emotional history of the individual and the family system. It gives the clinician a framework in which to promote clinically relevant and useful emotional work during the treatment process. Clinicians can use it to facilitate the constructive expression of emotions by clients.

The purpose of Emotions Genograms is to help the client become more aware of patterns of emotional expression in the family in terms of both pleasure and pain, so that effective and satisfying emotional experiences can take place in the present. The pleasurable emotions of interest-excitement and enjoyment-joy, and the painful emotions of sadness-anguish and fear-terror are explored in this chapter. Love, as the experience of pleasurable emotion, is also discussed in this chapter. However, romantic love and love life patterns are explored more fully in the chapter on Gender and Sexuality Genograms. In Chapter 9, anger and rage are discussed. Anger has been allocated a separate chapter because of the volume of information now available and because of the serious effects anger has on both relationships and personality. This chapter explores the psychobiological aspects of emotion, affect theory, and a method for helping clients develop their emotional intelligence.

☐ Constructing Emotions Genograms

Attitudes and decisions about expressing feelings usually are learned during childhood and adolescence. Emotions Genograms can help uncover the reasons for these attitudes and beliefs. Questions about how feelings were handled in the family, which feelings were acceptable or not acceptable, and how different feelings were expressed elucidate the historical basis of these attitudes. Attitudes that may have been functional and useful in growing up may not be functional in someone's life today. Brian's mother was extremely volatile and critical and he learned from his father that the best way to deal with her was to keep his feelings to himself so that there would be less provocation. Today, however, Brian continues the same emotional response toward his wife, placating her in the same way his father placated his mother. The consequence is that Brian does not communicate his feelings toward his wife, and their marriage is suffering from a lack of intimacy and connection.

Preparing for Emotions Genogram

There are several steps in the process of conducting Emotions Genograms. First, awareness of various feeling states must be created. Second, emotional patterns within the intergenerational family system must be identified. Third, specific feeling states and emotional scripts must be addressed. After these steps are completed, an Emotions Genogram can be completed in two ways: a general exploration of emotions within the family systems, or an exploration of specific feelings, such as sadness, loss, and grief; fear; and pleasure. In order to help clients become comfortable talking about their emotional experiences, two exercises, in particular, help the client review, evaluate, and discuss his or her emotional experiences: "My World of Feelings" and "Pain and Pleasure in My Family."

Disclosure of negative emotions is linked to relief of stress and improvements in health (Pennebaker, 1995). In contrast, those people who work to put on a positive impression and do not reveal emotion tend to have poorer health. The act of talking or writing (disclosure) alters the way events are stored in memory. Labeling an emotion reduces its intensity. Saying "I am angry" or "I am sad" reduces its intensity. Writing and talking about emotion helps in constructing coherent narratives that are vital in resolving traumatic and stressful experiences in life. Identifying and talking about negative feelings and experiences is often essential in order to end treatment successfully.

The process of expressing emotion should not be confused with acting out of emotions. If emotions are acted out through attacks, provocation, or manipulation, the emotion is being used for power and control in a relationship. In contrast, the "expressions" process aims to enhance interpersonal relatedness.

Some people are more emotionally repressed than others, and these people need more help and support to become aware of their feelings. Gordon (1993) identified three levels of awareness of feelings: level one: "I am aware of my feelings and I can share them with you;" level two: "I am aware of my feelings but I choose not to share them with you;" and level three: "I am not aware of my feelings, so I cannot share them with you." Hof and Miller (1981) developed an exercise called "My World of Feelings" as a communication exercise with couples. This exercise has been modified here for use with individuals, as well. The purpose is to help a client become more aware of the whole range of his or her feelings, to begin to express them appropriately, and to accept these feelings in himself or herself and in others. This exercise can be done verbally in the clinical setting, or the client can do it alone and in writing outside of the therapy session.

Those clients who are emotionally repressed can begin the Emotions Genogram process by keeping a diary of feelings for a period. Two weeks is often a good starting point. During this time, they are encouraged to pay attention and make note of their emotional reactions in various situations in their life. The feelings diary can help differentiate thoughts and judgments from feelings. The "My World of Feelings" exercise then can be incorporated into the diary. This exercise is useful because it helps a client become aware of his or her level of awareness of feelings and emotional states. It is difficult to explore the intergenerational patterns of emotional expression and mood if the client is blocked in his or her own emotional expression. Although clinicians might proceed without this level of conscious awareness, our experience suggests that this is an important step in the process of developing Emotions Genograms. This step also can help if anger is a predominant emotional state within the family, because the client often will recognize imbalances that exist in emotional expression.

The "My World of Feelings" exercise helps the client become more aware of feeling patterns that he or she experiences and provides the therapist with useful clinical information about the client-family systems level of emotional development. The client is asked to complete the following statements:

1. My favorite interests are...
2. I am happiest when...
3. I am excited when...
4. I am saddest when...
5. I am angriest when...
6. I feel most afraid when...

loved when. . .

reatest fear/concern about my life is. . .

t I like most about myself is. . .

10. What I dislike most about myself is. . .
11. Who I feel closest to in my life is. . .
12. What I like about the person I feel closest to is. . .
13. The feelings I have the most difficulty sharing are. . .
14. The feelings that I can share most easily are. . .
15. Right now I feel [blank] towards myself. . .
16. I feel [blank] sharing these feelings with you [the therapist]. . .

The Importance of Emotional Congruence

A clinician has a crucial role in monitoring and clarifying feelings that are expressed during treatment. As the clinician listens and resonates to the client's situations and self-reports, she or he may notice a lack of affect or an affect that does not seem to fit. Empathy between clinician and client is crucial. Emotional resonance fosters self-awareness and attunement as the self-other dialectic is processed through treatment. Empathic skills can aid the clinician in exploring feelings with the client. The therapist could say, "If I were in your place. . ." or "I would imagine that you felt. . ." If the client agrees with the feeling, and they discuss a shared meaning, the clinician knows that he or she is successfully tracking the feeling or mood of the client. It is also helpful for the clinician to use active listening, mirroring, or shared meaning techniques to reflect back to the client what he or she is hearing. There is a saying: "I know that you believe that what you heard is what I said, but what you don't understand is that what I said is not what I meant." Repeating back to the client, using feeling words, can help him or her deepen self-awareness.

Special Issues in Constructing Emotions Genograms

Anger, fear, sadness, joy, and excitement are broad families of emotion and each one has a range of intensity. Within each emotional sphere are many different terms to describe a particular feeling. Focusing on these basic emotional states helps the client begin to differentiate one feeling from another. Interest is the mild form of excitement. Enjoyment ranges from contentment to joy or bliss. These two emotions are the positive affects and often form the state named *pleasure* or *happiness*. The negative affects form the pain nexus of human emotional experience. Fear and terror share the same continuum. Distress and anguish form the continuum for what is often called *sadness*. Anger and rage share another emotional continuum. Because of anger's crucial role in family conflict, we devote a separate chapter to Anger Genograms.

Hope has received very little attention, although it has an important place in the emotional repertoire. Izard (1977) places hope on the interest-excitement continuum. Hope, like love, guilt, shame, and jealousy, is an affective-cognitive interaction, that is, the combination of an attitude, belief, or decision and the emotion. Weeks and Hof (1995) defined hope: "[it] is to entertain in the mind, deeply and resolutely, a conscious impulse toward something that promises enjoyment or satisfaction in its attainment, with the expectation that it will happen." Hope generally is considered to be related to goal attainment, in that one has hope if there is more than a zero chance of achieving a particular goal.

Shame is also a misunderstood emotional state. Tomkins (1962) defined shame as the emotion of indignity, transgression, and alienation. According to him, shame is the most reflexive of the emotions—an experience of the self by the self, in which the phenomenological distinction between the subject and the object of shame is lost. Guilt, on the other hand, results from wrongdoing (related to shame but more powerful). The experience of guilt binds the person to the source of the guilt and does not subside without reconciliation that tends to restore social harmony. While guilt hangs heavy (mainly with internal sanctions), shame befuddles (with real or imagined sanctions from others). Guilt complements shame in fostering social responsibility. Stosny (1995) proposes that guilt is a result of what we feel about what we do and shame is a result of what we feel about who we are. Pride is related to shame because it is an affiliative response. Pride emerges in the second year of life and also is based on the positive affects. Pride is explored in the Basic Genogram in the areas of self-esteem and mastery.

Love is also an affective-cognitive orientation that includes emotions but is more. Nathanson (1992) proposes that love is based on the experience of positive affect, both excitement and joy, and that love scripts precondition the experience of love. Similarly, Wheat (1980) identified five forms of love based on the Greek language. They are distinctive but overlap one another: *epithumia* (a strong desire), *eros* (romance, passion, sentiment), *storge* (security, emotional refuge), *phileo* (friendship, companionship, cherishing), and *agape* (unselfish love without expectation, valuing and serving, a choice of will). Each of these can be seen as variations in the constellation of the positive affects of enjoyment-joy and interest-excitement.

In developing Emotions Genograms, each of these feelings—anger, fear, sadness, joy, and excitement—can be explored with the client. Because of the roles they often play in family systems, romantic love is explored

| List People in Your Genogram | PAINS | | | PLEASURES | |
	Anger	Fear	Sadness	Joy	Excitement
(Make a note/check which emotions were prevalent/notable)					
Spouse					
Children:					
Parents(Step-parents):					
Grandparents:					
Aunts/Uncles/Other Relatives/Important Family Members:					
Friends:					
Teachers/Employers/ Mentors:					
Family Myths/Stories:					

FIGURE 7.1. Pain and pleasure in my family system. A format for exploring emotions in the family system.

in the Romantic Love Genogram (Chapter 9) and anger is explored in the Anger Genogram (Chapter 8). Otherwise, Emotions Genograms can become completely unwieldy and repeat the problems of the traditional genogram format.

As part of an Emotions Genogram, the client can begin by identifying the members of the family system and the predominant feeling states of pain and pleasure that characterize their different patterns of emotional expression. Another step in the Emotions Genogram process is to explore what feelings are predominant or unexpressed within the family system. The "Pain and Pleasure in my Family" exercise developed by DeMaria is a way to help explore themes in the family system (Figure 7.1).

Pain and Pleasure in My Family System: A Format for Exploring Emotions in the Family System

Once the client has obtained information about these areas by reviewing personal history with the therapist or discussing family history with other members of the family, he or she can complete the process of preparing for Emotions Genograms. At times, clear themes and patterns emerge and can be combined with other Focused Genograms. Gender patterns, in particular, can be addressed in greater depth by combining Emotions Genograms and the Gender Genograms. During the Emotions

Genogram process, many themes can be revealed. For example, Sue was the youngest of three children; however, both of her sisters had died. One sister had died as a very young child, and the oldest sister died of leukemia in her 20s. Within the past 8 years, both her mother and father had died. Her father was an only child, and one brother with whom Sue had very little contact survived her mother. Sue had been experiencing depression for several years without relief. In developing her Emotions Genogram, the theme of sadness and loss was readily apparent. Treatment focused for some time on addressing unresolved mourning.

Once the client is comfortable talking about his or her feelings, the specific process of exploring feelings within the family can begin. Emotions Genograms, first developed by Weeks and Treat (1992) (called the Feelings Genogram), can be used to collect considerable information about feelings in the family and may take several sessions to complete.

General Questions for Emotions Genograms

1. What were the dominant feelings for each member of your family (the family you grew up with)?
2. What was the predominant feeling in your family? Who set the mood?
3. Which feelings were expressed most often, most intensely?
4. Which feelings were not allowed? How were members punished when an unallowed feeling was expressed?
5. What happened to the unexpressed feelings in the family?
6. Who knew or did not know about how others felt?
7. What happened to you when you expressed the taboo feeling or feelings?
8. How did you learn how to deal with these so-called unacceptable feelings?
9. Did others try to tell you how you should feel?
10. Did you ever see anyone lose control over his or her feelings? What would happen? Did anyone get hurt? How?
11. If corporal punishment was used in your family, what feelings did parents express? What feelings were allowable for children?
12. Do you find yourself having feelings that you cannot explain but that seem like feelings you have had in the past?

In one case a young woman, Mary, was feeling chronically anxious and depressed. She was under a lot of stress at work and was the mother of three children. In constructing Emotions Genograms, it became clear to Mary that she came from a family in which complaining was unacceptable and both of her parents emphasized the importance of duty. In

Mary's marriage, she kept her complaints and concerns to herself; she did not want to "burden" her friends either. As Mary began to talk about her stresses with her husband and a friend, she began to receive support, but she also found that she was uncomfortable when emotional intensity increased. Comfort with emotional intensity is an important part of working through the issues raised through the Emotions Genograms. When someone grows up in a family that is conflict avoidant, emotional intensity can be very uncomfortable. Likewise, those who grow up in volatile families are more likely to be volatile themselves.

Sadness, Loss, and Grief

In the footsteps of Freud and Bowlby, Paul and Grosser (1965) espouse that unresolved mourning is a crucial factor in personal and interpersonal distress. Identifying deaths, abandonments, adoptions, immigrations, and other emotional cut-offs in the family can assist clients and therapists in accessing sadness, loss, and grief and understanding their impact upon the individual and the family system. The biological features of sadness foster emotional shut-down that allows grieving to proceed in a natural, and normal, fashion. If someone is sad, attention turns inward and he or she loses interest in daily living. This is an important and natural part of grieving. During grieving there is a progression from mild emotional intensity (distress) to anguish and on to anger and acceptance. However, grieving is not a linear process and during the early stages of grief and loss emotional intensity is often variable, with huge dips in intensity of sadness. Over time, as the person intellectually and practically reorganizes his or her life to live without someone who has been important, emotional intensity diminishes and becomes more sporadic. During these more sporadic episodes of sadness, emotional intensity can build up. However, the ebb and flow is more manageable emotionally than in the early stage of grief. This is the process of normal grieving, which is an important clinical assessment. Sally's emotional volatility seemed to be related to her mother's sudden and unexpected death several years before entering marital therapy. Before her mother's death, Sally and her husband were not aware of the cycles of emotional calm and distress that were now so much a part of their relationship.

Loss in childhood has repercussions that are more serious because the child's cognitive abilities are not able to support and bolster the emotional intensity that accompanies loss and grief. Often, this leads to incomplete and unsatisfying mourning. Future emotional expression is often more volatile and confusing. Rosen (1990) provides a model to help structure the exploration of loss in the genogram. He describes four types of death during the family life cycle: normative death: death of an elderly person; *premature death*: death of a middle-aged person; *cut-off in the prime of life*: death of a young adult; and *the unthinkable loss*: death of a child. If deaths are anticipated, there is more time to prepare than if deaths are sudden. Identifying which patterns are functional or dysfunctional is an important part of Emotions Genograms.

Prolonged illnesses also create stress for individuals and families as well and affect the grieving process, often interfering with normal grieving. In addition to the basic types of loss, Rosen (1990) describes four types of grief: abnormal grief, unresolved grief, interminable grief, and socially unsanctioned grief. He proposes five indicators for abnormal grief. Abnormal grief is evident if a family member is idealized or demonized, if there is lack of agreement about what caused illness and death, if a family member is talked about incessantly or barely mentioned, if there is incessant complaining about the health care as if better care would have created a better outcome, or finally if anger or resentment toward someone's death or illness defies explanation or resolution. Grief also can be unresolved because of either short-circuiting of the grieving process or interminable and inconsolable grieving. In either situation, grieving interferes with reorganization of personal and family life. Socially unsanctioned grief is mourning that does not receive social support. There are several examples of socially unsanctioned grief: perinatal death (miscarriage, stillborn, or first few weeks of life) and AIDS-related and other disenfranchised grief, such as the death of a friend, a distant family member, an ex-spouse, a pet, a secret lover, a coworker, or a patient. Rosen also recommends taking into account ethnic attitudes toward life and death and the expression of pain, suffering, and grief.

Questions About Sadness, Loss, and Grief

1. What are the patterns of loss in the family? What are the circumstances of these losses?
2. How was grief expressed or not expressed in the family and by whom?
3. Are there secrets surrounding any of the losses? Who has information? How is it shared?
4. Are there family or religious rituals for going through the grieving process? Were they followed?
5. Are both positive and negative feelings expressed about deaths or other losses? Are pictures, mementos, and stories shared openly, or are there no signs or perhaps "shrines" to someone who has died, abandoned, or been cut-off from the individual or the family?
6. Are there patterns of illness in the family?

7. What are the historical and contemporary patterns of normal, abnormal, unresolved, or interminable grief?
8. Have there been perinatal deaths in the family? How were they handled?
9. How are deaths of friends, distant family members, ex-spouses, pets, or coworkers addressed?
10. Are there cultural (religious, ethnic, or socioeconomic) considerations regarding loss and grief?

Eunpu (1997) recommends the use of the "grief genogram" to help individuals and couples to reduce a sense of isolation and constructively involve other family members in their grieving process.

More Questions About Grief

1. What were your experiences with grief in your family?
2. Who was allowed to grieve?
3. When was grief permitted (i.e., which losses are acknowledged as deserving grief)?
4. How was grief displayed and expressed in your family?
5. What were the family's attitudes about how long grief may last (i.e., what length of grieving is too long or too short)?
6. What does it mean to express grief differently than expected by your family?
7. How have children been involved in the grieving process?
8. How has the family viewed the use of outside support services such as support groups or mental health professionals?

Fear

Neuroscientists are tracking the effects of fear and terror within the emotional circuitry of the brain. The symptoms of post-traumatic stress disorder—hypervigilance, disturbing dreams, anxiety—become emotional allergies, the result of disregulated brain chemistry. Emotional allergies have been defined as acute emotional sensitivities to past emotional experiences (Gordon, 1993). Emotional allergies can result in excessive immersion in the emotional state or in excessive behaviors to avoid the emotion. The emotional circuitry of fear and helplessness triggers a biochemical storm that puts the body on general alert and fixates attention on the potential or actual threat. If trauma is severe enough, brain research now suggests that the biochemicals released in response to extreme stress set in motion a long-lasting and worsening disregulation of the body's complex biochemistry (Butler, 1996). Wolpe and Wolpe (1988) suggested that people develop useless fears that result under two circumstances. First, in a frightening situation, a highly emotional person will experience higher anxiety, and therefore more anxiety is attached to the situation. Second, an individual exposed to an earlier fearful experience is more vulnerable to the later development of several fears arising from similar circumstances. Wolpe believe that fears can spring up virtually anywhere, at any time, in connection with almost anything; susceptibility is not affected by intelligence or physical prowess (Wolpe & Wolpe, 1988).

Since 1986, Pennebaker (1995) has studied the effects of writing and talking about traumatic events. He found that if individuals are asked to write or talk about traumatic events, significant improvements occur in physical health. Similarly, Herman (1992) has outlined three steps to recovery from trauma: attaining a sense of security and safety, remembering the details of the trauma and grieving the loss and destruction to one's life, and reestablishing a normal lifestyle. This process allows for emotional relearning. The foundation of emotional reeducation is in teaching the neocortex, more specifically the prefrontal lobes, to inhibit the amygdala (LeDoux, 1989), but not at the expense of disarming the neocortex. Preliminary research and program evaluations suggest that teaching skills to identify, manage, and effectively express feelings is essential. The cognitive capacities of the human being, a delicate balance between the prefrontal lobes and the amygdala, are essential to stability of personality and interpersonal relationships.

Questions About Fear

1. What do you recall about being fearful in your life?
2. Did you experience traumatic events in your life? How was the fear expressed?
3. What frightened you as a child?
4. What frightens you today?
5. How do you react when you are frightened? How do you react when others are frightened?
6. What are your worries or phobias?
7. General screening for post-traumatic stress disorder (sexual abuse and severe posttraumatic symptoms are discussed in Chapter 8): Do you have particular fears or phobias; psychological numbing; difficulty concentrating; repetitive thoughts, feelings, or images; night terrors, waking in the night?
8. Did other family members suffer traumatic events during their life? What happened? How did they deal with or express their fears?
9. Are there patterns of anxiety disorders within the family?

Pleasure

"Life, liberty and the pursuit of happiness..." These words have different meanings to different people. Defining happiness is as difficult as defining love and many other values. Casriel (1972) suggested that pleasure results from the fulfillment of biological needs. Pearsall (1996) proposes the "pleasure paradigm" which rests on the concept of "enlightened hedonism." There is an emotional and physical basis for pleasure. The expression of the affects of interest and enjoyment combine to form the experience of pleasure and fulfillment in life. "Alert, active, energetic, clear, quick, logical, learning, gains knowledge, participates, accomplishes something, did something well:" These are the descriptors of interest. Interest is a crucial emotion that promotes and sustains motivation. Izard (1977) suggests that interest is the most prevalent motivational condition for the day-to-day functioning of normal human beings. Without interest, life has little meaning.

Joy, on the other hand, is a by-product of efforts that have other aims (Izard, 1977). Joy is described as a sense of confidence and importance that is coupled with contentment with self and others. Schutz (1967) defined joy as the fulfillment of one's potential. In Schutz's theory, obstacles to fulfilling one's potential are also obstacles to realizing joy in life. Some of these obstacles include the following: institutional rules and regulations that squelch creativity and impose mediocrity; hypercritical social relationships; dogma relating to child rearing, sex, and personal options in life; confusion and uncertainty about gender-role expectations and demands; high values placed on material success and achievement; and poor physical condition that diminishes sensation and experience.

Identifying the patterns of pleasure in the client's family system is a useful way to address generalized anxiety and depression. In individuals and families who are anxious or depressed, pleasure and enjoyment of life is often minimal. If the focus on pleasure reveals a dynamic, exciting family system, then an individual's depression and anxiety can be explored in relation to a wide range of choices. If the focus on pleasure reveals a suppressed, unhappy, unfulfilled family system, then the client's depression and anxiety can be explored by examining the fewer choices that are available. People often have expectations regarding the degree of happiness they can expect in life based on what they have learned in their family of origin. Exploring these patterns is often a useful exercise in moving toward balancing an individual's range of emotional experience.

Questions About Pleasure

1. What kinds of creativity are evident in your family?
2. Are family members generally viewed as lovable and important? Is affection shown regularly?
3. Do people in the family participate in hobbies? Social activities? Sports? Community activities?
4. What kind of social network is available? Family? Friendship? Work or career associates? Social, religious, or civic memberships?
5. How are physical health and well-being addressed? What are the patterns of general health? What are the patterns of physical exercise and nutrition?
6. Do you have "fun" in your life? How? Do members of your extended family have "fun?" How?
7. Do you have a sense of humor? Do other members of you family have a sense of humor?
8. Do you set goals? Have a positive mental outlook? How about other members of the extended family, now and in the past?
9. Do you take vacations, short trips, and schedule activities? How often? Was this something your family did when you were growing up? How often?

In addition to these questions, Pearsall's (1996) Aloha Test (aloha is the instinctive drive toward pleasure and healthfulness) explores five dimensions that contribute to a pleasurable lifestyle: patience, unity, agreeability, humbleness, and kindness. Clinicians may ask how the family system rates on these dimensions, as well.

Managing Affect While Constructing the Emotions Genograms

A clinician has a primary responsibility for creating a safe environment during treatment. At times, clients can behave inappropriately in the expression of their feelings. At other times, they are detached and seem emotionally unavailable. Constructing Emotions Genograms can amplify these behaviors, and the therapist must be prepared to attend to inappropriate and intense expressions of feeling as well as to support someone who is struggling. These patterns of expressions are learned and reinforced through life. Feelings are not the problem. Feelings are essential to personal happiness and interpersonal satisfaction. However, the behavioral patterns of expression or containment are the focus of exploration in Emotions Genograms.

If anger is being expressed through inappropriate behaviors such as snide remarks, criticism, shouting, or demanding, the clinician must establish baseline rules for communication. An Anger Genogram may be a more appropriate place to begin in these cases. Many clients have no idea about alternate modes of expression. Basic principles about "I messages" and clear communication are essential, and the clinician must be prepared to model these behaviors as well as establish the ground rules.

Conversely, if the clinician wants to intensify affect, role playing and Gestalt techniques can be very useful methods of fostering greater awareness of feelings. L'Abate's writing exercises (1992) can foster this process before and during the Emotions Genogram process. Gray's feeling letter (1984) is another method that can be used to address emotions. Stosny (1995) has developed a technique, called "Heals," that he proposes to foster emotional regulation. Many clinical models have similar methods for addressing affect in the clinical setting.

The clinician's use of empathic listening during the process of discovery not only can help the client become more aware of feelings but also provides a corrective emotional experience for the client. Often, repressed clients have experienced deprivation of appropriate emotional attunement early in their lives. The therapist also must be aware that a client may have difficulty accepting or dealing with "positive" emotional experiences. Corrective emotional experiences often are experienced as incongruent with previous relationship experiences. Most clients look to the therapist for reeducation and reframing of their emotional experience. This requires the therapist to move comfortably between cognitive and affective dimensions of emotion.

The Emotions Genogram process also can evoke painful memories, and the clinician must be prepared to provide support and reassurance during these times. The clinician should become familiar with literature on post-traumatic stress disorder symptoms, family violence, and effects of child abuse and neglect and have his or her own peer support or ongoing supervision.

The Emotions Family Map

The Emotions Family Map depicts the emotional tone and quality of important relationships. Along with the Internal Models Map (described in Chapter 6), it gives the clinician an important way to determine a helpful, and potentially emotionally corrective, therapeutic posture. Because the Emotions Family Map highlights contemporary relationship experience, and the Internal Models Map examines childhood experience, the clinician can examine similarities and differences between the two. A control-

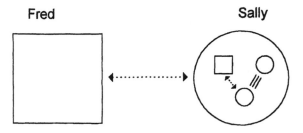

FIGURE 7.2. Illustration of an Emotions Family Map with wife's Internal Models Map.

ling and critical mother and a hostile and distant father who was often away from home characterized Sally's childhood relationships. Her marriage to a police detective, Fred, was similar to her relationship with her father and her mother. Her husband worked long hours and was often unavailable. Although he was generally supportive of her, John's detective work in homicide made him generally distrusting and hostile regarding the outside world. Consequently, John monitored Sally's whereabouts and discouraged her from being "out in the world" more than necessary. Sally's attachment style to her mother could be characterized as "preoccupied," and her attachment style to her father could be characterized as "dismissing." A moderately high level of anxiety characterized here relationship with her husband. Figure 7.2 illustrates how these relationships can be mapped.

The Emotions Time Line

When constructing an Emotions Time Line it is important to track and note emotionally traumatic experiences, especially those that occur from birth to age 10 years. These are critical years for brain development (turns out Freud was off by about 5 years!). Because stress produces cortisol, which effects the emotional center of the brain, intense emotional experiences early in life must be examined. Traumatic experiences throughout life also are responsible for post-traumatic stress disorders, which range from mild to severe depending on the traumatic emotional event. Corporal punishment, various forms of child abuse, and family violence are especially damaging to a child's developing emotional capacity; these are explored further in the next chapter. Tragedies also can effect emotional experience in significant ways. The Time Line is an effective way to track the duration of emotional stress experienced by the client system.

Making Sense of Emotions Genograms: Theoretical Underpinnings

Working with Emotions in Clinical Practice

The Emotions Genograms yields a great deal of information and can guide therapeutic strategy. Often, material gained during the process helps the clinician and client to go beyond the issues of the presenting problem and identify essential family issues that may be contributing to contemporary personal and family problems. Goleman's research (1995) suggests that helping people better manage their upsetting feelings—anger, anxiety, depression, pessimism, and loneliness—is a form of disease prevention and that many health problems can improve measurably if psychological needs are attended to along with medical needs. Greenberg and Safran (1987) specify four reasons for attending to emotional experience during treatment:

- Discharge or expression of emotion is important for mental and physical well-being.
- Emotional insight and awareness are key in becoming more "objective" about reactivity and responses to life experiences.
- Facilitating adaptive emotional expression is important in maintaining interpersonal relationships.
- Emotional processing is essential in alleviating distress from traumatic experiences. The importance of congruent emotional expression in maintaining satisfying interpersonal relationships cannot be overstated.

Emotions Genograms can begin a process of self-awareness and emotional congruity that can help clients change and improve many facets of their lives. The use of Emotions Genograms is dependent on the clinician's use and comfort with affective models of intervention. If a therapist is unfamiliar with affective models of intervention, Emotions Genograms may not be indicated or may be conducted in a very brief manner. Emotions Genograms are also inappropriate if anger management and anger self-regulation are the focus of treatment. As with other genograms, it is usually important for the clinician to address the presenting problem before exploring family history in any depth.

Although understanding emotional process is important in clinical process, attending to emotions during the treatment process has been controversial. Johnson and Greenberg (1994) identify eight reasons why emotion is relevant in interpersonal relationships and, consequently, in family treatment:

1. Emotional experience and expression is the primary building block of adult intimate relationships.

2. Emotions, such as love, are adaptive in human functioning.
3. Emotion is a primary signaling system.
4. Emotion primes and organizes people for action in general, and for interpersonal responses in particular.
5. Emotions play a powerful role in structuring interactional positions.
6. Experienced emotion provides access to needs and desires.
7. Emotions organize perceptions of self and other.
8. Emotion links self and system.

Greenberg and Safran (1987) identify three specific reasons for addressing emotion in psychotherapy: Processing information in an experiential manner produces productive client involvement in some forms of therapy; emotional arousal and expression are related to change in specific circumstances; and anxiety can be reduced by maintaining a high level of emotional arousal in specific circumstances. Although research is mixed on the importance of catharsis (intense emotional expression) as a means to resolve emotional or behavioral problems, advances in neuroscience, neuropsychology, and psychoneuroimmunology suggest that addressing emotions in the treatment process is extremely important. Emotions buffet our immune system; emotions may be the biochemical links between body and mind. Pert's research (1997) has led her to conclude that consciousness of emotional experience is essential for healing. In brief, emotion may be the heart of interpersonal communication and the foundation for personal well-being.

Satir (1967), one of the pioneer family therapists, emphasized that feelings that are not allowed, not expressed, or out of control often come out as incongruent communication styles, which lead to decreases in self esteem. Self-esteem is fostered by open communication of thoughts and feelings. However, cultural influences, family patterns, social conditioning, and psychological process often discourage expression of emotion. If congruent emotional expression is stunted, unclear and incongruent communication is often the result.

Satir (1988) identified four "stress styles" of communication that result from incongruence. These styles are designated as: (1) placating, (2) distracting, (3) blaming, and (4) superreasonable. In each of these stress styles, some aspect of emotional experience is negated. In the placating stress style, the person negates his or her own needs, thoughts, or feelings and overemphasizes the situation and the other person's needs. In the blaming stress style, the person is focused on his or her needs, thoughts, and feelings in the particular situation at hand and negates the other person, demonstrating a lack of empathy. In the superreasonable stress style, the person negates both his or her own needs, thoughts, feelings and those of the other person; only the situation matters. In the distracting stress style, the person negates himself or herself, the other person, and

ation. These stress styles are a consequence of unexpressed and
ated feelings and needs. Satir emphasized that suppressing feel-
___s a great deal of energy and attention and that people who either
cannot or do not express their feelings constructively and productively
are very lonely people. She believed that being able to communicate
about feelings leads to high levels of self-esteem, good communication
and problem-solving skills, and successful relationships.

The New World of Emotions

Neuroscientists are making exciting discoveries about the nature of emotion and the role of emotion in health and illness. Emotional intelligence
is a concept that suggests that knowing and managing our emotions, as
well as having emotional self-control, empathy, and relationship skills
are crucial for success in all areas of life (Goleman, 1995). Feelings are
indispensable for rational decision. Without access to emotional memory, everything becomes gray. Research is showing that chronic anger
and anxiety are health risks. Emotions that are beneath our threshold of
awareness have a tremendous impact on our perceptions and reactions
(Sotile, 1992).

Joseph LeDoux has been studying the architecture of the brain's emotional systems (Goleman, 1995), and his work is overturning longstanding ideas about emotional functioning. His work suggests that our
emotions have a "mind of their own" and specific neurological pathways
(Goleman, 1995) and that, in fact, experience in life is processed emotionally before intellect and reason can respond. Candace Pert, a highly respected neuroscientist interviewed by Moyers (1993), believes that emotion is not fully expressed until it reaches consciousness and that unexpressed emotions (through the accumulation of neuropeptides) are physically present throughout the body (Pert, 1997). Pert has identified and
studied the movement of amino-acid chains (called *neuropeptides*) in the
human body. She believes that these neuropeptides are the biochemical
correlates of emotions. These peptides are found not only in the brain but
also in the stomach, muscles, glands, and major organs. (There seems to
be some scientific basis to "gut" reactions.) Consequently, Pert has found
that every peptide can be found in the autonomic nervous system, and
therefore emotional memory is stored not only in the brain but also in
the body.

The mind-body link is not a new concept. However, strong scientific
evidence for these linkages is new. Research demonstrates that patterns
of emotional expression can have physical as well as psychological rami-
fications. Pennebaker (1995) found that if people talk or write about up-

setting experiences there are significant improvements in physical healt. Studies also show that loneliness and lack of social support result in low levels of natural killer-cell activity (Pennebaker, Kiecolt-Glaser, & Glaser, 1988). Research also demonstrates that marital conflict turns on the hormones (epinephrine, norepinephrine, and cortisol) that turn down the immune system. Not only do men and women respond to arguments with decreased immune-system function, but also when husbands withdraw during arguments, women's levels of epinephrine, norepinephrine, and cortisol skyrocket. The divorce experience also has been shown to suppress the immune system and should not be overlooked during the treatment process.

Casriel (1972) developed a system of therapy, called the *New Identity Process*, which considers emotion to be a whole-body experience. Although he developed his model during the 1960s and 1970s, his concepts are relevant to new findings about emotional expression. Casriel emphasized the interplay between affect, behavior, and cognition. His work is based on Rado's Adaptational Psychodynamics (1969), which emphasized the importance of emotions. Rado's central theme is that organisms move toward a source of pleasure and away from a source of pain. Casriel took this concept and combined it with his experience with confrontational emotional therapies used in therapeutic communities for treatment of addictions and so became one of the pioneers to explore the territory that emotions are physical, not psychological. His work incorporates both verbal and full-bodied physical expression of emotion. As Johnson and Greenberg (1994) suggest, intervention at the level of emotion helps the clinician create a necessary bridge among the intrapsychic, the interpersonal, the social, and the biological. Recently the American Psychological Association added body and movement therapies as recognized psychological services. Therefore, it would appear that the chasm between mind, body, and emotion is closing.

Emotion is not only universal, as Darwin noted so long ago, but also essential to human relationship. Darwin was actually the first to note that emotional expression was universal in many of its features. His primary interest, however, was in the universality of facial expressions as they related to emotional experience. Today, clinicians and researchers have built on this framework and are now working to define and understand the basics of emotion (Ekman & Davidson, 1994). Goleman (1995) describes a case of a young man whose amygdala (a structure in the brain that is sometimes called the "emotional brain") was removed in order to control a seizure disorder. He no longer recognized close friends, relatives, or even his mother, and the result was a complete loss of feeling. This condition is sometimes called *affective blindness*.

Frijda's laws of emotion (1988) are an attempt to summarize what is known about emotional functioning:

1. Interpretations of events influence emotional response.
2. Emotions arise because an individual determines that an event or situation is important to his or her goals, needs, or concerns.
3. Perceptions of events influences emotional response, and intensity corresponds to these perceptions.
4. Continued pleasures wear off; continued hardships lose their poignancy. Expectations about changes affect emotional response, and the intensity of emotional response depends on the person's frame of reference.
5. Pleasure is contingent upon change and variety and disappears with continuous satisfaction. Tolerance is developed to excitement, but pain persists under persisting adverse conditions.
6. Emotional events keep their power to elicit emotional responses indefinitely, unless counteracted by repeated exposures.
7. Emotions have a life of their own and are not always subject to rationality.
8. Every emotional impulse elicits a secondary impulse that tends to modify it in view of its possible consequences (anger-fear).
9. Individuals tend to view the world in ways that minimize negative emotional responses.

Pain and Pleasure: Naming the Feelings

Based on the research and work of Tomkins, Nathanson (1992) developed a model called *affect theory*. Affect theory is a useful clinical model describing affect, feeling, emotion, mood, and mood disorder. In this model, *affect* is the term describing the strictly biological portion of emotion, the unvarying patterns of physiological arousal. Although there is no universal agreement about the basic affects, most models of emotion incorporate these seven: excitement, enjoyment, surprise, fear, anger, distress (sadness or grief), and disgust. Excitement and enjoyment comprise the feelings commonly called *pleasure*, and fear, anger, distress, and disgust comprise the feelings commonly called *pain*. A *feeling*, according to Nathanson describes a person's level of awareness that an affect has been triggered. If someone experiences a sudden twinge in his or her stomach, for example, he or she might say to himself or herself, "I'm scared." This awareness and cognitive process bring affects into consciousness and, in many cases, into an interaction with another person. Assessing how a client has learned to express and name feelings is often an important part of assessment and treatment planning.

So what does the term *emotion* mean? What is the difference between *feelings* and *emotion*? How do these distinctions help with Emotions Genograms? According to Nathanson (1992), emotion requires yet another level of complexity beyond feeling. An emotion, he suggests, is a complex combination of affect, memory, and life scripts or biography. To understand someone's emotion called *anger* you need to know something about how anger was expressed in the family system; how anger socialized the culture of his or her peers; how anger was socialized in the school, community, and larger environment; and what particular kinds of incidents trigger anger in the person's individual life. Emotion is about the biography and history of affective experiences. This is the emphasis of Emotions Genograms: understanding and identifying the patterns of feelings in a client's life and family system.

Another contribution of affect theory is the notion of moods and mood disorders. *Moods* and *mood disorders* are defined as persistent states of emotion that may be tied to past experience and that also can be tied to biological disturbances. A child who lives in a chronic state of fear and who is growing up in a violent family or neighborhood can develop an adaptive emotional state that can become a fixture of his or her personality. This person might well have measurable changes in his or her biochemistry that might be assisted by psychotherapy as well as medication. The emotional mood state is both tied to past and present experience and is, ultimately, a biological disturbance as well.

Mood patterns can be identified using Emotions Genograms. For example, Linda presented her four-generation genogram and noted an extensive family history of alcoholism. Although alcoholism runs in families, in this genogram almost every individual had difficulties with alcohol. The clinician inquired about the emotional life of the family system and learned that in addition to the alcoholism these family members also had serious difficulties with anxiety disorders. Some studies of alcoholism suggest that one biological marker for alcoholism is the undersecretion of GABA, a neurotransmitter that regulates anxiety; this undersecretion results in a craving for calm (Goleman, 1995) Upon learning about the anxiety disorders in Linda's family, an Emotions Genogram was initiated and conducted to examine the influences upon Linda and her relationships.

Emptying the "Emotional Jug"

An important by-product of Emotions Genograms for the client is that emotional/feeling expression is encouraged. A number of clinical models support the expression of emotion as an important clinical intervention.

Similarly, suppressed feelings often are referred to as the "emotional iceberg," the "emotional jug," or the "emotional trash can." Gordon (1993) developed the concept of the emotional jug to describe the multilayered effect of emotions. The cork in the emotional jug is indifference, the attitude that develops after years of repressing emotions. Gordon suggests that once anger, fear, and sadness are confided in a safe and validating relationship there is room in the emotional jug for love and tenderness. Gray (1984) developed the *feeling letter technique* and identified five levels to emotional experience: level one: anger and blame, level two: hurt and sadness, level three: fear and insecurity; level four: guilt and responsibility; and level five: love, forgiveness, understanding, and intention. Working through these various levels of emotion can be an important consequence of the Emotions Genogram. For clinicians who emphasize this approach to treatment, emptying the emotional jug of negative feelings is an important clinical intervention.

The *museum tour* is a specific, and often-cited, technique developed by Bach and Goldberg (1974) to explore positive and negative memories and experiences, as well as traumas. The museum tour is a technique for exploring past hurts whether they are in the current relationship, past relationships, or childhood or adolescent experiences (Crosby, 1989). It can be followed by an exploration of these same themes in the family system. Additionally, it is often useful in conducting museum tours to talk with siblings, parents, relatives, and family friends. As a child, Beth's family-of-origin moved frequently because her father was in the army. In constructing Emotions Genograms, she and her sister got together to talk about the many moves and, in one case, they drew floor plans of several of the homes. This exercise helped each of them recall memories and experiences about the emotional themes in their childhood. After this step is taken further exploration of emotional themes and moods in the family can be pursued using "Pain and Pleasure in My Family" as a tool.

Other techniques for helping clients empty the emotional jug include recalling and sharing emotional memories through the use of old photographs, videotapes, and other memorabilia. Family albums can be a very helpful resource. The lack or loss of these kinds of materials also can help clients address past hurts. Melinda was the youngest and only female in her family. When photographs were suggested as a method for recalling family memories, she recounted how there were few, if any, pictures of her during her childhood. However, there were many pictures of her two brothers displayed throughout her parent's home. This step helped Melinda begin to explore her sense of loneliness within her family.

☐ Summary

The Emotions Genograms is a format for exploring the emotional intelligence of the family system. In this Focused Genogram, the emphasis is on understanding patterns of expression across the broad range of emotions—sadness, fear, loss, love, and pleasure. Patterns of individual and family emotional expression have important implications for adjustment, satisfaction, and health. Emotional intelligence is to social skills what IQ is to cognitive skills. The degree to which Emotions Genograms are employed in a specific clinical situation is determined by the clinical model of the practitioner. If the therapist uses an affective model of intervention, Emotions Genograms are an important tool for exploring the variety and range of affect expressed by the individual as well as the family. Neuroscience and other medical research indicates that the mind-body link via emotion is stronger than prior research suggested.

This chapter provides a model and guidelines for addressing the emotional features of individual and family functioning. Emotions Genograms help identify patterns of emotional expression and inhibition. Emotionally traumatic or stressful life experiences are noted on the Time Line; in contrast to the identification of themes, the Family Map examines the emotional quality of interpersonal relationships. Emotions Genograms follow the Attachments Genogram and give the practitioner an even better understanding of the individual and the family system. With the inclusion of the Anger Genogram in the next chapter, the clinician has a complete and in-depth view of the interpersonal world of the client system. This perspective helps the therapist target interventions that can provide corrective emotional experiences within the clinical settings as well as in family relationships.

☐ Recommended Readings

Goleman (1995), *Emotional Intelligence*
Izard (1977), *Human Emotions*
Nathanson (1992), *Shame and Pride: Affect, Sex, and the Birth of Self*

Anger Genograms

In the previous chapter, the Emotions Genogram was presented. Anger was excluded because anger is a powerful, important, and complex emotion. Anger can create havoc in human relationships and has both psychological and physical effects on the individual and family. The hot-reactor type A personality can lead to heart illness (Sotile, 1992). The destructive ways in which aggression and anger in the family can effect personality are discussed in this chapter. At its worst, anger can lead to the cycle of violence that destroys personal and family security through domestic violence, crime, and even death.

Anger results from physical or psychological restraint, or from interference with goal-directed behavior (Izard, 1977). A universal trigger for anger is the sense of being endangered—not just physical threat but also symbolic threats to self-esteem or dignity. In contrast to sadness or fear, anger is energizing. Some researchers believe that anger can, and should, be prevented entirely. Their research suggests that as anger builds on anger, unhampered by reason, people can erupt into violence. Others believe that expression of anger in appropriate contexts and relationships is crucial to mental health. Williams (1989) believes that we need to distinguish between anger that lets us know that a change is needed and a hostile, aggressive personality. His research shows that those who have a hostile personality are five to seven times more likely to die between the ages of 25 and 50 years.

☐ Constructing Anger Genograms

Anger Genograms are an important part of the MFG. The purpose is to help the client system connect current attitudes and behaviors about anger to experiences in the family. Patterns of hostility and conflict among the generations also are explored in Anger Genograms, along with an examination of the styles and intensity of anger and conflict within the family system. Did the family avoid and negate conflict or was anger violent and hostile? How were family members affected by anger? What messages did children receive about the expression of anger? As these questions suggest, the effects of anger can be seen throughout the family system, in both individual and relationship contexts.

The earliest experiences with anger occur in the family of origin. In some families, anger is handled in an appropriate and healthy way; members are allowed to be angry and encouraged to express the feeling openly and constructively. If someone is unfair, they apologize and even make amends if needed. These families rarely present for treatment.

In some families, anger is a forbidden feeling. These families attempt to suppress and deny anger that leads to emotional distance. Children do not see their parents fight openly or talk about angry feelings. Children in these families grow up learning how to express their anger indirectly. They learn that anger is a bad feeling, too horrible and frightening to talk about or express. Anger is feared because no one knows how to deal with it and it must be so terrible that it has been banished. These families also may intellectualize, and their members often have obsessive-compulsive, superreasonable personality styles. Individuals from these families will equate anger in a relationship with a relationship that is a mistake. In other words, one cannot be in a relationship in which anger exists. It was not allowed in the family; consequently, it should not be allowed in adult relationships.

In another type of family, anger rules the day. These families are conflict-habituated. Anger is a pervasive feeling in these families. Everyone is allowed, even encouraged to join the game of being angry with everyone else. Cognitive control in these families is poor. Members are overreactive, and there is a great deal of emotional fusion. As long as members are angry with each other, no one has to look at himself or herself or take personal responsibility. In the blaming style, the other person's needs and feelings are not taken into account.

Gender is another factor to be taken into consideration in examining anger styles. In many families, patriarchy is the rule. Father is the dominant member and he uses anger and active control styles (Miller, Nunnally, & Wackman, 1975) to maintain compliance. The mother takes on the submissive role, not confronting her husband. Children may become the objects of father's anger and of mother's anger toward her husband. The children feel powerless and fearful and often suppress their anger, knowing that the consequence of getting angry is more punishment. This type of family encourages the development of gender-specific emotional roles and emotional powerlessness. In extreme cases, this pattern is the foundation for domestic violence and battering.

Preparing for Anger Genograms

Anger Genograms are appropriate in most cases. Understanding the underlying intrapsychic, interpersonal and familial patterns and themes is important in the following situations: over- and underexpression of anger, ineffective conflict-resolution skills, gender-specific expression, and cognitive distortions about anger (anger is bad). In practice, Anger Genograms usually are needed in all cases. The exception can be if a client is able to handle anger appropriately and can discuss it constructively. However, marital therapy often reveals deficits in an individual's ability to self-regulate anger responses. If a client is knowledgeable about anger patterns within the family, Anger Genograms can be used to clarify the patterns.

The timing of Anger Genograms is important. If a client were coming to therapy in a crisis, it would not be appropriate to move to Anger Genograms immediately. The beginning stage of treatment focuses on problem solving. Once the client system has made progress in addressing the presenting problem, the therapist can begin to create Anger Genograms. If the presenting problem is intimate violence, the Anger Genogram is a very important step in getting an accurate assessment of the scope of the problem.

Anger Genograms seek historical information in order to help make sense of current attitudes, emotions, and patterns of behavior. Doing Anger Genograms without the current context would not make a great deal of sense. The first step in the process is to gain some understanding about anger in the here-and-now. Weeks and Hof (1995) have developed a series of questions to help acquire this information. These questions should be covered slowly and thoroughly. Questions 1 and 10 frequently require entire sessions or more to be answered. Question 1 is not just about the definition of anger, but the attitude, beliefs, and feelings about anger. Question 10 is the most complex. Because of its physiological power, anger fills up the "emotional jug" referred to in Chapter 7. The other feelings that are connected, interrelated, and underneath it become suppressed.

Questions About the Meaning and Function of Anger

1. What is anger?
2. What does it mean when you are angry?
3. What does it mean when you are angry with your partner or someone else?
4. What does it mean when your partner (or someone else) is angry?
5. What does it mean when your partner (or someone else) is angry with you?
6. How do you respond to you partner's (or someone else's) anger?
7. How do you respond to your own anger?
8. How do you let your partner (someone else) know you are angry?
9. How long does your anger usually last?
10. What are the feelings that are associated with your anger?

As this information is collected, it is important to help the client discern thoughts and judgments from feelings. Many clients have trouble focusing on the feelings. They confuse a thought ("I told her to go to hell"), which is a statement of action, with a feeling ("I was furious with her"). Judgments also become confused with feelings. Saying "I feel fine" or "I felt bad" are actually judgments about feeling states and are difficult for many clients to separate out from the feelings. Once this work has been done, and the current emotional context established, Anger Genograms then can be done. Anger and conflict go hand-in-hand. Therefore, Anger Genograms uses both terms.

The next step in the process is to address the various expressions of anger. Expression of anger can sometimes be clear and up-front and other times very subtle. Learning to recognize personal patterns of anger is an important step in developing emotional literacy, a crucial social skill (Goleman, 1995). The repression of anger, and other emotions, is rooted in communication styles and patterns learned in the family. Patterns of corporal punishment and family violence often affect attitudes and feelings toward anger. Despite anger's powerful physiologic makeup, many people learn to suppress their anger. Others exhibit type A personality or narcissistic rage, both of which are discussed in the section on theoretical underpinnings later in this chapter.

Consequently, a client may not always recognize anger when it is present, and it can take some time for the clinician to identify the anger style. Lee grew up in a family in which children had no voice. However, the adults screamed, yelled, and were emotionally and physically volatile. Mother, father, grandmother, grandfather, aunt, or uncle as deemed necessary administered corporal punishment. There was no recourse, no ally. Lee learned to accept anger and aggression from others but did not feel her own.

Bach and Goldberg (1974) developed a useful model for identif
ferent styles of anger and aggression. They categorized eight diffei
terns of styles. The first method is what they called "hidden agg:
In this category, the person and his or her partner deny they are angry but
act in hostile ways toward each other. In some cases, one person may facilitate another's self-destructive behavior such as drinking or using drugs.
A second method is quite familiar to therapists. This expression of anger is
"passive-aggressive." The specific techniques include forgetting, procras-
tinating, misunderstanding, and attributing meaning to another's behavior that was not intended. A third approach is "moral one-upmanship."
The angry person takes a position of being morally right or superior in
an attempt to put the other person down, create guilt or self-doubt, or
cast doubt on the person's character. In the fourth method, the anger is
difficult to see because it is hidden behind a behavior deemed socially
acceptable. The angry person "intellectualizes" the feeling and presents
himself or herself as the rational one. By implication, the other person
is cast as the irrational or "crazy" player. Being "nonrewarding" is the
fifth method. A nonrewarder will withhold praise or acknowledgment of
something done well or appreciated, even if it is appropriate. The underlying message seems to be that the other person can never be good
enough. In the last three methods, anger is expressed from a position of
expressed weakness or helplessness. The "helpless aggressor" uses fears,
hurts, and weakness to avoid responsibility and control the relationship.
The "sickness tyrant" uses physical illness in the same way. The "Red
Cross nurse aggressor" overtly offers to help others by keeping them dependent and helpless, which actually perpetuates their weakness. When
the "victim" does not get better, the person can feel justified in getting
angry.

The value of understanding such patterns is that they help clinicians
characterize behavior patterns that are not going to lead to constructive
expression of anger or to relationship satisfaction. The patterns become
warning signs that the client is entering a cycle that can not lead to problem resolution. Satir (1988) suggests that identifying stress styles and patterns gives choice, increases awareness, and helps promote understanding.

When assessing the client's current state relative to anger, as well as
anger in the family system, it is important to go beyond simple statements
and descriptions. It may first be useful to work with the client in the here-
and-now to help him or her learn more about how to recognize his or her
anger. Then he or she can connect these patterns to how his or her parents (and grandparents; sometimes even great-grandparents) expressed
anger. Stan, for example, reported in therapy sessions that he did not get
angry. If there was conflict with someone in his life, he avoided the per-

son or got out of the relationship. Stan prided himself on his rationality. However, he was on the verge of leaving his wife because he "didn't love her anymore." As the marital problem was explored, it became apparent that Stan had avoided conflict with his wife for many years and that by avoiding conflict he also had avoided expressing his needs and concerns to her. Her attempts to be kind or supportive, which became feebler over the years, often missed the mark, and Stan believed that she only cared about her needs and desires. Anger Genograms would reveal that Stan grew up in a family filled with hostility and violence and that Stan had decided that conflict would not be part of his life.

After diagnostic information has been gathered, different therapeutic strategies may be implemented. In general, the clinician can think of the work in terms of the cognitive, the affective, and the behavioral. Antidepressants sometimes are used as well. In the past, much of what was written about anger has been from a behavioral perspective. The behaviorists stress learning new skills to resolve conflict and address the anger. L'Abate and McHenry (1983) provided an excellent review of the major behavioral interventions. Learning new skills is certainly part of the work that needs to be done. However, learning fair fighting skills first requires a readiness. Most clients are not ready because they do not possess the proper attitude toward anger (defined as compassion by Stosny, 1995), have a number of cognitive distortions about anger, and are not in touch with the feeling complex that surrounds anger. A comprehensive approach to dealing with anger and conflict has been described (Weeks & Hof, 1995). Stosny's work with family violence is also a resource (Stosny, 1995).

The family-of-origin material helps the client gain appreciation of the impact of his or her early experiences and what he or she internalized about anger. The client should begin to recognize how he or she acquired behavioral patterns based on modeling of his or her parents (or other significant figures) and the cognitive distortions learned from each parent. Once he or she is cognizant of these facts, he or she is freer to choose his or her own beliefs about anger and conflict. The therapist then has a better chance to offer new and positive perspectives on anger and have these ideas accepted. In some cases, the first step is to stay with the family-of-origin material for some period until it has been assimilated consciously and altered. If the anger is toward the parents, it might be useful at some point to hold sessions involving the parents so the adult child can express these feelings, experience validation from the parents, and understand the parent's difficulties in dealing with the feeling.

Another technique for addressing anger toward family members is to write a "letting go of grudges letter" or "feeling letter." In this format anger, resentment, fears, regrets, hopes, and wishes are explored. After writing this letter, usually unsent, the client writes the letter he or she would like to receive in response. This is often a very clarifying experience for the client. Sometimes the spouse can be the reader of the wished-for response. In this format, a bond of empathy is created between the partners, which can provide a satisfying experience for the client dealing with the anger.

The information derived from the meaning and function of anger and the subsequent Anger Genograms needs to be processed at an affective level. Allowing oneself to experience anger free of guilt and other emotions that have blocked it is a first step. The expression and clarification of anger can be channeled into healthy self-assertion, self-expression, and congruence, short-circuiting the impulsivity of misunderstood anger. It then is possible to access the anger at deeper levels, such as underlying sadness and fear. The therapist wants to facilitate a deeper awareness of the anger using whatever techniques fit the client. Some clients respond well to keeping an anger journal. Clients write down the event that triggered anger, thoughts about the event, feelings about the event, and what the client could do to resolve the event. Other clients do better with in-office techniques such as dream analysis, feedback, and a variety of Gestalt techniques used to amplify emotion. However, emotional-release strategies should not be entered into without specific training in these methods.

Once there is an awareness of the anger feelings, it is possible to do some cognitive therapy that fosters greater emotional self-awareness and empathy. As early as 1976, Ellis was writing about how to deal with anger more constructively using a rational-emotion approach. His basic idea was to identify the irrational thoughts that created the angry feeling and change the thoughts. For example, he believed thinking in terms of shoulds, oughts, and musts generated a good deal of anger.

In addition to the techniques offered by some of the major approaches to therapy, three other techniques are useful. One is focused writing; another is a cathartic method that addresses not only emotion but attitudes around the emotion as well; and the third is a cognitive technique. Focused writing involves writing about a particular event or feeling in a thematic way. In many cases, it involves describing the feeling in detail, what led to the feeling, and what one can do to change the feeling. The procedure normally requires four 15 minute sessions and has been found as effective as one session of psychotherapy. L'Abate (1992) has further developed the idea of writing for anger by developing a program on anger. The program consists of a series of questions designed to elicit new thinking in the client. There are six topics: identifying personal anger style, direct and indirect expressions of anger, practicing direct anger, practicing indirect anger, feeling angry versus expressing anger, and distinguishing anger from other feelings.

The second technique, the New Identity Process is an experiential method with the goal of emotional reeducational and attitude reassessment (described in Chapter 5). The New Identity Process allows full-bodied emotional expression in a safe environment while addressing attitudes and beliefs that effect anger, hostility, and aggression.

The third technique, developed by Stosny (1995), is called "Heals" and provides a technique for self-regulation of anger through compassion.

The purpose of this book is not to present comprehensive treatments for areas explored by the Focused Genogram. Anger, in particular, has been written about from a therapeutic perspective using the intersystem model (Weeks & Hof, 1995). The reader who needs to learn more about the various therapeutic options and how to implement them can use that book as a resource. Once the clinician has laid the groundwork for exploring anger in the family, the Anger Genogram questions can be explored.

Questions About Anger

1. How did you parents deal with anger and conflict?
2. Did you see your parents work through anger and conflict?
3. When members of you family (name each one) got angry, how did others respond?
4. What did you learn about anger from each of your parents? Would you identify any family members as type A personalities?
5. When a parent was angry with you, what did you do and feel?
6. When you got angry, who listened or failed to listen to you?
7. How did members of your family respond when you got angry?
8. Who was allowed or not allowed to be angry in you family?
9. What are your best and worst memories about anger in your family?
10. Was anyone ever physically hurt when someone got angry?
11. How were you punished as a child? How were siblings punished?
12. Did you witness violence in your family? Between whom?
13. Did you witness or participate in violence in your community?
14. What sibling rivalry experiences did you have with your siblings? How physical was the rivalry?

Questions About History of Abuse

Assessing child abuse, child neglect, sexual abuse, corporal punishment, and family violence and neglect is another important facet of Anger Genograms. Interpersonal aggression and violence affect attachment style in extremely negative ways. In addition to dismissing and disorganized attachment styles, narcissistic rage can become a component of the person's personality. These patterns become intergenerational, and child-abuse victims grow up with a higher likelihood of abusing their children than those who were not abused as children.

Child abuse is the intentional use of physical force that hurts or maims a child and/or use of emotional and verbal tactics that cause emotional harm. *Child neglect,* on the other hand, is the intentional omission of care for a child that results in physical or emotional harm. *Sexual abuse* is molestation of a child; whenever a parent or primary caregiver perpetrates the molestation, sexual abuse is called *incest.* Often clients may be reluctant to discuss the details of physical violence that took place during his or her childhood. In many families, corporal punishment was considered acceptable. Questions about corporal punishment often provide the clinician a foundation for exploring family violence and physical abuse.

1. Was corporal punishment used in your family? To what extent and how often? Were parents in-control or out-of-control? Were there differences in the ways boys and girls in the family were punished? Were there differences between the way the older children were punished compared with younger children? Do you think that the level of corporal punishment in your home was too severe?
2. Was corporal punishment also used in the homes of cousins, other relatives, or friends? Did you ever receive corporal punishment in school or any other setting outside your family?
3. Did child abuse ever take place in your family or your extended family? Was it reported to the authorities? Who reported if? What happened?
4. Have you witnessed violence or child abuse? What were the circumstances and details?
5. Has anyone ever touched you in ways that made you feel uncomfortable?
6. Did you ever have any difficult or frightening sexual experiences? Did you have any childhood or adolescent sexual experiences that you think were wrong or were upsetting to you?
7. Has anyone in the family been sexually abused? What do you know about the circumstances?

The Anger Family Map

The Anger Family Map (Figure 8.1) shows to whom and to what extent anger is expressed in the family. An arrow is used in mapping anger to indicate the aggressiveness of anger. The degree of volatility is indicated

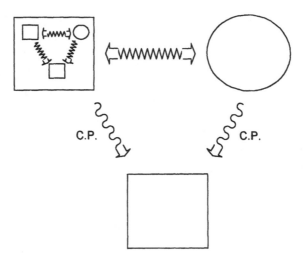

FIGURE 8.1. This Anger Family Map indicates interpersonal violence between spouses and mild corporal punishment is noted as "C.P.". Father's Internal Models Map (IMM) reflects a similar Family Map with more serious corporal punishment.

by the height on the peaks and valleys of the arrow line. The Anger Family Map can reveal gender patterns of anger in particular. It also shows families that are emotionally distant. The anger map is extremely important because it shows the clinician whether anger-management strategies must be addressed. The use and extent of corporal punishment also is graphed on the Anger Family Map.

The Anger Time Line

The Anger Time Line provides a way to track experiences with anger. Developmentally, anger, expressed as rage in infants and young children, becomes increasingly manageable through parental guidance and modeling. Unfortunately, corporal punishment, family violence, and emotional volatility within the family do not teach the child how to deal constructively with his or her anger. In many cases, the family reinforces unhealthy ways of expressing anger. Corporal punishment is a model for use of aggression to achieve one's ends. Many families are mild in their expressions of anger; other families are extreme. Some families are nurturing with young children and stricter with adolescents. Families differ in many ways in the expression of anger. Gender is also a factor in the expression of anger.

The Anger Time Line tracks the client's experiences with anger throughout his or her life and the life of the family. For example, Suzanne did not experience corporal punishment but watched as her y brothers were subjected to severe corporal punishment "becau were boys." She found herself particularly sensitive to her husband s dis cipline of her son. The Anger Time Line addresses the "when" of experiences with anger, corporal punishment, and family violence. Frequently, there are periods of calm and periods of stress in families. The client's age at these periods can affect his or her response.

☐ Making Sense of Anger Genograms: Theoretical Underpinnings

Anger in the Family

"Don't suppress it; but don't act on it" (Chogyam Trungpa, a Tibetan Teacher)

Conflict and anger are intimately connected and inevitable in close relationships. Marital and family therapists know that one of the most common problems in treatment is unresolved conflict. There tend to be two extreme patterns: conflict avoidance and conflict escalation. Conflicts erupt over a myriad of issues, ranging from in-laws, to children, to sex, to how the toothpaste is squeezed. Some people do everything they can to avoid these conflicts; others confront, attack, and ambush at the slightest provocation. The fact that conflict exists means that the people involved have different expectations, desires, or needs. The problem is that many people are uncertain how to effectively address their complaints and differences, and consequently they become frustrated and express their anger in destructive ways.

Anger is a signal that a need is being unmet or that an injustice has taken place. Part of the therapist's task is to help the client understand what his or her anger is telling him or her. One of the healthy functions of anger is to signal that someone feels constrained, frustrated, or insulted. The interactions that stimulate anger may be related to the self, a partner, the family system, or the social environment. Every individual has certain rights and needs that should be respected, acknowledged, and dealt with in an empathic way. If a boundary is violated, anger is often the reaction. For example, Keith had developed a number of close male friendships through a men's group. Following the group meeting, he spent time with the men in social situations and would sometimes get together with various members. In these meetings, he shared intimate details about his marriage with these men. Initially, he did not realize his wife would not want him to share certain facts, although he knew his wife was a person who had a high need for privacy. She was angry when she learned that Keith had shared what she considered private details of their relationship with other people.

Anger can also be an expression of unmet needs for a secure and safe relationship and is a normal human response to separation and abandonment (Bowlby, 1973). Those who have felt abandoned more in their life than they have felt supported often will react angrily in anticipation of lack of support and caring. One result is that anger becomes a regulator of distance in the relationship. Rather than request and negotiate for physical and emotional closeness, the person attempts to manage the stress of unmet attachment needs through the expression of anger. However, anger is not the only feeling that is aroused by separation and abandonment. Sadness and fear are also parts of the process. Habitual expression of anger can interfere with the expression of these other feelings and sometimes substitute for them.

If someone has experienced rejection or abandonment in the past, the belief is often that the same experience will happen again. If attempts for reassurance, comfort, or reparation are thwarted, fears of abandonment and rejection combine with anger and result in pushing others away in order to see whether they stay in the relationship or return after being rebuffed. This behavior pattern is characteristic of insecure attachments.

Anger, and the conflict that inevitably goes along with it, can be used to influence the degree of closeness in a relationship. Unfortunately, the angrier someone becomes, the less aware he or she is of the underlying need to have a safe and reliable relationship. Anger is a powerful physiologic response that short-circuits the thinking process. Not only does the person "forget" that she or he is trying to get a need met, but she or he also loses awareness of the ways in which early experiences shaped beliefs, attitudes, and emotional allergies. If rage takes over, it is impossible to "think straight."

Family and social relationships require a tremendous amount of negotiation. Everyone has different needs and sees and hears things differently. Many people lack the necessary skills to talk with each other in assertive and congruent communication styles that foster effective emotional expression and facilitate conflict resolution. In addition, many people have not learned to accept, recognize, and work with their anger. Unattended anger tends to perpetuate itself, creating more anger, resentment, and hostility, and guarantees that there will be relationship difficulties.

Bach (Bach & Wyden, 1968; Bach & Goldberg, 1974) was one of the first to suggest that the argument over the innate nature of aggression was moot to the discussion of how to modify the instigation and expression of aggression. His work addressed the how-to of separating the feeling of anger from the behavioral expression of anger. This approach is useful because it provides therapists with a foundation to help clier their anger and aggression. As with other emotions, the feeling not the problem; the problem is how anger is expressed. Ange aggression when it used as a force for power and control. Izard (1977) ... fined aggression as hostile actions or behaviors, which intend to do harm to, embarrass, or demean another through physical means, including verbal attacks. Type A personality is an example of how aggressiveness affects personality and interpersonal relationships. Narcissistic vulnerability is a conceptual model to describe the intrapsychic effects of criticism and hostility on the child's ego development.

Type A Personality

Type A personality is a coping style, a set of habitual responses. Two cardiologists, Friedman and Rosenman (1974) first identified type A personality. The characteristics of this coping style include excessive striving for achievement, competitiveness, and impatience. Research supports the hypothesis that hostility may represent the "toxic" element of type A behavior. Hostility is fueled by efforts to constantly prove oneself. Self-worth is unstable and must be demonstrated repeatedly. Underlying attitudes toward life are that life is a zero-sum game and that resources are scarce.

Sotile (1992) believes that insecurity and anxiety, not anger, grandiosity, or confidence, are the factors that underlie the type A personality. This is an important distinction. The interplay between physiological reactivity and psychosocial experiences is central to understanding the type A personality. When faced with a stress, type A personalities evidence an exaggerated autonomic nervous system alarm reaction and an impoverished calming reaction. Hot-reactor type As have spikes in their alarm system, which take a greater physiologic toll on them. Type A individuals tend to come from families with demanding, critical parents fostering negative self-esteem and pervasive anxiety.

Narcissistic Vulnerability

Narcissistic vulnerability is a construct that helps explain the psychosocial dimensions of aggression. Feldman (1982) developed the concept of narcissistic vulnerability to describe the process of how the effects of aggression can become a deeply rooted and pervasive part of an individual's psyche. Narcissistic vulnerability stems from the relative weakness of internalized positive introjections and the relative strength of internalized negative introjections (Feldman, 1982). These introjections are conceptually similar to Bowlby's concept of internal working models. In Feldman's model, anger is narcissistically driven and expressed as rage. The narcissistically vulnerable individual is self-fragmented, has a poor sense of self-esteem and identity, and is developmentally delayed in his or her emotional development. Feldman, like Sotile, believes that this intrapsychic problem results from interpersonal problems in the family-of-origin, especially chronic overt or covert disapproval by one or both parents. Narcissistic vulnerability leads to hypersensitivity, narcissistic behavior, and blocked empathy toward others. If narcissistic expectations (that others will automatically fulfill all one's needs) are not met, frustration sets in and leads to narcissistic rage. In turn, narcissistic rage leads to cognitive distortions and projective identification and results in conflict escalation. Most often, such conflict erupts over insignificant issues.

If anger is expressed aggressively in a relationship, there is often an underlying need to dominate or control the relationship. Anger is used as an instrument of intimidation, in order to force the other into submission. The repeated and irrational expression of anger to silence the other can eventually condition the other person that there is no way to reason, so he or she gives up and withdraws, or gives in and placates. If rage becomes violent, the lesson is learned more quickly. On the other hand, in some relationships, the battle for control is mutual and hostile and the relationship becomes chronically volatile. In this cycle, neither partner addresses the underlying sense of dependency (Mack, 1989) and the reasons for frustration are never addressed. Sometimes these patterns lead to ongoing, overt, physical violence within the family.

Family Violence

If anger is left unchecked, the rage, hostility, and aggression often leads to physical violence. Gelles and Straus (1989) have researched family violence extensively and suggest that violence is part of the fabric of intimate relationships. They conclude that people are violent at home because they can be violent. Like others, they emphasize that the social restrictions on domestic violence are limited (Gelles & Straus, 1989, Pleck, 1987). When Gelles and Strauss began their research on family violence in 1973, violence was defined as an act carried out with the intention, or perceived intention, of causing physical pain and injury to another person, with a range from the slight pain of a slap to murder. After more than 20 years of research, they believe that the true nature of domestic violence cannot be separated from the attitudes and beliefs we have about child rearing and corporal punishment.

Further, Gelles and Strauss (1989) believe that private violence is at the root of public violence. The taproot for violence in the home comes from a person's earliest experiences with spankings and physical punishment from parents. Repeated exposure to family violence leaves scars on the human psyche. Gelles and Strauss outline nine forms of victimization in the family, in addition to violence towards women and children: sibling violence, teenage victimization, parent victimization, elder abuse, courtship violence, sexual abuse and victimization, marital rape, emotional abuse, and neglect. These forms of family violence often are overlooked but are important in assessing the degree of violence within the family. Sibling violence, in particular, is commonly dismissed and assumed part of normal sibling relationships. However, the effects of a bullying and aggressive sibling can be profound. Steve had an older brother, Jack, who harassed and intimidated Steve from his earliest memories. Jack would punch, push, and shove Steve and then play victim if Steve dared complain. If Steve complained, Jack's retaliation became more violent. Steve found that as he grew older he was placating in work and team sports. At work, he struggled for recognition. He continually tried to "look over his shoulder," and his relationships with other men were nonexistent.

Walker (1979) has described the "cycle of violence" that takes place in domestic violence and applies to both physical and emotional abuse. The first stage is the tension-building stage, characterized by emotional and verbal abuse and threats and minor battering. In response, the woman becomes compliant and accommodating to keep the minor incidents from escalating. Stage two, the acute battering incident that Walker characterizes as an "uncontrollable discharge of tension," is often brief but in severe cases can continue for a more extended time period. During the battering episode, serious physical harm often takes place and often doors, walls, furniture, and other objects are broken or damaged. The battering episode is followed by the third stage of contrition and compensation. The batterer tries to make up for the outburst. Nevertheless, the cycle soon begins again.

Children from violent homes experience a wide range of personal problems (Gelles and Strauss, 1989), including temper tantrums, troublemaking friends, school problems, failing grades, discipline problems, and aggression with other children. The long-term impact of family violence suggests that there is an intergenerational transmission of abuse. Egeland's Mother-Child project at the University of Minnesota, which began in 1975, found that 70% of the mothers who had been abused as children mistreated their own children (Egeland, Jacobvitz, & Papatola, 1987). One of the most serious effects on children who experience violence is a warping of the child's natural bend toward empathy (Goleman,

1995). Empathy is crucial to the formation of mature, loving relationships.

Family violence was not a subject of public discussion from the turn of the century until the late 1960s (Pleck, 1987). According to Pleck, the *Journal of Marriage and the Family* (a major scholarly journal in family sociology) did not publish one article on family violence from the time it was established in 1939 until 1969. Consequently, there is often a tendency to overlook patterns of hostility and violence in the family by practitioners as well as clients. Slowly, attitudes toward intimate violence—spouse abuse, child abuse, corporal punishment, and emotional abuse—have been changing. However, the effects of anger, aggression, and family violence are intergenerational.

Corporal Punishment

Straus (1994) has become a harsh critic of corporal punishment. He defined corporal punishment as the use of physical force with the intention of causing a child to experience pain, but not injury, for the purpose of correction or control of the child's behavior (Straus, 1994, p. 4). He believes that corporal punishment affects psychological development of children, legitimizes other forms of violence, and is traumatic for young children. In addition to producing psychosocial dysfunction, corporal punishment is inconsistent with humane values. Whether Strauss is right about the conspiracy of silence around this form of family violence, examining patterns of corporal punishment is very helpful when conducting Anger Genograms. Mild, moderate, and severe patterns of corporal punishment often can be linked to "anger styles." The client may present with Type A characteristics or features of narcissistic vulnerability. The patterns of corporal punishment provide clues to understanding underlying attitudes and beliefs about one's own anger as well as that of others. Discussing forms of corporal punishment also gives the clinician an opportunity to open discussion about the possibilities of spousal abuse and child abuse within the family. The client's response provides further information to aid in developing hypotheses and treatment strategies.

Child Abuse, Child Neglect, and Sexual Abuse

The true incidence of child abuse and neglect is not known and cannot be separated from attitudinal changes and reporting requirements, but more than two million cases are reported annually. It is important that the clinician distinguish between physical abuse and corporal punishment as discussed in the questions regarding abuse and neglect. However, child abuse is not a new social problem. It has afflicted Western civilization since antiquity. Infanticide and beatings have been common treatment of children through the centuries. In the 17th century, things began to change when the souls of children became a focus of concern. However, flogging and whipping of children was customary and based on the idea that children would learn to control their wills. In the 18th century, Jean Jacques Rousseau was the first to suggest that parents stop their practice of swaddling and beating their children. However, these changes in philosophy also were taking place at the dawn of the Industrial Revolution; childhood then was filled with forced labor. Children were forced to work on behalf of their families, at sometimes 4, 5, or 6 years of age. Boys, in particular, were rented and sold. In response, the first child labor laws were enacted in England in 1802. Further social concern for the welfare of children led to societies for the prevention of cruelty to children. Since the beginning of the 20th century, advances in medicine, psychology, and social welfare policy have led to greater and greater attention and understanding of children. Social reforms during the 1960s paved the way for current attitudes, policies, and programs concerning child abuse and neglect.

Polansky (1981) studied child neglect for over 15 years before he published *Damaged Parents: Anatomy of Neglect*. This study defined child neglect as a condition in which a caretaker responsible for the child either deliberately or by extraordinary inattentiveness permits the child to experience avoidable suffering or fails to provide one or more of the ingredients generally deemed essential for developing a person's physical, intellectual, and emotional capacity. Polansky's research led to the finding that the "main etiological lead was that [the parents of neglected children] had been deprived in early life, quite probably in their first year, by their own parents." The cycle of neglect derives from a cycle of infantilism and severe emotional immaturity. The stunting of parenting instincts because of early experiences is supported by Harlow's studies (1958) and attachment theory.

Although the 1960s and 1970s were a time of attention to child abuse and neglect, Crewdson (1988) calls 1984 the year of the sexually abused child. The term *child sexual abuse* first appeared in the federal Child Abuse Prevention and Treatment Act of 1974. Sexual abuse covers a variety acts. Russell began a study in 1978, a nonclinical sample, to determine the extent of child sexual abuse. Just as in the case of child abuse, there are no specific numbers about the extent of sexual abuse. However, Russell's study suggests that 16% of the population had experienced sexual abuse. Other studies go as high as 30% of the population. The effects of child sexual abuse are emotional (guilt, anger), physical, and sexual (over- and premature eroticization, dislike of sex, counterphobic reaction).

Russell's study identified many elements that result from child sexual abuse. There are a number of factors influencing effects of child sexual abuse including age of onset of abuse, prior emotional health, duration of the abuse, who the perpetrator is, coercion used, type of sexual activity, involvement in pornography, reactions of others after the abuse, and the effect of court appearance. Behavioral responses of child sexual-abuse victims include aggressiveness, antisocial behavior, sexually aggressive behavior with other children, running away from home, suicidal behavior, fear of being left alone with adults, fear of bathrooms or showers, and refusal to change clothes for physical-education classes. The physical cluster of effects varies and includes stomach aches, headaches, urinary-tract infections, and lack of appetite. Psychological effects include difficulty sleeping, nightmares, and minor mood swings. Socially and behaviorally, victims show declining grades or erratic attendance, increases in fighting or stealing or both, refusal to attend social activities, withdrawal, and inappropriate sexually focused behavior. The interpersonal effects include isolation, shame, and ineffective coping (Haugaard & Reppucci, 1988).

Verification of abuse can be difficult. Goodwin (1989) suggests that a detailed sexual, psychosocial, violence, and family history should be obtained from each parent, keeping the typical family profile in mind as well as personal and professional biases. Family violence often is considered a secret; however, the impact of experienced or witnessed violence can be significant. Goodwin's *Sexual Abuse: Incest Victims and Their Families* (1989), is an excellent resource for understanding and assessing serious sexual abuse. Posttraumatic assessment of child sexual abuse also must include questions about child abuse and family violence. The intensity of posttraumatic symptoms is often a clue to identify the severity of failures in environmental protection and the extent abuse. In Goodwin's experience 5% to 10% of incest accusations are fictitious.

A study by Russell (1986) found that although fathers, uncles, and brothers were perpetrators of sexual abuse, the majority of perpetrators (60%) were not relatives. Perpetrators are evenly distributed among social class, age, and ethnicity, although the group under 18 years of age is the largest. Fathers and grandfathers are the most frequent abusers, with fathers perpetrating the most serious abuse and grandfathers being the least likely to abuse once. Uncle-niece incest is both serious and widespread, followed by abuse perpetrated by brothers-in-law, first cousins, and other relatives. Brothers, first cousins, and other male relatives were those most likely to use physical force. However, physical force was not used in two thirds of the cases. Fathers, grandfathers, and uncles do not seem to need force. The number of female perpetrators is small. Most incest happened around ages 11 or 12 years. Stepfather-daughter incest is more prevalent and severe than biological father–daughter incest. In cases of brother-sister incest, girls are less likely to marry, more likely to be subjected to physical violence, and more likely to defect from religious upbringing.

These facts help the clinician organize the information he or she receives from the client. Assessing the severity of sexual abuse is an important part of the Anger Genogram. Family violence is widespread and must be assessed in each family system.

☐ Summary

This chapter examines patterns of anger and its expression. Based on a psychobiological model that recognizes the power of anger, methods for addressing anger in clinical practice have been discussed. Both anger management and anger self-regulation are important techniques. Anger management addresses interpersonal expression of anger, anger self-regulation includes cognitive and self-soothing strategies. Both are important in helping clients work with and understand their anger.

The importance of assessing aggression, corporal punishment, and family violence has been emphasized. Physical aggression in the family and in the community can have significant effects on the formation of personality and sensitivity to stress. Clinicians are encouraged to explore these areas in order to help clients understand the roots of their own aggression. The effects of early experiences with anger often lay the foundation for difficulties with expressing or containing anger in adult and family relationships. Early experiences with anger can influence parenting behavior, marital intimacy, and peer relationships as well. Because anger also feeds and reinforces itself, overt expression of intense hostility is destructive, and sometimes dangerous, in interpersonal relationships.

Hostility has significant negative effects on health, marital relationships, parent-child relationships, sibling relationships, and personal and work relationships. Consequently, assessing anger with clients is a crucial part of conducting the MFG. Aggression and violence are widespread throughout society; therefore, the effects must be considered on a case-by-case basis. Unless the clinician is willing and comfortable enough to explore anger, clients may be uncomfortable admitting that they, their spouses, or their parents are physically aggressive. If anger and its expression are not examined, clinicians may miss assessing a crucial area of interpersonal experience.

☐ Recommended Readings

Bach & Wyden (1969), *The Intimate Enemy: How to Fight Fait in Love and Marriage*

Gelles & Straus (1989), *Intimate Violence*

Hyman (1997), *The Case Against Spanking*

McKay, Rogers, & McKay (1989), *When Anger Hurts: Quieting the Storm Within*

Straus (1994), *Beating the Devil Out of Them*

Tavris (1989), *Anger, The Misunderstood Emotion*

Trepper & Barrett (1986), *Treating Incest*

9

CHAPTER Ellen Berman, M.D.

Gender, Sexuality, and Romantic Love Genograms

This Focused Genogram provides a way to examine issues of gender, sexuality, and romantic love with clients. For both men and women, gender probably influences rearing, opportunities, and life structure more than any other factor. From the first question asked at birth—is it a boy or a girl?—life experience is gender linked. This is true not only in love and sexuality, but in male and female psychology, and in the countless differences in role, opportunity, and power offered to men and to women. From this sense of gender difference flow different kinds of love for the essential people in our lives, and our construction of sexuality and its meanings. The Gender, Sexuality, and Romantic Love Genograms give clients a mechanism for understanding intergenerational influences on their sexuality, loving, and everyday experiences of being men and women. Each of the components of these genograms— Gender, Sexuality, and Romantic Love—contains elements of the others. A Time Line contains elements of all these components, as the person moves developmentally from childhood to adult love relationships.

Issues of gender must be examined from both the individual and the family's patterns and beliefs, and from the cultural aspects of what is acceptable for a boy or girl of a given culture. Cultural patterns include both sex-role behaviors and rules about how power and responsibility are partitioned by gender in that culture. Although American culture is at base patriarchal, each subculture has its own specific rules.

The biological givens and tendencies of gender are also critical factors in understanding this complex issue. The major questions that focus this issue are how the primary sense of gender identity is developed, whether and in what ways women and men differ in regard to aggression, nurturance and leadership ability, and how sexual choices and behaviors develop. Our knowledge of the genetic givens of gender is not great, but many assumptions have been constructed around supposed facts. In general, it is fair to say that although physical differences do occur and seem to suggest that men and women come into the world with somewhat different tendencies, these can be in large measure overridden by culture (Halperin, 1996). Men and women's abilities form two overlapping bell-shaped curves, not two separate ones.

It is helpful to consider separately gender, sexuality, and romantic love, because each has its own definitions, issues, and problems. Gender is wider category and includes identity, roles, preferences, and sexuality. Maleness and femaleness in human society comprise wide varieties of psychological tendencies and socially prescribed behavior, of which sexual attraction and behavior is only one aspect. The specifics of sexuality and reproduction, however, have their own critical domain of knowledge. Love is a phenomenon we are just beginning to understand. It contains elements of attachment, sexuality, and male and female psychology. If gender and sexuality have sexual reproduction as one key function, love is the glue that makes it possible to raise the children produced through these unions. In this chapter, separate genograms for gender, sexuality, and love are presented so that the reader can focus on one set of issues at a time.

In the family, the parents may choose to impart the dominant cultural messages about gender or to resist them, but they must in some way deal with them. A family who believes that intelligence matters more than appearance in girls may support a daughter's intellectual development but not pay any attention to her clothes. This might put her in conflict with her school culture. In many families, male and female children are treated very differently. Boys, in general, are given more freedom, encouraged to dream of an occupational future, and expected to separate from their mothers and bond with fathers and other men (which is problematic if Dad works all the time and is not home). This model tilts toward a psychology of separation, toward a focus on task rather than emotional process, and at times toward the devaluation of women. Girls are more often (but again, not always) raised to see themselves as caretakers and relational people, more interested in people than things. This tends towards a personality structure valuing intimacy over independence and a sense of relational responsibility towards all members of the family (Jordan, Surrey, & Kaplan 1991). A search through the Gender Genogram often discovers alternative role models if one is trying to help a client develop more flexible behaviors. If the family is very rigid, people who do not follow cultural norms will often be members who have been regarded as eccentric or silenced in some way. For example, in the 1950s, a woman who left her abusive husband and worked to raise her child alone may have been seen as an embarrassment rather than a symbol of strength. For her young niece, seeking a model of toughness in adversity, this aunt may be an important resource.

In some families, personality traits or behaviors seem to be gender-specific on one or both sides of the family. For example, most of the men in the lineage might be passive or alcoholic, or most of the women might be angry or appearance-obsessed. This is repeated down the generations, as each child considers behaving in prescribed ways or chooses someone just like Dad or just like Mom, or behaves in a way that elicits that behavior after marriage. This is an intergenerational legacy to which each new boy or girl born into the family must react in some way, either by avoiding, identifying with, or denying it.

Beliefs about gender may vary dramatically between the families of two people marrying, which may create major conflict within the new couple. For example, a woman from a home in which men admired women married a man from a family in which women were second-class citizens. In spite of his intellectual desire for an equal partner, the husband's basic conditioning made it impossible for him to be the adoring and admiring spouse she wanted and that he wanted to be. His instinctive reactions from years of watching his parents and his basic gender schemata made it a constant fight for him to truly value her.

All of these issues are considered in the Gender Genogram, which examines the fit among beliefs and practice about gender among the culture, family, and person.

☐ Constructing Gender Genograms

Because Gender Genograms cast a wide net, family interviews with many family members, as well as self-assessment data, are helpful. Most family members are quite clear about family beliefs about gender and can label those who bought, or fought, the family's legacy. The Gender Genogram questions focus on general beliefs about men and women, family patterns of closeness and dominance, issues around work and money, sexuality, reproductive events, sexual orientation, and physical and psychological dysfunction.

Questions for Gender Genograms

Many people have developed gender questions and genograms, and this set represents a composite of that work. Some specific questions in this genogram were suggested by Ed Monte and Cynthia Shar, the second half of the Gender Genogram questions come from unpublished work by Peggy Papp.

1. Family beliefs about being a man or a woman: What does the family believe about what men and women should do in the world? (For example, become educated, become rich, become tough, become beautiful.) Does this change over the life cycle? Is one gender considered superior to the other? On what basis? What defines masculinity and femininity? What do you have to do or be to become an adult man or woman in the family? What are family beliefs about marriage, and the roles of men and women in marriage? What are family beliefs about money? Who earns it, who controls it, who spends it, saves it? How gender-specific are these patterns? Are the messages given by men and women in the family contradictory or consistent? If mixed messages are given, who says what? How gender-stereotyped are the messages?

2. Gender and work: What is the educational level and occupation of all members of the family of origin? (One must be sure to include all aunts, uncles, cousins, etc., because one is looking not only for patterns but also for unconventional role models.) Are there gender-specific patterns of jobs or career choices? For those with careers, were they successful? How is success or failure at work defined in the family? Are the men or the women in the family, as a group, considered more successful at work? Is child-care or volunteer work valued, or considered a career? If there is inherited wealth in the family, are men or women more likely to inherit? To be given control over the money?

3. What are family patterns of relationships in terms of closeness or distance, showing emotions, taking, giving, or sharing power? Do men and women show their needs for closeness and distance differently? Do relationships generally tend towards an egalitarian model?

4. Who does most child care and house management? Historically, have the men in the family been emotionally present to the children? Have the women? Which are stronger, the bonds between the adult partners, between same-sex parent and child, or between opposite-sex parent and child?

5. What are the patterns of affairs, divorces, abandonment, loyalty, and sacrifice by men and women in the family?

6. Who are the family heroes and heroines? For what are they honored? Are there more men or women who are honored? Are the family villains male or female? What are their "crimes?"
7. Are there gender-specific patterns of migration to different cities or countries in the family's history? Who is allowed to leave home and for what reasons?
8. What is the role of men and women in sex (liking it, initiating it, avoiding it, and talking about sexual matters)? Who is most accepting of sexuality as a positive force? Who is most negatively judgmental about it?
9. Are there gay or lesbian members of the family who are out to the family? How do men and women in the family feel about this?
10. Are there patterns of reproductive events or problems (infertility, abortions, stillbirths, difficult or dangerous pregnancies)? How are men and women seen as contributing to these?
11. What are the patterns of psychological and physical problems in the family, and are they mostly or completely limited to one gender? One should look for common psychological difficulties, including alcoholism, drug abuse, depression, anxiety disorders, psychotic illness, eating disorders, aggressive behavior, and being a victim or perpetrator of abuse. Are there gender-specific patterns of physical illness? (For example, many men but no women have heart disease in this family.) Are there gender-specific patterns of early death? Of survival from life-threatening situations?

In addition to these questions, the clinician also can examine the impact of family, peer, and cultural expectations on current gender issues.

Questions About Family Impact on Current Gender Behavior

1. How close do you come to fulfilling your family's expectations for your sex?
2. How have you gone about trying to conform to or rebel against these expectations?
3. What positive or negative effects have these expectations had on your life?
4. How have you struggled to overcome the negative effects?
5. If you are married or in a serious relationship, how close do you and your partner come to meeting expectations of marriage, of being a husband or wife? How have family expectations regarding gender affected your relationship?

6. Under what circumstances do you have the most positive image of yourself in your relationship? The most negative? In what ways does your partner live up to your ideal wife, husband, or partner?

Questions About Peer Expectations

1. How have the standards of your peer group concerning male and female roles affected your life? Have there been different peer groups with different standards over the years to which you have related? When these groups are in conflict, which set of standards is most compelling to you?
2. How have you dealt with the pressure to conform to these standards?
3. Which standards do you consider desirable or undesirable?
4. How is your self-image affected if you fail to attain these standards?

Questions About Cultural Expectations

1. Who were your idols growing up (real or fictional)?
2. What did they model as desirable male or female qualities?
3. Which did you try to emulate, and how did this affect your life?
4. What effect did these models have on your expectations of relationships?
5. What impact are they having on your current relationship?
6. What is the effect of mass media (television, films, books, etc.) on your ideas about male and female roles and your current relationship?

The Importance of the Gender Lens

Because gender issues are so pervasive, some questions from Gender Genograms should be done routinely, even if not obviously directly linked to the presenting problem. Many of the most common problems in clinical practice are to some extent results of gender conditioning. It is a great help to realize that, in many instances, one is fighting cultural norms, not just one's personal dynamics. Realizing that one's attitudes are being imposed from the outside is the first step in changing them. For example, a man who is trying to learn to be more in touch with his and other's feelings needs to realize that his fear of emotion is partly because he was taught by his peers that to be emotional was to be a "sissy." A woman who finds herself continually protecting her alcoholic husband needs to know that it is not masochism that drives her, but a belief that "a woman should stand by her man," and that "the love of a good woman will straighten a man out."

Some problems that clients face are almost entirely gender-linked. For example, eating disorders are seen almost exclusively in women except among male dancers, performers, or athletes who are particularly involved with body appearance. Particularly with eating disorders, which may appear as psychodynamic problems with self-hatred, it is important to look for a history of body anxiety and eating anxiety in the family, and to point out the constant barrage of media messages about female bodies and beauty with which the client is coping. For people moving between cultures or classes, the clash between their old gender norms and the new ones may leave them acutely confused. For the therapist, gender and culture awareness are crucial steps in understanding the client's issues, and the Gender Genogram is an essential step.

☐ Constructing Sexual Genograms

Erotic energy, sexual attraction, and sexual behavior are powerful forces in everyday life. Although therapists have stopped seeing sex as the only primary motivating force in human behavior, it is certainly a central organizing force, hardwired into our nervous systems as a source of pleasure in order to ensure survival of the species. Sexual development takes place within the family and is deeply influenced by family messages and behaviors, although some aspects of sexuality, such as a period of increased sexual awareness around age 6 years and sexual desire in adolescence, develop because of physiologic hormone shifts regardless of family dynamics. Less obviously, issues of specific physical attraction, such as a preference for certain body types or odors, are connected to early nonverbal learning experiences in ways that we are just beginning to understand but that are out of conscious awareness.

Sexual development at the physical level develops on a very well laid out timetable that occurs in the presence of adequate nutrition regardless of family dynamics (Craig, 1996). The Sexual Genogram is most helpful in defining and deconstructing family attitudes and beliefs about sexuality, which result in the development of specific love maps or scripts in the child. The Time Line is most helpful in focusing on the child's increasing conscious knowledge of his or her own sexual response and his or her parents' response to his or her developing sexuality, as well as sexual traumas (rape, surgery) in childhood and adult life.

The past 30 years have seen enormous changes in sexual norms, from the sexual revolution to AIDS. The major changes of the sexual revolution took place in the late 1960s and early 1970s. People born before 1955 grew up in an era in which it was shameful not to be a virgin when one married; now this norm is mostly gone in American popular culture (Bromberg, 1997). Cohabiting is now a norm; about 25% of those living in the United States have cohabited. A study in Oregon found that cohabitation with a future spouse rose from 13% to 53% between 1970 and 1990 (Cunningham & Antill, 1995). Sex is spoken about far more frequently and taken for granted more than when Masters and Johnson began their pioneering work in the late 1960s. In therapy offices these days, money is the last secret—and people are far more willing to talk about their sex life than their money.

People born after 1970 grew up in the age of AIDS, which has made any unprotected sex with a nonmonogamous partner potentially deadly. This has forced sexually active nonmonogamous adults of all ages into a much riskier situation and produced a complex change in the way sex is viewed. It also has produced changes in sexual practice as each sexual pair struggles with the concept of what constitutes safe sex. Therefore, the Sexual Genogram and Time Line are particularly helpful, because they help people understand what sexual norms have been handed down through 40 years of cultural change, and how the family and client have experienced the multiple rapid shifts in sexual experience and meaning.

Incest or sexual abuse in the family is the ultimate and most destructive sexual secret. Other sexual secrets in the family also can have serious impact on later generations. For example, a rape or abortion in the generation before can lead to a great fear of sexuality. A series of affairs by a parent, particularly if the child is made a confidant, provide yet another confusing series of messages. Homosexuality may or may not be considered a family secret. Particularly for clients struggling with their own sexual identity, it is useful to ask about whether others in the family are known to be homosexual.

Preparing for the Sexual Genogram

Sexual Genogram usually is not done in the first session or two, before client and therapist have developed trust in each other and decided to work together. Even with couples who enter with specific sexual difficulties, it is best to give them a chance to get acclimated and give the therapist a chance to know their nonsexual histories and personalities. It is often best to start by asking the person to take the Sexual Genogram questions home and answer them in private, in preparation for sharing with a partner or the therapist. If there is a partner it is helpful to get his or her sense of the family's sexual issues.

When the decision is made to acquire information from the parents, a cautious approach is in order. Because this is difficult material for parents and adult children, it is helpful to start with questions to the parents about beliefs and education. "What were you taught about sex when you were a child? How did you feel about sex when your son or daughter was a child? What did you want him or her to know about sex? Were you able to talk about it?" It is not necessary or advisable to get the details of one's parents' sex life or to share one's own with a parent, although some parents and children eventually share some information. If an adult child has a specific sexual dysfunction, it is sometimes helpful to know if the parent had the same problem and how he or she solved it. What is important are the beliefs, behaviors, and secrets that shaped the family. Sexual behaviors that are part of the family's self-definition are also important, for example, a relative who was a philanderer, or a pregnancy out of wedlock that resulted in panic, shame, or cut-off. Some parents are comfortable sharing information about their own sexual development, at least regarding timing of early sexual thoughts and puberty and how early sexual messages shaped their first sexual experiences. The age of parent and adult child make a difference here. It is easier for a 40-year-old child to speak of these things to a 65-year-old parent than a 21-year-old child to a 45-year-old parent. The latter have not had as much time of shared adulthood, and the level of discomfort may be higher.

Questions for Sexual Genograms

1. What are the overt and covert messages in this family regarding sexuality and intimacy? Regarding masculinity and femininity?
2. Who said or did what? Who was conspicuously silent or absent in the area of sexuality and intimacy?
3. Who was the most open sexually? Intimately? In what ways?
4. How were sexuality and intimacy encouraged? Discouraged? Controlled? Within a generation? Between generations?
5. What questions have you had regarding sexuality and intimacy in your "family tree" that you have been reluctant to ask? Who might have the answers? How could you discover the answers?
6. What were the "secrets" in your family regarding sexuality and intimacy (e.g., incest, unwanted pregnancies, or extramarital affairs)?
7. What do the other "players on the stage" have to say regarding these questions? How did these issues, events, and experiences impact upon them? Within a generation? Between generations? With

whom have you talked about this? With whom would you like to talk about this? How could you do it?

8. How does your partner perceive your family tree or genogram regarding the previously mentioned issues? How do you perceive your partner's?

9. How would you change this genogram (including who and what) to meet what you wish had occurred regarding messages and experiences of sexuality and intimacy?

10. Were there inappropriate sexual behaviors by family members, for example, sexual fondling by relatives, nudity in the home when children reached adolescence, detailed discussion of sexual preferences in the presence of small children?

11. Are any family members known homosexuals? How were they treated? How could one express nonsexual love for same-sex people?

The Sexual Genogram was developed by Hof and has been discussed in several publications (Hof & Berman, 1986, 1989).

The Importance of Sexual Genograms

Because family norms and values affect sexual scripts, a person's sexual style and beliefs are usefully traced through the genogram even if things are going well sexually. In addition, many people coming into treatment have some sexual concerns, even if they do not have sexual dysfunction. These often are gender-linked, which brings us back to Gender Genograms. In general, women allow themselves to become sexual if they feel in close emotional contact, and they have difficulty if they are angry or distant. For most women, sex is more possible if they are in connection. For many men, sex is the only way in which they can allow themselves to be in emotional contact, so they are more apt to try to use sex as a way to get back together if there is disconnection. This infuriates many women. Men are more apt to split-off sex from their emotions, and to use it for other functions than connection, for example, as a sleeping pill, to ward off anxiety, as sport, or to prove themselves as men. In the famous study of sexuality in self-defined happily married couples, women had far more sexual complaints than men, about lack of foreplay, tenderness, and so forth (Frank, Anderson, & Rubinstein 1978). These issues are deeply embedded in gender conditioning about what sex should be, and therefore questions must be asked specifically about the intersection of sex and gender. For example, "What is your image of what a real man and a real woman are like in bed?"

Because historical time and culture affect sexual patterns, it is helpful to know specifically the age of parents, and the decade of the client's childhood. For example, a client who was an adolescent in the early 1950s may have a very different set of values than one who was adolescent in the 1970s, and the disjunction with parental values may be most intense in people born from 1960 through 1984 to parents whose sexual values are 1950s models. Children born to baby-boomer and later parents may share many more sexual values but still struggle with their own value systems. Never again, post-AIDS, will sexual freedom (or sexual anarchy, depending on one's value system) be the same as in the pre-AIDS days of the sexual revolution.

In addition, if the parents or the child were immigrants, it is helpful to compare the cultural attitudes on sex from the country of origin with American culture. For example, a couple moving from India or from an Islamic culture, with arranged marriages and emphasis on female virginity, to America in the late 20th century may develop family conflict about male and female roles and sexuality.

Sexual Genograms are helpful if the issues of the couple include a wish for personal growth in this area and should always be done if sexual concerns or dysfunctions exist. Homosexual clients may find them particularly helpful to work on around coming-out issues. Homosexual clients, of course, are subject to the same range of sexual concerns and dysfunctions as heterosexuals.

Self-assessment genograms are relatively easy to do. The client should be encouraged to do them at home in private first, because so much anxiety often is attached to sexual issues. Family journeys to collect information should be carefully planned in advance. Sexual information is best collected from family members after a more general discussion of family history is begun and it is clear that family members are amenable to answering questions. The main contraindication to working on these issues in therapy is a very high level of anxiety or suspicion about confronting sexual material. With incest survivors, although the material must be dealt with, it is critical that a safe therapeutic environment be developed first.

☐ Constructing Romantic Love Genograms

Love in adults usually consists of some combination of commitment, passion, and attachment (Farber & Kaslow, 1997; Sternberg, 1986). It differs from friendship in its intensity, the presence of sexual attraction, and dependence on the other for need fulfillment. Love involves feelings (affection, passion), cognition ("I am labeling this feeling love rather than friendship"), and behaviors (which will vary with age and style but usually involve physical closeness and often marriage). Love that is for some reason unacceptable, because culture or family restrictions, is often framed as friendship, a crush, or so forth so that one can avoid acting on it. Sexual love must be differentiated from love of other family members, love of friends, and love of abstract things like country. Because we only have one word in this language to define what is actually a broad spectrum of feelings, people often have very idiosyncratic definitions of how they should feel. Love can be further explored using the Emotions Genograms (Chapter 7).

Patterns of unrequited love, loss, abandonment, or divorce are important as well. It is remarkable how many people recreate their parents' patterns in this area. For example, a person deciding to divorce at 40 often has a father or mother who did so as well. Sometimes a person whose parents endured a difficult marriage and did not divorce feels compelled to divorce to prove he or she is not like the parent. A parent whose great love was an affair partner, rather than a spouse, leaves the child questioning whether real intimacy is possible within marriage. Of course, patterns of divorce in this century have been affected profoundly by the changing norms of marriage and divorce. Many people with no family history of divorce embraced the idea of self-fulfillment as opposed to sacrifice and left their partners in the years following the 1960s. Thirty years of experience have taught us that divorce is frequently not an answer to personal pain, but in this country there is a strong belief that passionate love is a necessary component for living.

Love genograms are relatively easy to do, and family journeys are essential. This kind of information usually is hidden from young children if possible but often is given willingly to adult children.

Questions for Romantic Love Genograms

Love and Intimacy in the Family

1. How were intimacy and love displayed in your family by men and women?
2. How did your parents show love toward each other? Toward the children? How were children expected to show love? What did you have to do to receive love (perform academically, be beautiful, be a loving family member)?
3. Did loving involve primarily caretaking, listening, saying loving things?

4. Who was the most and the least loving in your extended family? Who was the most and least loved in your family?
5. Who in the family was abandoned, or abandoned others?
6. Were loved ones lost through death or tragedy?

Romantic Love

1. How was romantic love shown in the family?
2. What is the story of your parents' courtship? Are there other well-known stories of courtship in the family?
3. Are there family patterns of divorce or abandonment during court-ship or after marriage?
4. Did the family believe in "love at first sight," or did "true love" develop slowly? Was being in love a good reason or the only reason to get married, or were other reasons more powerful?
5. In order to be in love, were you supposed to be passionate, jealous, demanding, or more of a good friend?
6. Was love seen as logical or beyond logic?
7. If you were in love with a person of the wrong cultural background or your parents did not approve, were you expected to give up the lover or the parents?
8. If a person fell in love, could one still be loyal to friends, other family members, and so forth?
9. Was falling in love considered an acceptable reason to have an affair?
10. If you loved someone who did not love you back, was this cause for despair?

The Importance of Romantic Love Genograms

Love relationships in the family-of-origin provide a powerful template for future behavior. This is particularly true in the area of ongoing intimacy. Persons struggling with intimacy need to know what their family legacy is. If a family journey is done as part of this genogram, these questions can be used to explore areas in which an adult child has felt deeply unloved by a parent. It is an excellent chance to see how parental projections got in the way of love ("you remind me of the sister I hated"). It is also a possibility that a parent or child who has never expressed it will be able to say "I love you" during the process of exploration.

☐ The Gender, Sexuality, and Romantic Love Family Map

This Focused Family Map for Gender, Sexuality, and Romantic Love reveals patterns of gender identification, love, and conflict, which provide a template for further experiences. Patterns of closeness and distance with parents or significant others of the same sex and of the opposite sex are an important focus of this Family Map. Masculinity and femininity, romantic love and attachment, and sexual behavior provide powerful examples for the developing child. The ability to fuse lust and tenderness, love and commitment, and kindness with assertiveness is learned in the family. The family that holds to rigid rules of gendered behavior or love behavior may produce children ill suited to the basic complexity, even messiness, of adult sexual love. A search for warmth, flexibility, and human connection between same- and opposite-sex people allows for finding strengths in the client and family.

☐ The Gender, Sexuality, and Romantic Love Time Line

It is most helpful to create a Time Line in which gender development, love, and sexuality are graphed together, in order to see the relationships among them. Information of particular importance includes issues around birth—was a girl or a boy wanted, how did parents and grandparents feel about the sex of the patient, what role models were available at birth, were the parents loving toward each other and the child? As the child develops, questions include relationships with parents and siblings, first awareness of crushes or special friendships, how the child acquires sexual information, and any particularly positive or traumatic events related to sexuality, love, and abandonment or one's masculinity of femininity. With puberty, the issues of sexuality and love become paramount, and as the person develops into adulthood, both sex and love experiences should be listed, as well as issues related to gender such as sexual harassment, gender and related privileging or oppression, and reproductive issues.

Homosexual clients should be questioned about how or when they first became aware of the same-sex interest, how they came out to themselves, to whom they have come out in the family and community, and what their love and sexual experiences have been. The degree to which they have been closeted, or "out," is often important in determining their sense of themselves as competent and acceptable. In addition, parental and family response to the announcement of orientation should be examined.

☐   Making Sense of Gender, Sexuality, and Romantic Love Genogram: Theoretical Underpinnings

Gender

Seven areas are included in Gender Genograms. In this section key issues for each area are described, followed by discussions of gender differences and similarities, gender development, gender issues in parenting, sexual development, sexual dysfunctions, and romantic love.

General Beliefs About Men and Women

There are often considerable differences between marital partners in their respective attitudes toward men and women, which may result in contradictory messages to the child. (For example, father may not want to spend the money to send a girl to college because he believes that women do not need an education; his wife, who gave up her own career for marriage, may be determined that her daughter take a different route.) This set of beliefs may include the roles of men and women in marriage, what their roles should be in the wider world, and who makes and controls the money. Sometimes, spoken beliefs are at variance with actual family dynamics. A mother may insist that Dad is the head of the household, while she is actually making both home and business decisions. Gender-based beliefs are transmitted from the culture but often have their roots in family events. For example, a girl child may be taught by the culture that men are stronger and better than women and watch her mother treat her father like a king. On the other hand, a girl whose grandfather deserted her grandmother, and whose father died of alcoholism, is unlikely to believe men are strong, stable, and permanently available, so her family experience will be at variance with the culture.

Family Patterns of Closeness, Distance, and Dominance

In general, the cultural set is that women are in charge of closeness and men in charge of setting the rules. In fact, families vary greatly in their specific patterns. In the wider world, however, most men have more access to power than women do. The culture privileges men in many ways, assuming that in return for giving protection, both financial and otherwise, they should be granted deference. Because men have more access to money and leadership positions in the outside world, and generally make more money than their wives, feelings and behaviors often are skewed by the wife's relative lack of power should she leave the relationship. Women, who see themselves as less powerful, and are taught to take care of relationships, very often marry men who are most concerned about autonomy and work focus. As a result, in marriage, in this country, men and women often fall into patterns in which the woman is the emotional pursuer, the person wanting more intimacy and discussion of feelings, and the man tends to prefer more "alone time" and prefers talk of solutions to talk of feelings. In general, women do more child and house care regardless of how many hours they work (Rasmussen, Hawkins, & Schwab, 1996).

House and child care are deeply linked to other issues of power. A truly egalitarian lifestyle hinges on equality in earning, and most especially in who does what in the "second shift": the maintenance work for their lives together (Hochschild, 1989). In traditional families, men support the family by working outside the home, although they may do some designated house tasks involving the car, the garbage, and the lawns and gutters. All the rest of the house and child care jobs belong to the woman, although the man may "help" if he is willing. In such marriages, the wife tends to feel less powerful. Couples who develop a more egalitarian or role-reversed lifestyle may suffer from family or cultural scorn. Excellent books to help couples deal with this issue are *Chore Wars*, by Thornton (1997), and *The Second Shift*, by Hochschild (1989).

Issues Around Work and Money

Men still are taught to focus on money and power as central to their self-definitions and their value in the culture. Women, at this point, are in a more ambivalent situation, because work is now more acceptable and even approved of in many circles. Women, however, are paid less and still must balance work and children, a concept seldom discussed for men. The highest leadership positions in government and business are still almost entirely male.

Because for many women money is still a man's area, we see many women who earn money, or do most of the purchasing and bill paying, who have left all the investing and basic financial planning to their husbands. These women often feel helpless and disempowered around money issues. Women alone, who have learned to do these things, often develop greater self-esteem when they realize they can handle their own support and finances. For an interesting, unusual and helpful discussion of money, see *The Secret Meaning of Money*, by Madanes (1994).

Sexuality

Sexuality is also included in Gender Genograms, although it is covered more specifically in Sexual Genograms. In this culture, sex still often is seen as something men take and women give. Because sex is more dangerous for women, both in terms of reputation, emotional vulnerability, and possible pregnancy, women tend to be more conflicted between the recent messages that they have a right to be sexually desirous and the older messages that they better watch out and be careful. Because women also are subject to more abuse and rape than are men, sexuality feels more conflicted. Initiation of sex still is considered the job of the man, although this has been changing in recent years. Because men in this country have been taught to separate from their mothers and to have few women as friends, men often make friends only with their lovers and use sex as a primary way to be close. (Zilbergeld [1992], in *The New Male Sexuality*, discusses these issues at length.) This confuses many women who need to feel safe and close before sex in order to feel open and sexual. Nevertheless, in any specific family, either the man or the woman may be the one to most appreciate and discuss sexuality. Alternatively, everyone in the family may agree on their feelings about sex.

Sexual messages are complex, and very different for men and women, both at the cultural level and at the family level. At the cultural level, there is tremendous confusion about sexuality. Although the media focuses constantly on sex (music, television, and movies all have sexuality as a constant and overt text), we still are arguing over whether we should provide sex education in the schools. Both men and women are seen as very sexual in the media. However, in plot-driven media (television and movies), the nice girls are seen as more monogamous and the bad girls (read, "more sexual") are more likely to be killed off. Men, on the other hand, are still more likely to be admired for their sexual prowess.

Reproductive Events

Reproductive events are included in Gender Genograms because issues around pregnancy and birth, both positive and negative, are experienced by men and women as powerfully tied to their senses of themselves. Reproductive events such as infertility affect both men's and women's senses that they are "real men" or "real women." Men and women may experience some reproductive events very differently. For example, in an early miscarriage the woman, who carried the child in her body, may grieve longer and harder than her partner and is likely to need to talk about it, while the man is often in less acute pain. Even if he is sad, he also is more prone to feel that he must be strong for his wife, therefore keeping his grieving from her and perhaps appearing cold.

Sexual Orientation

The sense of being an acceptable man or woman is separate to some extent from one's sexual *orientation*. For example, it is possible to see oneself as a masculine man and still have a love and sexual orientation toward men. (It is also possible to have deep fears about one's masculinity and still be attractive to, and attracted by, women.) There is a great deal of fluidity in homosexual behavior and in people's definition of self as homosexual; many people are capable of having both male and female lovers, or changing sexual orientation late in life. People who are capable of bisexual arousal patterns nevertheless may have love relationships preferentially with same- or opposite-sex people. There is still a great deal of scientific controversy as to whether preferential homosexuality is genetically determined, learned, or a combination of both (Falco, 1991).

Physical and Psychological Illnesses

Physical and psychological illnesses have gender components to them. For example, men are prone to earlier heart disease, partly because estrogen protects against heart disease (women's risk increases after menopause) and partly because they are under different kinds of stress and less likely to take care of themselves. Women are more prone to get depressed than men, partly because of female gender-role conditioning, and men are more likely to become violent or alcoholic because of male role training. If men are supposed to be tough, they will be more likely to act out or try to medicate away sad feelings. Women are far more prone to eating disorders. In some families, the genogram explains much of the behavior. For example, Beverly's grandmother was seriously obese. Her mother hated her grandmother and swore she would never gain weight and was very compulsive about food and appearance; Beverly grew up with the idea that weight gain was terrible. Faced with her history, plus the cultural demand in the past 20 years for extreme slimness in women, she developed anorexia.

Gender Differences and Similarities

Gender-linked cultural norms affect everyday behavior at the macro level (most jobs are still differentiated by gender, and men earn more money) and at the micro level (women are expected to smile more than men do). Almost all known cultures today, and certainly all Western ones, are patriarchal in nature. Patriarchy has been defined as the systematic privileging of men over women within a hierarchical structure (Stacy, 1993). The fact is that women do more of the world's work, gain less of its money, and, with a very few exceptions, are not among its leaders (Humphrey Institute of Public Affairs, cited in Taylor et al.). The assumption that women are less important than men are, except in areas of home and family, affects men's and women's senses of self-worth and their life opportunities. Any culture, however, has areas of conflict and ambivalence built into it. Within broad cultural boundaries, many roles are possible and many beliefs can find expression. At present, for example, our culture is engaged in a serious struggle to become more egalitarian, with both opportunities and confusion built into it that affect both genders.

Families are not only integrated into a culture but also transmit it, with editorial comment, to their children. Within a particular family, the broad possibilities of cultural norms meet specific family dynamics, and a variety of different messages may be given. Boys and girls will be treated differently, but the ways in which they are treated vary and may be very subtle until the children reach their teens. Men or women may be the preferred or admired gender.

In the family, children first learn what personality and behavioral traits are acceptable for boys or girls. This varies by situation and class. A specific father, for example, may be concerned that his boy succeed but may define success as a brilliant batting average in little league or a brilliant report card. Whichever he chooses, however, he will probably see it as a way for his son to be strong, tough, and able to take care of his family in the future. A girl may be encouraged to be outspoken and aggressive, or quiet and passive, but she almost certainly will be encouraged to make herself attractive and marriageable. Because families and family members differ widely in their beliefs and practices around gender, some being very sexist and some egalitarian, it is important to get a sense of the family's patterns over time, and how the client internalized or fought them. Thinking through the set of family and cultural messages allows clients to form a more flexible gender story for themselves.

As the family teaches the child about gender, the messages are deeply internalized as part of psychological development. This forms one of the most central areas of the person's psychological makeup. Men's and women's self-worth, ability to work in the world, and patterns of love relationships all are related to what messages they have internalized about gender and how they believe that they "measure up" to those standards. Because these beliefs are so deeply internalized, they feel natural, as if they are biological givens, and may be followed even if the person intellectually disagrees. For example, well-paid career women, strong and financially successful, may allow themselves to be controlled, even hit, at home and accept this if they have internalized the message that women are subservient to their husbands. Men may strongly believe in equality but find that they leave most of the child care to their wives. Schwartz (1994) suggests that more couples are finding ways of developing truly egalitarian marriage, but they are attempting this in a culture that makes it very complex. Groups such as Promise Keepers, for example, while encouraging men to be more active in the family, based on biblical interpretation, believe that men should be the leaders and women the followers (Promise Keepers, 1994).

The subject of gender differences and gender similarities has fascinated researchers for years, as has the question of whether they are biologically fixed or socially learned. This usually is framed as an either-or question—nature versus nurture. More sophisticated studies have shown that the answer is a complex mix, and that feelings and behaviors are shaped both by biology and learning. Unfortunately, the research has become highly politicized because of its implications for the allocation of money and power (Fausto-Sterling, 1985). For example, parents (and scholarship donors) who believe that women biologically are programmed to be wives and mothers are less likely to pay for advanced schooling. People who believe aggression is biologically programmed into males tend to be more pessimistic about teaching boys peaceful means of conflict resolution (or letting girls into military school). (For a good review of this literature, see Fausto-Sterling, 1985, chapter 5.) Efforts to protect women often have unintended consequences that inadvertently privilege men. For example, a decision was made in the military not to allow women in combat positions in this country. However, a female nurse, a noncombatant and therefore lower paid, can be in more danger if she is working in a land-based combat zone than if she is working as a higher-paid "combat" officer on a submarine.

It appears that in areas not related to reproduction the absolute differences between the sexes, be they academic, physical, or social, are relatively small, given equal opportunities and training. Even in areas of physical strength, women are coming closer to men's abilities, as it becomes more possible for women to train and compete in sports events. Even at the highest Olympic levels, the differences, although real, are not huge. However, differential rearing can produce very large differences in test scores. For example, girls' math scores on standardized tests used to be noticeably behind boys. Years of working to discourage math phobia in girls have succeeded to the point at which the scores are relatively equal, except in the top 1% (New York Times, May 6, 1994). It seems that women can be taught math, and we know that men can be taught peace.

Whether women are by nature more interested in people, and men more in things, is still a subject of considerable debate. Gur and Gur (1995), for example, have shown that men and women show dramatic metabolic differences in the regions of the brain controlling motor function and emotional responsiveness, with men having more action in the limbic system, an area responsible for action-oriented responses including aggression, and women having more in the cingulate gyrus, a region processing symbolic communication by way of facial expression and speech. Some child-development experts have seen evidence of more aggression in young boys compared with young girls. However, it is clear that men still can be ministers, teachers, and psychiatrists, all of which require intense attunement to communication and an absence of overt aggression. We, as therapists, certainly assume that biology does not prevent men from learning effective ways to communicate. We also assume that women can find their voice, become assertive if they are not already, and focus on outside work as well as children.

In areas involved with sex and pregnancy, biological elements are present, but the interpretation of their importance is complex. Sexual attraction is a basic animal phenomenon programmed into us for species survival. We do not know why particular humans are attracted to each other, although both rearing and pheromones probably play a part. We can understand the issues of psychological attraction from genograms, but we cannot always predict from that why love or attraction arise or die.

Obviously, the fact that women become pregnant and give birth gives rise to biological differences in anatomy and physiology, but research on fathers thrust into the primary caretaking role by unemployment or by the loss of a partner shows that men are perfectly capable of acquiring the necessary skills (Hochschild, 1989; Lamb et al., 1987). (This is reflected in TV sitcoms in which the most active fathers are single fathers.) Even male rats, placed with newborn rats when no female rats are present, exhibit caretaking behaviors with newborn rats, suggesting that the ability to parent is built into mammalian anatomy (Money & Erhardt, 1972). However, if men and women in the same household parent, women are more likely to do the bulk of the child care and carry almost all of the managerial responsibility (Hochschild, 1989; Lamb et al., 1987).

Although men and women are capable of greatly similar behavior, it does not change the fact that one's gender is a critical fact in society and that it is impossible to function as a person independent of gender. It is a fascinating subject of speculation that all societies program gender-specific behavior, although the specific behaviors of each culture vary enormously. Even within a culture, behavior varies with situations. For example, until recently, women were expected to be the cooks for the family and husbands did not prepare dinner, but all the chefs in restaurants were men.

Gender Development

Gender identification, the knowledge that one is a boy or a girl, is a gradual process that seems to begin very early, perhaps around 1 year of age, and is in place by age 2, the point of object constancy and language development. For most (although not all) persons, it is absolute. Some persons who are known as transsexuals believe that they are trapped in the body of the wrong sex; some have surgery to change their bodies. It seems likely there is a heavy biological component to one's sense of oneself as male or female, because it is so early and definite, but we have not elicited the mechanism. On the other hand, a wide variety of studies suggest that girl and boy babies are treated differently by parents and visitors from birth, so a good argument can also be made that much or all gender identification is learned. Studies done in the 1960s suggested that it was possible to reassign the sex of children below the age of 2 years successfully (Money & Ehrhardt, 1972). However, now that those children have reached adulthood, things are less clear. In the famous case of a boy child reassigned as a girl after he lost his penis in a medical accident, the original reports suggested that he was successfully reassigned and was happy as a female (Money & Ehrhardt, 1972). Follow-up reports indicate that in adulthood he has not accepted his imposed identity is currently married and living as a man. Other cases turned out similarly (Diamond & Sigmondson, 1997).

As their sexual identities consolidate, children participate in developing a picture of what that gender identity implies in terms of how they should think and behave. In the beginning, these are very black-and-white schemata. School-aged children concentrate on gender roles and how to be masculine or feminine in our culture. By puberty and adolescence, boys and girls begin to imagine a future that is heavily influenced by what they have learned is possible for the men and women they will be.

Gender roles are the set of behaviors considered appropriate for a man or woman in a particular culture. In mainstream American culture, the stereotypic male is supposed to be tough, strong, logical, aggressive, and brave. New demands for tenderness and a willingness to be more egalitarian have complicated male role models. The stereotypic female is supposed to be nurturing, gentle, intuitive, emotional, deferent to men, involved with her appearance and somewhat dependent, except when she is supposed to be strong, assertive, logical, and so forth. (Role be-

havior is particularly complicated and confusing at this point in historical time.) Each individual person learns what the rules are but may or
may not follow them. For example, women but not men wear makeup.
Some women, however, refuse to wear any makeup, even if their friends
and neighbors encourage them to do so. Men may wear makeup if they
are acting, or sometimes if they are homosexual and flaunting it. Some
teenaged boys wear makeup as a way of "gender bending," or playing
with gender roles.

Because male development demands that men constantly prove their
masculinity, and because men are more valued in the society, it is easier
for women to flout convention and adopt male roles (assertiveness at
work, wearing pants) than for men to adopt female-identified behaviors
(wearing makeup, gentleness). Some roles are in the process of change
but show evidence of traditional roles. For example, even though both
men and women are now equally entitled to enjoy their sexuality, men
are still supposed to call women for dates, and women are supposed to
wait to be asked. Compared with many other countries, however, notably
Arab and many Asian countries, gender roles are fairly flexible in North
America.

Within cultures, sex roles are profoundly class and culture bound.
Women from most Asian countries are expected to be subordinate and
nondemanding, both in and out of the family (Lee, 1982). African American women are supposed to be strong and nurturing, usually are expected to work, and often have very central roles in the community
(Boyd-Franklin, 1989). Traditional Caucasian women in this country are
given a great deal of power in the family but are expected to behave in
a sweet, gentle, and nondemanding way outside it. This has changed in
the past 30 years, but women still are expected to be more nurturing and
less tough than men are. Until recently, it was assumed that women in
this country should not wish to work outside the home and that it would
make them hard and unfeminine, but in practice this applied most to
middle- and upper-class women. Poor and single women were expected
to work because the family needed the income. Even now, welfare mothers are castigated for not working, but middle-class working mothers are
blamed for deserting their children. For men, masculinity is culturally
linked to performance and strength, but in working-class situations this
might mean being good at sports or feats of physical strength, while in
intellectual circles this might mean a brilliant academic career, with little
interest in physical activities.

In the animal kingdom, gender roles and arrangements also differ
widely by species; even among primates, some live in male dominant
groups, some with female and children together with males basically absent except during breeding season, and some in situations in which fe-

males or couples are dominant rather than males. In general, in mammals, females do most of the child rearing, but in some species males take an active part. Our culture, of course, is in the midst of a massive argument as to how we should conduct ourselves around these issues, and the animal kingdom offers no absolutes.

Each family conveys key cultural messages, passing them down the generations. Most family messages are a complex mix. Mothers and fathers give the earliest information about expected behavior of boys and girls, but the peer group, the media, and the extended culture rapidly reinforce this.

Homosexuality is prevalent throughout all human societies, regardless of the culture's attitude toward it. The causes of homosexuality are still obscure. Current thinking seems to be in the direction of biological underpinnings for obligatory homosexuality. Homosexual people have a sexual identity congruent with their biological sex but an erotic preference for members of their own sex. Some people seem to have a truly bisexual sexual preference and have lifelong concurrent or consecutive relationships with both men and women. Homosexual people may prefer androgynous or traditional gender-role behavior. The old stereotype of the male homosexual may be the queen of *La Cage Aux Folles*, but there are many homosexuals who serve in the armed services and embody all of the most traditionally masculine role behaviors.

Violence and rape are common in this society, with men being the perpetrators most of the time. Sexual violence against women, both among strangers and within the home, is a major psychological and public-health problem. Violence is associated with poverty and alcohol, low self-esteem, and narcissistic rage, but it is also a product of cultural norms that devalue women and give cultural permission for it to occur. Until recently, women who were raped were assumed to be "asking for it"; marital rape was not a crime, and in some subcultures it was considered normal for a husband to hit his wife occasionally to keep her in line. Women can also be violent, although if they kill their partners it is more likely to be in self defense (Gelles and Strauss, 1989).

Gender Issues in Parenting

Boys and girls are treated differently by mothers and fathers, in ways heavily influenced by the parents' beliefs about men and women. For the child, parental relationships are the first experience of learning how to behave with one's own and the opposite sex and learning what boys and girls are valued for. Depending on temperament, same-sex siblings may receive different treatment; for example, the artistic quiet son becomes

"Mom's kid," while the more aggressive son becomes "Dad's kid." This will, in turn, affect their sense of themselves as men in adulthood, and their treatment of women.

Mothers

Although the mother is usually the primary caretaker for boys and girls when they are young, the girl is more likely to be seen by mother as an apprentice, someone like her, who will at some level share her life experiences. The little girl usually shares this feeling and while little wants to be like her mother (although when she becomes a teenager trying to establish her own identity this may be a frightening thought). A boy child tends to be treated as different or other, someone who must ultimately separate to become a man. Most women remain deeply emotionally connected to their mothers and involved in their lives. According to the Stone Center, this is how girls learn to develop greater empathy (Jordan et al., 1991).

If mothers are devalued by fathers or devalue themselves and other women, this is passed down to their daughters as well, and their sons learn that men do not need to treat women with respect. Blaming of mothers is still very common in academic and medical circles; mothers often are blamed by doctors, fathers, and children (and themselves) for any problems in the family, regardless of the father's behavior, or his presence or absence (Bograd, 1990).

In many families, boys are seen as belonging to the father. Many mothers are so afraid their boys will be "sissies" that they distance themselves emotionally from them very early (Silverstein & Rashbaum, 1994). Many boys learn to tune their mothers out very early, in order to become more independent, more separate. This disconnection teaches them to block certain empathic responses. However, this pattern is not repeated in all cultures. For example, in India, the mother-son bond is the closest family bond into adulthood. Mothers who are psychotic, depressed, narcissistic, or drug-addicted may elicit either caretaking or avoidance responses in boys, which likely will be repeated in their relationships with other women. Daughters of such women, especially oldest daughters, frequently end up as parentified children.

Fathers

Until the 1970s, the culture encouraged fathers to see their role primarily as breadwinner and to disregard or devalue much direct contact with younger children. Even now, many men, when pressed, see their role as wage earner as more important, and serious work in the "second shift" as less interesting, if not unmasculine. As a result, many children grow up with psychologically absent fathers, making up "how it should be" from the media. For some boys, this experience of being underfathered leads to a sense of false masculinity and a sense of never being good enough (Pittman, 1993). Available fathers usually provide effective role-models and foster high self-esteem for their sons. Through their positive relationships with their wives and daughters, available fathers also teach their sons that females are important and valuable. Some fathers, however, are disinterested in their daughters, afraid of their beginning sexuality in adolescence, or overly concerned with their appearance. This leaves many girls ill prepared for finding a warm, nurturing mate, because their normal, familiar male figure is unavailable. However, well-functioning fathers teach their daughters that they are worthy human beings and model functional male-female relationships in their marriages.

Boys are praised more often for being tough, unemotional, angry rather than sad, people who "do" rather than "be." Girls are praised more often for nurturing, caring for the family, being obedient, and being depressed rather than angry. This is the beginning of the things-versus-people split mentioned earlier. Girls also are trained by their families and the media to be enormously body conscious in a way that boys are not. Being thin and pretty has become a major cultural obsession, as the rapidly rising rate of eating disorders indicates (Bromberg, 1997).

Sexuality

Our sexuality is deeply connected to sex-role learning and cognitive-belief systems, as well as biology. Both men and women experience sexual desire and arousal, but they think and feel differently about sex and have a different relationship to it, messages that they take from both the media and their families. Many men see sex as conquest or right. More women see sex as giving something. Love relationships also show both differences and similarities: Men and women have similar responses of falling and remaining in love, but women are more likely to make this the centerpiece of their life focus, whereas men are apt to give more or equal weight to occupational success. Women, who have been trained to be the emotionally connected ones, are more likely to experience love and connection as proving that they are successful human beings, and feel responsible for the emotional quality of the relationship. They also are more apt to want to talk about it. Men, who have been trained to be autonomous and to separate from their mothers, may need the connection of love just as badly but be afraid that it will compromise their autonomy. This often complicates their responses to women, because it feels as if love is taking something away.

Erotic response is a complex mix of poorly understood biological factors and psychological-developmental ones, which develop in complexity as the child grows older. Sexual desire has three components: drive, motivation, and wish (Levine & Rosenblatt, 1997). Sexual drive is the biological component, recognized by genital tingling, heightened responsivity to erotic environmental cues, plans for sexual behavior, and increased erotic preoccupation. This is a biological process, requiring a modest amount of testosterone, dampened by medication, illness, and depression. Falling in love heightens it, as well as joy from any source and low doses of alcohol and drugs. There is some biological variation in drive level, in that some people, consistently from childhood, show more interest in sex than others do. Motive is the psychological aspect of desire, recognized by willingness to bring one's body to the partner for sexual behavior. This has much to do with the person's perception of the context of the relationship. Wish has to do with the social component, cognition: "I wish to have sex but I'm too tired to want it." Intergenerational factors can decrease drive by increasing sexual anxiety, and increase or decrease motive and wish by casting sex, or the partner, in a particularly good or bad light.

The concept of sexual script or love map has been used to describe the set of erotic responses and sexual preferences developed from early life that are most consistent in the person's everyday life (Money, 1986). This may include the type of partner ("I am only turned on by unavailable women") and the type of lovemaking ("I can mostly be turned on by men who are physically very strong, and I prefer to be the passive partner and not try too many new things"). The person's adolescent and adult experiences may or may not allow the person to alter their sexual script. Although one cannot understand the chemistry of attraction from a genogram, we can learn why, at the psychological level, a person might, for example, be uninterested in a kind and loving lover and prefer a cruel and withholding one. The ebb and flow of desire within a couple results form the changing intensities of its components.

Children's sexual development begins early (Craig, 1996). The awareness of their own and others' sexual selves is based in biological changes that, we are learning, begin far before puberty. Even in infancy, children learn that stimulation of the genitals feels pleasurable. Recent studies indicate a rise in sexual hormones by age 6 years (probably responsible for increased sexual feeling which Freud called *oedipal*). It is at this time that children probably develop the beginning of body preferences in sexuality (for a particular body type or smell). Some paraphiliacs report paraphilic responses at this age. (Paraphilia is a disorder of sexual aim, a sexual pre-occupation with unusual, dehumanized eroticism, such as masochism, pedophilia, preoccupation with items of clothing such as shoes, particular body parts, or behaviors such as exhibitionism.) Young children may develop crushes as early as age 6 or 7 years, and in one study, the mean age for first recalled sexual attraction was 9.6 years for men and 10.1 years for women (McClintock & Herdt, 1996). In the earlier years, there is sense of attraction, a vaguely sexual valance. Sexual desire begins later, around 11 years old, with relational sexual behavior later still, after anatomical maturity had been reached. This pattern is true for both homosexuals and heterosexuals. Most children learn to masturbate early (boys more than girls).

Within the family system, sexual attitudes and behaviors are modeled for children, and modeled very differently for men and women. Although sexual interest and expertise are properties of both sexes, it is a rare family that conveys to both sons and daughters that sex is a wonderful thing and that one's partner in sex must be treated with respect and care. It is more likely that daughters are told to be wary because of the dangers (reputation, pregnancy, diseases), that boys are told that it is fine to be sexual if you protect yourself, and that the more sexual members of the family tree are denigrated if women and admired if men. For girls, active sexuality may be discouraged, encouraged, or conflicted. For boys, the messages are that tenderness and sensitivity are less important than overt sexuality, and that sex is one of the places in which one must prove one is a man. Many parents who are having serious sexual difficulties themselves convey information to the children that sex is no fun. Few parents convey the real pleasure of sex even if they talk about the mechanics. Homosexual or sexually conflicted teenagers seldom receive any positive information and often are made miserable by their peers. However, many high schools now are providing more support and programs for such young people, and many more parents now are learning to be comfortable with teenagers who are unsure of sexual orientation or are self-defined as gay.

How the child understands these feelings also is determined culturally. For example, in Freud's time, any suggestion of sexuality was ignored or punished, so sexuality went underground and the period was seen as latent. Today, the media, especially television, introduces sexual behaviors and practices far earlier than in previous generations. Children's knowledge of adult sexual behavior is often very much at variance with their ability to process or understand it or relate it to their own bodies. In our culture today, in some schools, sexual teasing may begin at age 9 or 10 years, and boy-girl pairing and overt dating may begin as young as 11 or 12 years (McClintock & Herdt, 1996). In some areas, genital sexuality may begin around 12 or 13 years, and with the decrease in age of puberty to 10, 11, or 12 years in girls, we are seeing more 12- and 13-year-old girls who are pregnant. In other areas, sexual experimentation may begin much later. Baby-boomer parents, often very confused over the question of sexual rights of adolescents and whether they think their children should be sexually active, sometimes have left adolescents confused about sexual behavior, with few rules and less protection than in previous times. Because parents vary so widely in their beliefs about proper sexual behavior, it is important to ask about this on the genogram.

In adolescents, a complex mix of cultural norms, sexual drive, and opportunity determines the timing of the first sexual encounters. Children are very apt to repeat parental patterns in this area as well, because it is seen as normal, (e.g., "Dad started having sex at age 14, so should I") or as a response to parental anxiety. Often, parents convey confusing and mixed messages because they are so anxious and worried about the when and how of their child's sexual experience. Mothers who have early out-of-wedlock pregnancies and are unhappy about it may try to influence their daughters to begin sexual experience later in life. The daughters may hear and take this message to heart, or may find themselves, for a variety of reasons, including rebellion, self-hatred, or identification, repeating their mother's pattern.

Children whose parents are sexually inappropriate or overstimulating (e.g., insisting on washing a child's body at age 9 or 10 years, constantly making sexual comments or jokes about the parent's own sexuality) may become overly sexual or very inhibited. Children subject to fondling or sexual behavior (incest) by an older sibling or an adult in the house are apt to develop dissociation and a sense of betrayal and lack of trust in people, as well as other symptoms of trauma syndrome, such as flashbacks.

Sexual Dysfunctions

Sexual dysfunctions include problems of desire, arousal, and orgasm. Any of these components can be problematic, separate from the others. It is possible, for example, to have sexual contact, and even orgasm, without desire. It is possible to have desire and arousal without orgasm. It is possible to have all three and still feel that the encounter has been emotionally distant. Sexual dysfunctions listed in the *DSM-IV* (1994) include hypoactive sexual desire disorder, sexual aversion disorder, female sexual arousal disorder, male erectile disorder, female orgasmic disorder, male orgasmic disorder, premature ejaculation, dyspareunia, vaginismus, sexual dysfunction due to a medical condition and substance-induced sexual dysfunction. For a discussion of sexual dysfunctions in detail, see Leiblum and Rosen (1988) or Levine and Rosenblatt (1997). The practice of sex therapy has gone through many permutations in recent years. Dysfunction has been linked to lack of information and skill, to issues of couple problems of intimacy or control, as well as to problems in individual dynamics. A helpful book, which considers the emotional and psychological issues of sexual function rather than the mechanics, is *Passionate Marriage*, by Schnarch (1997). Particularly with problems of erectile dysfunction, organic causes are common and often overlooked. A genogram is very helpful in looking at family dynamic causes of dysfunction, but a full assessment of the problems requires a detailed consideration of current patterns and a careful physical examination. The recent success of Viagra demonstrates how frequently erectile dysfunction has an organic component.

Sexual addiction, or compulsion, is not described in the *DSM-IV* (1994), but many people believe strongly that it exists (Carnes, 1991). This is a constant preoccupation with sexual material, coupled with a need to masturbate or have sex on an extremely frequent basis with high anxiety if this need cannot be filled. For patients with this problem, it is helpful to look for similar patterns in family members, as well as a history of affairs, inappropriately stimulating early environment, and other compulsive symptoms, such as gambling or rituals.

Romantic Love

The *feeling* of being in love, that is, the first initial burst of romantic attraction, is extraordinarily powerful, and partly biologically based (Crenshaw, 1996; Walsh, 1991). Romantic love seems to involve physiologic arousal (energy, excitement, decreased appetite), sexual longing, intense focus on the loved one, and a particular kind of idealization. Interestingly, one recent study of romantic love found that a number of people feel in love in the first few hours of acquaintance (Willi, 1997). Many, although not all, of these continued the relationship into marriage. Those who did had marriages equally stable as those who reported that they fell in love slowly. It is also possible to have a feeling of love without participation of the loved person (e.g., in unrequited love, or love of a public figure). Romantic love seems to involve a connection to an idealized object and is a change in the self. That is how love at first sight occurs, because the person, who is unknown at a basic level, seems to fit the romantic ideal. Companionate love, which requires both partners and has more to do with the attachment system developed in early childhood, seems to involve other neurotransmitters and is more related to a sense ~~of~~ and safety when the other is nearby or available. This kind of a~~ttachment~~ cannot develop until the people have been together for some ti~~me and~~ usually involves a more realistic vision of the loved one.

Most people in this culture want to experience both romantic and companionate love, preferably with the same person. The ability to give and receive love in long-term or committed relationships, however, is deeply embedded in the family history. The question of how in the family one knew one was loved, and what one was loved for, is a central piece of heritage. For example, if a man comes from a family in which love is shown by fixing and doing things, and a woman comes from a family in which women are adored and given flowers and jewelry, she probably will not understand that his redoing the driveway after a hard day's work is truly an act of love. If a child's parents are unable to express enough love to make the child feel lovable, the child may spend much of his or her life searching for someone who can make them feel good about themselves. If the child was loved only for academic accomplishments, it is hard for him or her to believe any one would love anything else about them. Many people with this background develop workaholic, nonintimate lifestyles, believing they are expressing love by becoming famous or working hard.

Whether one believes it is safe to love anyone, or anyone who is kind to you, is another complex question embedded in one's history. A man whose mother was demanding, intrusive and angry, and whose father was unavailable to protect him from her demands, will not trust a woman, particularly if she wants to know where he is or wants emotional contact. It is also possible to love someone and treat them very badly. Many people who believe they love their partners do not let that stop them from constant criticism, neglect, or even violence. A search through the family tree for loving relatives, or for variant ways of expressing and receiving love, sometimes provides helpful guidelines for changing one's feelings and behavior. The relationship between love and power is complex. Although some believe that a love relation is impossible except between peers, the tendency of men in relationships to be older and physically stronger, with more money and political and social influence, makes true equality difficult. The complexity of managing a relationship that may feel emotionally equal but socially and politically unequal is a constant source of confusion for both partners. For some women, love fosters a relationship in which power is willingly given up so that the women can be "swept away" or protected by a strong man. For some men, serving as a protector is crucial for experiencing love. These are not issues to be solved but to be understood for each couple, in terms of their own idiosyncratic patterns.

□ Summary

Gender, sexuality, and romantic love present a complex pattern in which basic human emotions of love, sexual desire, and closeness interact in a cultural, social, and political milieu of gender-linked power inequity and biological and psychological gender differences. Sometimes the differences appear so large that we seem like separate species; sometimes the differences seem so small that we cannot understand what all the fuss is about. Using a gender lens is not the same as assuming all human problems exist because of gender. A willingness to explore the idiosyncratic understandings of how sex, love, and intimacy are connected in the individual person is critical to good therapy. As part of the journey home, each of us discovers that these are among the central questions and essential elements of family life: gender, sexuality, and romantic love.

□ Recommended Readings

Francoeur (1991), *Becoming a Sexual Person*
Schnarch (1997), *Passionate Marriage*
Walters, Carter, Papp, & Silverstein (1988), *The Invisible Web: Gender Patterns in Family Relationships*
Weeks & Hof (1987), *Integrating Sex and Marital Therapy*

CHAPTER 10

Culture Genograms

Cultural background and experiences determine attitudes and beliefs about life and what political, social, and economic options and opportunities people are likely to have. This chapter provides an introduction to the incredible diversity of various cultural patterns and influences. Unfortunately, most people are unaware of the cultural values and biases that their family systems and their environments impose upon them. Cultural experiences organize attitudes, beliefs, feelings, and behaviors both personally and intergenerationally. These attitudes, beliefs, and behaviors are particularly evident in prejudices, biases, and bigotry that exist among and between various cultural groups. Culture Genograms are a way of bringing these hidden values, expectations, and assumptions out into the open for review, clarification, and modification. The purpose is to examine the impact of race, immigration, and ethnicity, religious orientation, and class upon individuals. Culture defines one of the most important parameters within which family systems and individual personalities develop. Although they are presented last, Culture Genograms, like the other Focused Genograms presented in this book, are a fundamental and essential part of the MFG.

Culture Genograms provide the broadest perspective possible and encourage a systemic vista. A cultural sense of self is important to healthy self-esteem. Hardy and Laszloffy (1995) believe that culture is the broadest multidimensional concept, which incorporates, but is not limited to, ethnicity, gender, social class, and religious orientation. Others believe that gender and age are the defining parameters within families and that culture is a secondary variable. A separate Gender, Sexuality, and Romantic Love Genogram has been established, distinct from culture, in order to avoid making Culture Genograms too broad.

Culture is defined by *Webster's Dictionary* (1990) as the broad base of ways of living built up by people in a particular area and includes beliefs, roles, behavioral habits, ways of expression and feeling, rituals, meaning, and collective goals. In the United States, "mainstream" culture, primarily European American, encompasses a number of general beliefs such as that individual rights and responsibilities take precedence over duty to extended family; progress, optimism, and future orientation are central values; and consumerism and enjoyment of material advantage are good things. Cultures usually contain in them inherent strains and contradictions so that even those who are fully acculturated have areas of choice and areas of stress. The United States still values family ties very highly, in spite of its commitment to individual choice. However, a person may belong to one or many subcultures by birth (e.g., Italian American), by marriage (e.g., a Caucasian American who marries a Vietnamese American), or by choice (e.g., a fundamentalist religious group, Civil war enthusiast). The subculture may be all-encompassing or partial and may have values different from mainstream culture. Fundamentalist religious groups of all persuasions place loyalty to church and community over self-determination. In America, most people belong to a number of subcultures.

Culture Genograms are a method of uncovering and addressing the influences of cultural biases. An academically gifted African American teenaged male, for instance, faces conflicting messages in American culture. The white community assumes that he may not really be all that "bright," his peers may believe that studying and being academically successful is not the "tough" or masculine way to behave, his parents may value education above all else, and his grandparents may be concerned that he aim for a secure job. In large part, the family system's responses to these issues are determined by its unique legacy. If other males in the family are high achievers, then the stress within the family is likely to be high. If males in the family are varied and attitudes are flexible toward achievement, then the stress within the family will be lower. Cultural differences impact family dynamics in many ways. Cultural influences affect marital relationships, parent-child relationships, and expectations about kinship and community.

☐ Constructing Culture Genograms

The clinician can flexibly use Culture Genograms throughout treatment. In the beginning of therapy, there is the obvious issue of sameness and difference between the therapist and the individual or family member. Behaviors and attitudes of both clinician and client must be understood within the cultural context from which they emerge. If the therapist and the client are from different cultural backgrounds—racial, ethnic, religious, or socioeconomic—these differences create myriad opportunities for misunderstanding. If misunderstandings take place, interventions are unlikely to be effective. Next, the therapist must be aware of cultural differences within the family. Are there biethnic marriages or multiracial children within the family system? Are these marriages or children accepted by extended family members or are they a source of conflict and disharmony? Although cultural or racial family secrets are unlikely to emerge in the early stages of developing the MFG, developing Culture Genograms gives the clinician indications where information is sparse or inconsistent. Often, family members simply do not know facts about the family history.

Collecting Information

Collecting information for the genogram can be therapeutic for the client. The clinician's attention to the cultural dimensions of the client's social experience often is perceived as validating and affirming and is an important part of building rapport. If there are obvious cultural differences between the clinician and the client system, creating Culture Genograms can be essential in developing an atmosphere of empathy. Sensitivity to cultural themes and biases also can help the clinician overcome transferential and countertransferential roadblocks. For example, when an Asian client enters treatment, the shame of entering therapy for a troubled child or adolescent cannot be overlooked. A Culture Genogram is a tool that the clinician can use immediately to reduce resistance to clinical intervention.

Using the questions suggested in this chapter, the clinician could develop a thorough Culture Genogram that examines racial, ethnic, religious, and socioeconomic themes and patterns within the family. Biases and attitudes that constrict personal and family functioning can be exposed and discussed during treatment. Specific intervention strategies can be developed to effect cognitive or behavioral changes that will help the client address the problems that brought him or her into treatment. Analysis of the cultural patterns in the family system enables the clinician to assess in what areas client advocacy can be useful as well.

When developing Culture Genograms, highly motivated clients can find it useful to contact the National Genealogical Society. It provides support and assistance to people looking to trace their family history. Smith (1990) established the top 10 genealogy questions asked in public libraries, and a brochure is available from the Society. The pamphlet addresses questions such as where to find local history information; where to find birth, marriage, divorce, and death records; where to find church and cemetery records; where to find and how to use census records; where to find military records; and where to find immigration and passenger-list information. This kind of information can enrich the client's experience in putting together a Culture Genogram.

When the client and clinician are from different cultural backgrounds, it is important to develop rapport before initiating Culture Genograms. If the client is uncomfortable, in any way, about discussing racial, ethnic, religious, or socioeconomic issues, the clinician can use the opportunity to talk with the client about his or her comfort level with the clinician. There may be questions or beliefs that the client has that, when addressed, strengthen the therapeutic alliance.

Markovitz (1997) suggests that giving language to the larger cultural system that is part of clients' lives provides knowledge and understanding, which empowers clients to make better choices about their lives. A multicultural perspective expands the context of the treatment process. This aspect of Culture Genograms should not be underestimated.

Race, Ethnicity, and Immigration

The questions included for Culture Genograms examine both in-group experiences and norms as well as out-of-group biases and prejudices. The questions begin with an overview of racial cultural experience and then are expanded to include ethnicity and immigration, religious orientation, and socioeconomic status.

Questions for Culture Genograms: Race, Ethnicity, and Immigration (Modified from Hardy & Laszloffy, 1995, with permission)

1. What were the migration patterns of the group or groups that constitutes your family? How do family members define themselves racially and how do you define yourself?
2. If other than Native American, under what conditions did different family members (or their descendants) enter the United States? In what years did they arrive? If they came as a family, who in the

family wished to emigrate, and who did not? Were there ties to the homeland? Where and how were they maintained?

3. What were or are the group's experiences with oppression? What were or are the markers of oppression?
4. What issues divide members within the same group? What are the sources of intragroup conflict?
5. Describe the relationship between the group's identity and your national ancestry. (If the group is defined in terms of nationality, please skip this question.)
6. What significance do race, skin color, and hair play within the group?
7. What are the dominant religions of the group? What role does religion and spirituality play in the everyday lives of members of the group?
8. What role does regionality and geography play in the group?
9. How are gender roles defined within the group? How is sexual orientation regarded?
10. What prejudices or stereotypes does this group have about itself? What prejudices and stereotypes do other groups have about this group? What prejudices and stereotypes does this group have about other groups?
11. What role (if any) do names play in the group? Are there rules, mores, or rituals governing the assignment of names?
12. How is social class defined in the group?
13. What occupational roles are valued or devalued by the group?
14. What is the relationship between age and the values of the group?
15. How does the group define family?
16. How does this group view outsiders in general, mental-health professionals, and other professions?
17. How have the organizing principles of this group shaped this family and its members? What effect have they had on the client?
18. What are the ways in which pride and shame issues of each group are manifested in the family system?
19. If more than one group makes up the culture of origin, how were the differences negotiated in the family? What were the intergenerational consequences?

Religious Orientation

Religion is another powerful lens of Culture Genograms. In general, Caucasians of European descent tend to have a Judeo-Christian heritage. Buddhism and Confucianism, primary religions in Asia, often influence Asians who immigrate to the United States, although they frequently become members of Christian faiths in the United States. African Americans, although influenced by Christianity in the United States, are now reclaiming their African connections with Islam. Understanding the diverse nature and contradictions of Christianity, Judaism, Islam, Buddhism, and other religious influences provides a broad context for understanding a particular family system in political, social, and historical perspectives. The importance of including religion is illustrated by the example of a Caucasian, female university professor who grew up in the northeastern United States and came from a Protestant faith. She met and married another university professor of Arabic, Muslim background. Their relationship was comfortable until they had their first child. Their relationship became intensely conflictual around roles in the family, authority, responsibility, and decision making. The independent American wife was not an acceptable Muslim mother to the husband. The patriarchal Arabic husband was not an acceptable American father to the wife. This couple's conflicts must be understood not only from a clinical perspective that emphasizes the need to improve communication and conflict resolution, but also from the cultural perspective. In this case, conflicts centered on religious differences that established very different values and assumptions about family life, marital roles and responsibilities, and gender.

Although it is beyond the scope of this text, the clinician needs to have a basic understanding about the major religions and their influences on family systems. Although religions share many similarities, there are significant differences. Religions vary whether they emphasize faith or specific deeds, what behaviors are valued (self-abnegation versus achievement, pacifism versus warfare to spread God's word), and what traditions are established and observed. They also vary in how much of a place they give to psychological issues: For example, is psychotherapy acceptable or should prayer suffice? In clinical practice with couples struggling with one partner's extramarital affair, the clients' religious and spiritual orientations have important implications for dealing with forgiveness. Forgiveness is a very different process in Jewish and Christian traditions.

Questions About Religious Orientation

1. How important is religious practice or affiliation? What religious affiliations exist within the family?
2. Is there conflict within the family about religious practices?
3. How do religious beliefs influence self-esteem, marriage, parenting, sexuality, and familial responsibilities and loyalties?
4. What are the unique features of the religious orientation of the family?

5. Have family members married outside the family faith? What were the consequences?
6. Is religious affiliation a source of strength in the family system or a source of conflict?

Family rituals and traditions have various levels of importance within family systems and often are tied to religious beliefs (e.g., Christmas, Hannukkah, Ramadan). Other rituals and traditions can have ethnic origins. In order to provide the family with meaning and significance, these rituals and traditions must be repeated and must be coordinated in order to provide a sense of predictability, connection, and identity and a way to enact values (Doherty, 1997). Doherty identifies rituals of connection, celebration, and community. In order to enhance the power of the religious-orientation genogram, additional questions can be asked about family traditions and rituals.

Questions About Family Rituals and Traditions

1. How does the family system celebrate rituals of connection: family meals, rising and retiring, coming and going, going out and going away, couple rituals?
2. How does the family system observe these rituals of celebration and community: special-person rituals (birthdays, Mother's Day, Father's Day), Thanksgiving, Christmas, community and religious rituals, rituals of passage (weddings and funerals)?

Socioeconomic Status

Blended with race, ethnicity, and religion, Culture Genograms would not be complete without the socioeconomic lens. Socioeconomic status and experience influences important areas of life. For instance, socioeconomic background has a suppressive role on age of marriage and the number of children a couple is likely to have. Trend data suggest that the more affluent and better educated your parents, the less likely one is to marry, and the higher the average age at first marriage. Higher education also tends to be associated with lower levels of divorce. Lower level of education (high school and below) is associated with welfare dependency, divorce, illegitimacy, and father's absence. Socioeconomic status influences the availability and options for power and resources. In families with limited financial resources, issues and questions about who goes to college, where, and why have momentous implications within the family. Rachel, born in 1956, was not supported in her desire to go to college. Family resources were limited and college was an option only for her brothers. Rachel's resentments led to jealousy as her brothers achieved greater and greater success in their careers, while she felt left behind. Culture Genograms provide a structure to examine cultural biases and stereotypes as they interact with financial limitations in the family.

Questions About Socioeconomic Status

1. What did your parents teach you about social class? With what class did your parents identify themselves?
2. How did this fit or not fit with what they modeled for you by their behavior, where they lived, who they associated with, and so forth?
3. What possibilities do you think they felt they had to shift social class status? Would your parents agree or disagree with your perceptions?
4. How important was social class to them and to your siblings in the neighborhood in which you grew up?
5. Do you think your family was more or less concerned about social class than other families?
6. How might things have been different in your family if different economic possibilities had been available to it?
7. Do different members of your family belong to different social classes? Have members of your family changed class (up or down) due to marriage, making or losing money, illness, or bad luck?
8. When you were growing up, what messages did peers pass on about social class?
9. What ideas about social class do you want to pass on to the next generation? How are these the same or different from what your parents taught you?
10. What meanings do you think people ascribe to social class in our society?
11. Where do you see yourself in relationship to these kinds of assumptions?
12. Think back to when you first visited, lived in, worked in a neighborhood of a different social class. How did you think about social class differently/act differently, after that?

These questions are adapted from, and based on, Roberts (1991).

The Culture Family Map

The Culture Family Map often reveals patterns of closeness and distance between relatives. Distant relatives, who might have very little place in the client's life, may become resources once they are identified. A Cultural Family Map might include a nanny from another country who provided childcare for a period of time. The quality of these relationships can be graphed using the Culture Family Map. The affects of socioeconomic changes, religious practices, and immigration also are shown on the Cultural Map. Mary's cousin arrived from Russia. For the next year, Mary had a very involved relationship with the cousin that included several trips with him and his family back to Russia. Mary spent a great deal of time helping her cousin's wife, children, and family get established. During this period, her relationship with her husband and children became distant.

The Culture Time Line

As with other Focused Genograms, the Culture Time Line is a place to note specific time periods that uniquely identify the client's history. Noting when racial and ethnic issues and conflicts occurred can be very important to the construction of the client's narrative. When exploring his family's immigration from Italy, Anthony learned that his family had been landholders and that his grandfather maintained contact with his Italian relatives until World War II. The war devastated the family's holdings and the family had relocated to another part of Italy. During this time, his grandfather, who lived in the United States, lost contact with his family. His grandfather went into a depression and was a changed and unhappy man. Anthony's understanding and appreciation for the effects on the family for the next generation enabled him to make contact with local relatives and reconnect with cut-off family roots.

The Culture Time Line shows when significant changes took place and how these events related to one another. The level of stress on a family due to often-dramatic changes, as focused on by Culture Genograms, can be assessed for short- and long-term effects.

☐ Making Sense of Culture Genograms: Theoretical Underpinnings

Race

Race is an extraordinarily complex issue in this country, which is one of the most racially diverse and racially conscious countries in the world. Physical-trait differences in skin color or clear differences in features are the usual basis for differentiating race, but, in fact, race is, to a surprising extent, a social construction. For example, by the end of the American Civil War there was so much intermingling of Caucasians and African Americans (primarily due to white slave owners having sex with their slaves) that a socially constructed definition was created during the post-Civil War period: anyone with one eighth (or even one sixteenth or one thirty-second, depending on the state) of African heritage was considered Black. Many such people, of course, had Caucasian skin and features. Fear of "racial impurity" was so strong that it was a crime to "pass." The ability to "pass" and the concept of "passing" demonstrates the power of social construction of race.

Social construction of racial identity is fluid and affects a person's power and privilege within the culture. People of Caucasian European descent are privileged in the United States while people of color, or those defined as people of color, have fewer opportunities and less access to power. There is also a hierarchy of privilege among people of color. For example, people defined as Asian are, at this point in history, generally more admired than people designated African American. In general, voluntary immigrants have a higher social position than those who have a history of being enslaved or colonized by the dominant culture (e.g., African Americans or Native Americans) (Ogbu, 1978).

South America is a particularly interesting example of the interaction of race and ethnicity. Many South Americans are multiracial, the result of mixing of indigenous Indians, African slaves, and European conquerors. However, those with mostly European heritage are still privileged. Many North Americans tend to label anyone with a Spanish accent from Central and South America, Cuba, or Puerto Rico as Hispanic or Latino, which erases specific differences of race, class, and ethnicity. For example, a Puerto Rican man states that he defines himself as Puerto Rican but does not think of himself as a person of color. However, while in the United States he identifies himself as a minority and identifies with people of color. A well-to-do Argentinean woman identifies herself as white and upper class. She is troubled that in the United States, when among people who did not know her, she is treated with disrespect and seen as a person of color because of her accent. The term *Latino* or *Latina* tells very little about the specifics of class, race, or country. In conducting Culture Genograms, the therapist must explore the person's own construction of his or her culture and identity, as well as how he or she experiences racial and cultural biases.

In the United States, race is often a code word for black-white relations, which have their roots in slavery. There are people alive in this country whose grandparents or great-grandparents were slaves or shareholders, so that this heritage is still very real and alive today. The most obvious markers of segregation—the separate water fountains, the segregated neighborhoods, the laws against interracial marriage—were still the norms in the childhood culture of one of the authors. The consistent prejudice against African Americans and the impact of slavery has made it difficult for African Americans to become fully integrated and for Caucasians to allow them to participate in American life on an equal footing.

In the United States, "white skin" is privileged in a variety of ways, one of which is that one's actions are not considered to be a reflection on one's race. For people of color, the anticipation of and vulnerability to prejudice are daily facts. One of the most confusing situations to a person of color is that, in these days in which segregation laws do not exist but racism does, many situations are ambiguous. Advancements, problem relationships, or poor performance reviews may be about performance or related in some way to racial biases.

Despite often-hostile environments, many people of color do well in this country. This is due to both their own abilities and the abilities of their families to help them deal with prejudice in a nonrestrictive way. Unfortunately, mainstream prejudice often is integrated into family life, so that in some African American families light skin and straight hair are preferred and light-skinned children are treated better than dark-skinned ones (Pinderhughes, 1989). It is important to understand how the family supports the child in developing a positive racial identity and teaches her or him to deal with the daily problems of living in a highly stressful situation. Class also impacts the family. Middle-class African American families, like other middle class families, live in a different situation than those in poverty. Gender is also a factor. The experiences of African American women are different from those of African American men. Black men are perceived as more dangerous, and often have fewer academic and work opportunities, than women (Boyd Franklin, 1989).

Mary, a 15-year-old African American, shared this story with her therapist: "My family and I moved to this area and I am one of four blacks in my entire class. I was pretty much accepted by white girls but not by white guys. They made fun of me because my hair wasn't as soft and didn't move like the other girls. I didn't know what was more important, trying to fit in or being myself." Mary's report underscores the psychological conflict created by racial bias. There is much literature that discusses racial differences and their effects, and there is a wide range of racial biases. Unfortunately, racial bias and bigotry have not been eliminated from social or political research, and these biases are periodically reinforced. This occurred with the publication of *The Bell Curve* (Herstein & Murray, 1994), which created renewed controversy regarding racial differences in intelligence.

Ethnicity and Immigration

Ethnicity is a sense of belonging to a particular group that emigrated from a particular geographic place with its own culture. In the United States, many people have this type of dual identity—a sense of roots connected to the area of emigration as well as an allegiance to mainstream values. A vast number of Americans are within four or five generations of an immigration experience and have some connection to their country of origin. The process of acculturation—that is, the switch to predominant allegiance to and expression of the dominant culture—is difficult and normally takes a family about three generations. In any country, members of different races can be included in an ethnicity—for example, Jamaicans of Black, Indian, and British descent all will be seen as Jamaican if they move to Haiti.

Between 1820 and 1860 more than five million people immigrated to the United States. Ninety percent of these five million were from England, Ireland, and Germany. Furthermore, between 1860 and 1920, 29 million more people immigrated to the United States, and most of these people came from Russia, Poland, the Balkans, Italy, and Asia. As of 1990, the total Hispanic population was over 22 million people, and it is the second-fastest growing ethnic population (after the Asian population); the Native American population now totals more than 1.9 million. Twelve percent of the total population, almost 30 million people, are African Americans, almost all descendants of slaves. As of the 1990 census, 24% of the population in the United States is African American, Latino American, Asian American, Pacific Islander, or Native American. The Census Bureau estimates that by 2050 this percentage will increase to 40% of the population. At some point in the next century, it is likely that white European Americans will constitute a minority group (Olmedo, 1994).

These facts have important implications. First, there are differences in the legacies that are passed down through generations if a single individual immigrates due to poverty or if a family unit immigrates because an uncle has already made his way and now wants to help his brother and his family. Next, there are differences if someone immigrates with some education and financial resources or if someone comes as a child and soon loses a parent or parents to disease or an accident. Changes in immigration and patterns can affect different generations of a family system. The husband's great-grandparents may have immigrated in the late 1800s, while the wife's family immigrated during the 1920s.

Because of widespread immigration in the late 1800s and early 1900s, there will be few American families who can go beyond four generations in constructing their genograms. Sometimes it is difficult for people to go beyond their own grandparents. Often the fact of immigration represents a cut-off for a family from its ethnic roots. The circumstances that led to immigration become family myth, or lost to memory. By being knowledgeable about immigration patterns, clinicians can be more focused in constructing Culture Genograms. A basic knowledge of history helps the process as well. If a client does some background research on their family, he or she often finds out where the family tree stops. Asking historical questions during this process often can help the client gain a richer understanding of the impact of immigration on the family system.

Clients often report that getting and giving the cultural history reconnects them to their ethnic origins. Cheryl, for example, recalled that there was always a sense of shame that she felt because of her Slavic heritage. In constructing her Culture Genogram, Cheryl learned about her grandfather's loss of ties to his family in Hungary due to pograms, and his difficult immigration experience. She reconnected with an aunt, began to explore her heritage in more depth, and experienced a sense a pride about her roots. Incorporating these perspectives enriches clinical interventions. The therapeutic alliance is strengthened by increased empathy between clinician and client. Clients often state that learning about their family heritage is a significant and important experience as part of the treatment process.

McGoldrick, Pearce, and Giordana (1982) have detailed more than 30 different ethnic groups, grouping them by American Indian, African, Latino, Asian, Middle Eastern, Asian Indian, European, Jewish, and Slavic heritage. Landau-Stanton (1986) has developed "transitional mapping" as a method for assessing the level of cultural transition and integration into the community. She suggests that "transition conflict" emerges as a result of differential rates of adaptation. Some members of the family learn the new language and adapt to the new culture. Other family members yearn to return "home." Consequently, the therapist should establish how and when immigration took place and how the family system adjusted and adapted to the migration process. Susan, who was 14 years old when her family emigrated from Korea, spent all of her time watching television in order to learn the new language. Her father, on the other hand, struggled to come to terms with the changes brought about by the move to the United States. He reluctantly learned the language. Susan's social relations were constrained because she was reluctant to bring friends home. Her father's employment opportunities were limited. Ultimately, Susan became the spokesperson for the family within the new culture.

Immigration patterns are considered carefully in Culture Genograms. The United States is an ethnically diverse nation, and this diversity will be evident in many genograms. The majority of Americans are descended from Europeans who came to the United State to obtain religious and political freedom and economic opportunities. The circumstances of immigration are often important themes in the MFG and should be explored in detail. Jewish families who escaped Europe during the Nazi reign; a West African woman looking to escape from a patriarchal social system; a Vietnamese man who marries an American woman and never discusses his Vietnamese heritage: These are important circumstances with significant effects on legacies and family dynamics. These patterns suggest that clinicians cannot overlook the immigration and ethnicity of a family system and the impact on current family functioning.

The application of race, ethnicity and immigration Culture Genograms is illustrated by examining three different family systems based on the various foci of race and ethnicity. The families include an African American family, an Asian family, and one Caucasian family. These cases were selected to illustrate how patterns of migration, oppression, in-group and out-of-group differences, physical characteristics, religion, and gender are culturally affected.

African American Families

The unique issues faced by African American families are highlighted by Haley who, after 12 years of intense personal research, poignantly fictionalized his family's history to create the story *Roots* (1976). This story has been chosen because it demonstrates the profound influence of slavery on an African American family that often is overlooked in the genogram process (Figure 10.1). The capture and enslavement of Africans is a unique political, social, and moral history.

The history of African Americans is inseparable from the struggle and place of slavery in American history. The story of Kunta Kinte (Haley's ancestor) personalizes slavery. *Roots* is metaphorically, and historically, the history of every African American family. Because so much of their history is lost, Boyd-Franklin (1993) points out that African American genograms seldom conform to bloodlines. It is hard to identify bloodlines if the family unit was not a function of slavery. Kunta Kinte was brought to American as a slave and married Bell, who was 39 years old at the time of their marriage. Before she married Kunta Kinte, Bell's two children had been sold. Later, Kizzy, the daughter of Kunta Kinte and Bell, was sold to a slave master. The legacy of emotional and physical separation continued into the next generation. Kizzy's son George married Matilda, who, like her mother-in-law Kizzy, had been torn from her families. These losses established a legacy of emotional turmoil and struggle during even normal life.

The effects of slavery on bonding and attachment within African American families cannot be underestimated. It is rare that an African American family has many details about its family history. For example, Robin's family moved to the northern United States in the early 1960s, leaving behind the extended family network. In developing her Culture Genograms, she learned that her great-grandfather had been a slave, but no one in her family wanted to talk about the details. The elders in the family wanted to put the past behind them.

Identity confusion and biculturality continue to be important issues in working with African American families. These issues are intertwined with the darkest side of slavery. The rape of female slaves and the birth of biracial children created tremendous stress within each generation of Alex Haley's family. With freedom, however, came the challenge of developing a new identity, one different from African ancestry and one different from the life as a slave. Culture Genograms provide a unique opportunity for the clinician to assist African American clients to examine the impact of their families' unique experiences.

Asian Families

Culture Genograms are an especially useful tool in working with Asian families. Often Asian families drop out of treatment after one or two sessions. Acknowledging family and personal problems amplifies their shame.

Asian families are not alike. Koreans, Chinese, Japanese, Cambodians, Vietnamese, and other Asian groups differ not only geographically but also historically. These historical influences create differences and rivalries among the groups. However, in America "Oriental" is often used as a term to describe these divergent groups, even though each has a unique culture shaped by history, tradition, and customs. For example, Koreans resent the Japanese for the annexation of Korea by Japan in 1910. Today, two forms of government separate North and South Korea. Korean society has been influenced by the Confucian tradition, which emphasizes five distinct interpersonal relationships: leader to citizen, parent to child, husband to wife, elder brother to younger brother, and friend to friend. The emphasis on family obligation and filial duty remained unchanged for centuries. Marriages historically were arranged, and producing a male heir was a primary responsibility for a woman, although custody of children went to the husband. Polygamy was an old and historically acceptable custom. Displays of negative emotions were completely unacceptable. However, changes in Korean lifestyles began to take place with the Westernization of Korea, beginning in 1950. This kind of detailed information is very important in Culture Genograms.

In a consultation regarding a 13-year-old boy from Cambodia, Culture Genograms, in particular the immigration process, became a guiding in-

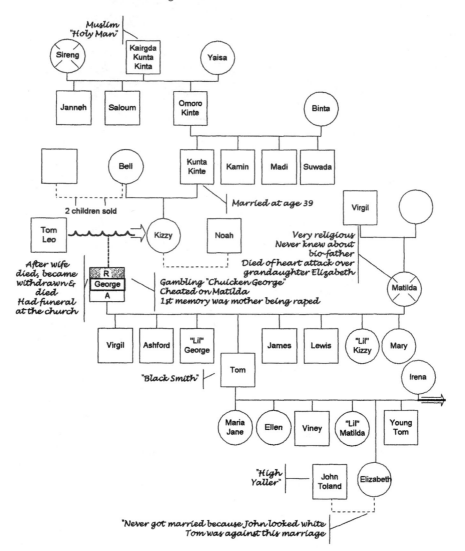

FIGURE 10.1. Alex Haley Family Genogram. (Genogram drawn by Linda Yoo Kelly [1996].)

fluence on the treatment plan. Chuiem had been brought to Philadelphia by an uncle who found him in a refugee camp in Cambodia. The conditions and life within these refugee camps were extremely impoverished. Chuiem suffered from school difficulties and depression. He had no recollection of his family in Cambodia. His uncle had been arrested for child prostitution and pornography and Chuiem had been placed in

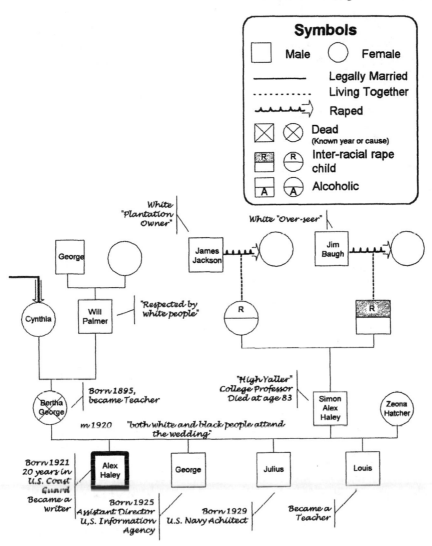

FIGURE 10.1. (continued) Alex Haley Family Genogram.

foster care. As the clinician explored the records of Chuiem's arrival in Philadelphia a picture emerged of a child who had been taken away from his poor family in Cambodia and been brought into a child-prostitution ring. The trauma of poverty within the refugee camps had been coupled with sexual violence and assault. Through exploring recollection of Cambodia and coming to the United States, Chueim began to share drawings with the therapist and began to address his history for the first time. Other therapy attempts to address school work or misbehavior had resulted in nonparticipation and noncompliance by Chuiem. This is an example of examining the effect of problems in Southeast Asia and the later effects on immigration.

Caucasian Families

Caucasian families can be different from one another. Culture Genograms underscores these differences. Mark and Debbie are a couple in their 30s with three children, expecting their fourth child. Mark's mother is Italian, his father Irish. His mother's family immigrated to the United States when she was a child and were very disappointed that their daughter did not marry someone who was Italian. His father was a factory worker who had a difficult time supporting the family financially. His paternal grandfather, who emigrated from Ireland, had been alcoholic and out of work much of his life. Fitting traditional stereotypes whereby Irish men are often seen as passive, Mark's father was very reserved while his mother was passionate, controlling, and concerned with the family's financial security. Debbie, on the other hand, defined herself as American, meaning she did not know her ethnic origins, although Debbie had a sense that there were many English descendants in her family tree. She felt her mother tended to be a cold and distant woman, although Debbie's family had a strong and stable educational and professional history. Consequently, Mark's lack of career focus and frequent job changes were a source of serious conflict in their marriage. Debbie was also distressed because she felt that his mother "babied" him and was more concerned with Mark visiting on a regular basis than with his work. Culture Genograms were used to help them understand the differences in their ethnic heritages and helped shift the focus from a conflict-withdrawal cycle to clarifying their needs and expectations with one another.

Religious Orientation

Clinicians tend to leave the religious and spiritual dimension outside of the practice setting (Raider, 1992). In many families, religion plays a central role in the family's values, traditions, and rituals. Marriage, parenting, community service, and attitudes toward work, money, and productivity can be significantly influenced by religious beliefs. Many religions are, in fact, practiced as a way of life (e.g., Islam, Buddhism).

Raider (1992) has suggested that the therapist, through specific questioning, can help the couple to assess ways in which religion influences their family structure (for example, "To what extent does the family's religion define family membership?" [p. 174]), their family processes (for example, "To what extent does the family's religion offer guidelines for family problem solving and decision making?" [p. 176]), their family boundaries (for example, "To what extent does the family's religion influence the degree of permeability of the family's boundaries with the neighborhood, community, and outside environment?" [p. 179]), and their family system equilibrium or integration (for example, "To what extent does the family's religion emphasize tradition, stability, and order?" [p. 180]). Careful assessment in these areas may uncover hopeful and helpful supports or guidance for the individuals and the family as they work together at problem solving and decision making.

Spirituality can be an important focus of treatment depending on presenting problems. In the case of extramarital affairs, for example, practitioners often explore issues of forgiveness as part of the treatment process. A client's religious beliefs often influence his or her attitudes toward forgiveness. Greeley's research (1991) suggests that religion plays a role in marital and sexual satisfaction. Examining interreligious marital patterns can reveal sources of conflict and tension within the family system. Consequently, examining religious beliefs and values can be an important Culture Genogram to explore with the client.

Socioeconomic Status

Social class is an important aspect of American life, yet it is frequently overlooked in the clinical setting. Ross (1995) calls attention to the importance of attending to issues of social class within the family system. She identifies three patterns of social class tension: one family member achieving significantly more or less than others within the family system, marrying someone who is "up" or "down" in social class (from "the other side of the tracks"), and divorce and remarriage, causing class differences between children and parents. Ross notes that upward or downward mobility of individual family members can be the basis for many tensions within the individual and the family and that, too often, these tensions go unacknowledged by clinicians. Social-class tensions effect individuation and differentiation, identity, and attitudes toward financial success. The social-class lens focuses the therapist to consider the influence of these tensions.

☐ Summary

Developing a Culture Genogram is an essential step in creating a client's MFG. Racial, ethnic, religious, and socioeconomic realities and experiences are powerful forces that shape personal identity and family traditions and expectations. Without examining these influences in detail, the clinician is developing intervention strategies that are biased by his or her own cultural experiences. Respecting and working with cultural differences enhances the entire treatment process.

One of the first steps in developing a MFG with a family is acknowledging its racial and ethnic origins. Both the client and the clinician bring biases, spoken and unspoken, to the interview. Initial impressions are racially and ethnically biased and based on personal appearance, language, or other attitudes or behaviors. It is a natural part of establishing relationships to identify sameness and differentness. For many people this is a crucial element in establishing trust and gaining rapport during the treatment process. Acknowledging differences and similarities between the clinician and client helps foster the therapeutic bond. The clinician may choose to begin with a Culture Genogram or wait for a more clinically relevant time. However, conducting Culture Genograms is considered a valuable part of the clinical experience for many clients.

☐ Recommended Readings

McGoldrick, Pearce, & Giordana (1982), *Ethnicity and Family Therapy*
Pinderhughes (1989), *Understanding Race, Ethnicity, and Power*
Raider (1992), *Assessing the Role of Religion in the Family*

CHAPTER

Conclusion: Using the Multifocused Family Genogram in Practice

The genogram is an essential clinical tool that helps practitioners obtain and maintain a broad systemic view of the client and the family system. The MFG, with the Basic Genogram, Focused Genograms, Family Maps, and Time Lines, organizes and expands the use of the genogram beyond its traditional bounds. Focused Genograms are an important assessment and clinical tool that can be added to the clinician's practice strategy. However, learning to use the structure and methods of the MFG is a gradual process for most clinicians.

The MFG format is flexible and permits the practitioner to use various pieces of the Focused Genograms as they become relevant. For example, if the therapist is working with a couple around a problem of power and control in the marriage, he or she may use a Focused Gender Genogram first with an accompanying Time Line and Family Map. As treatment progresses, the practitioner may focus on sexual difficulties and use the Sexuality Genogram to explore this area with the client. In turn, the therapist may realize it is useful to broaden the context by conducting the Attachments Genogram. With continued experience with the various components of the MFG, the clinician will become more familiar and facile with its use.

Once the clinician has mastered the techniques of constructing the MFG, it becomes an important clinical tool, used more frequently and consistently. Because of its overarching structure, the MFG keeps the clinician and the client focused on addressing symptoms and problems in the contexts of individual, interpersonal, family, and cultural functioning. Exploration using the broad range of Focused Genograms offered by the MFG offers a panoramic view of the client system. Without this comprehensive assessment process, the practitioner can miss important aspects of the client's life experience. The analysis of attachment patterns and emotional expression provides an important link among intrapsychic, interactional, and intergenerational patterns.

Systems theory and attachment theory share roots in biological theory. The genogram originally was developed as a method to study genetics. The MFG is an attempt to integrate these concepts with the practical day-to-day experience of interviewing clients and helping them explore with their intergenerational legacies and loyalties. From the viewpoint of family therapy supervision and training, all clinicians are encouraged to conduct the complete MFG with all clients on a regular basis. However, the MFG is designed to be used piece-by-piece and is adaptable, based on clinical setting and clinical model. What is most important is that practitioners explore the varied dimensions of their clients' life experiences in a focused way.

Family life is much too complex and diverse to avoid using a structured framework to assess family patterns. The Focused Genograms are an effective way to explore problem areas with clients and have been used for many years by the authors. Treatment may lose focus and cohesion as the therapist gets lost in the complexities of the client's life. Using Family Maps and Time Lines enhances the process by adding developmental and relational perspectives.

Attachment theory provides a model for understanding the foundations of interpersonal behaviors in the family. This model is particularly useful because it leads to an examination of the intergenerational transmission of internal working models, a complex process that family systems theory has been struggling to explain for many years. The MFG uses attachment theory and the Internal Models Map as ways to link intrapsychic, interpersonal, and intergenerational phenomenon. Patterns of distance and closeness, enmeshment and cut-off can be explained by describing the quality of secure attachment, anxious-ambivalent attachment, avoidant attachment, or disorganized attachment. Not only can these labels describe parent-child relations, but they also can explain intergenerational themes as well. Families filled with divorce, financial ruin, erratic personal success, and pockets of violence can be described as disorganized families. Enmeshed, chaotic families reflect the ambivalent attachment style. Working toward the creation of a secure therapeutic alliance, a secure family, and secure interpersonal relationships within the family fosters healthy functioning and personal fulfillment. The whole function of attachment is to insure safety and security and enhance chances for survival. Satir (1967) wrote and spoke for many years about the importance of the family as a secure base for the healthy development and self-esteem of all the family members.

The use of Family Maps to help develop and focus the therapeutic alliance is new. Other than Stanton's 1992 article, mapping has received little attention in the professional literature. Research suggests that mapping has been narrowly focused on cut-offs, conflict, and enmeshment. These patterns are so characteristic of so many families that these mapping procedures begin to lose their meaning over time. An overlooked function of mapping is to enhance the clinical relationship. Mapping family dynamics and internal models provides clinicians with a template for providing therapeutically directed corrective emotional experiences for the client system.

This book presents a method for constructing Focused Genograms that not only encourages a systemic intervention but also maintains focus on individual and family development. Maintaining a sense of time and fluidity of family structure and process is not always easy. The Time Line is an effective tool for helping the therapist maintain this perspective. Sometimes a family's functioning is healthy, but then tragedy strikes— a child is accidentally killed, a father is severely injured, a fire wipes out a family's home. Events such as these create stress that strains the family's and the individual's abilities to cope. There can be widespread systemic repercussions.

The MFG (with its Basic Genogram, Family Map, Time Line, and Focused Genograms) brings the genogram to a new level of development for both individually oriented and family systems oriented clinicians.

Bibliography

Aguilera, D. (1967). Relationship between physical contact and verbal interaction between nurses and patients. *Journal of Psychiatric Nursing, 5*, 5–21.

Ahrons, C. (1994). *The good divorce: Keeping your family together when your marriage comes apart.* New York: Harper Collins.

Ainsworth, M. D. S., Blehar, M. C., Waters, E., & Wall, S. (1978). *Patterns of attachment: A psychological study of the strange situation.* Hillsdale, NJ: Erlbaum.

Andersen, P. A., & Liebowitz, K. (1978). The development and nature of the construct touch avoidance. *Environmental Psychology and Nonverbal Behavior, 3*, 89–106.

Ansbacher, H., & Ansbacher, R. (Eds.). (1956). *The individual psychology of Alfred Adler.* New York: Harper & Row.

Bach, G., & Goldberg, H. (1974). *Creative aggression.* New York: Doubleday.

Bach, G. R., & Wyden, P. (1969). *The intimate enemy: How to fight fair in love and marriage.* New York: William Morrow.

Balint, M. (1979). *The basic fault: Therapeutic aspects of regression.* New York: Brunner/Mazel.

Becvar, D. S., & Becvar, R. (1996). *Family therapy: A systemic integration* (3rd ed.). New York: Allyn & Bacon.

Belsky, J., & Isabella, R. A. (1988). Maternal, infant, and social-contextual determinants of attachment security. In J. Belsky & T. Nezworski (Eds.), *Clinical implications of attachment.* Hillsdale, NJ: Erlbaum.

Benjamin, J. (1989). *The bonds of love: Psychoanalysis, feminism, and the problem of domination.* New York: Pantheon Books.

Blossom, H. J. (1991) The personal genogram: An interview technique for selecting family practice residents. *Family Systems Medicine, 9*(2).

Bograd, M. (1990). Scapegoating mothers: Conceptual errors in systems formulations. In M. Mirkin (Ed.), *The social and political contexts of family therapy.* Boston: Allyn & Bacon.

Bordin, E. S. (1979). The generalizeability of the psychoanalytic concept of the working alliance. *Psychotherapy: Theory, Research and Practice, 16*, 252–260.

Boszormenyi-Nagy, I. (1987). *Foundations of contextual therapy.* New York: Brunner/Mazel.

Bowlby, J. (1958). The nature of the child's tie to his mother. *International Journal of Psycho-analysis, 39*, 350–373.

Bowlby, J. (1969). *Attachment.* London: Tavistock Institute of Human Relations.

Bowlby, J. (1973). *Separation.* New York: Basic Books.

Bowlby, J. (1977). The making and breaking of affectional bonds. *British Journal of Psychiatry, 130*, 201–210.

Boyd-Franklin, N. (1989). *Black families in therapy.* New York: Guilford Press.

Boyd-Franklin, N. (1993). *Racism, secret-keeping, and African-American families*. New York: W. W. Norton.

Brazelton, T. (1984). *Neonatal behavioral assessment scale*. London: Lavenham Press.

Bromberg, J. (1997). *The body project*. New York: Random House.

Browning, D., Miller-McLemore, B., Couture, P., Lyon, K., & Franklin, R. (1997). *From culture wars to common ground*. Kentucky: Westminster John Knox Press.

Butler, K. (1996). The biology of fear. *Family Therapy Networker*, 38–45.

Byng-Hall, J. (1995). Creating a secure family base: Some implications of attachment theory for family therapy. *Family Process, 34*, 45–58.

Carnes, P. (1991). *Don't call it love: Recovering from sexual addiction*. New York: Bantam

Carter, E. A., & McGoldrick, M. (1980). *The family life cycle*. New York: Gardner Press.

Carter, E. A., McGoldrick, M., & Ferraro, G. (1989) *Changing family life cycle: A framework for family therapy*. New Jersey: Prentice Hall.

Casriel, D. (1972). *A scream away from happiness*. New York: Grosset & Dunlap.

Casriel, D. *The road of happiness*. Unpublished manuscript.

Clarke, J. I. (1978). *Self-esteem: A Family Affair*. Minneapolis, MN: The Winston Press.

Cotton, N. S. (1983). Development of self-esteem and self-esteem regulation. In J. Mack and S. Ablon (Eds.), *The development and sustaining of self-esteem in childhood*. New York: International Universities Press.

Coupland, S. K., Serovish, J., & Glenn, J. E. (1995). Reliability in constructing genograms: A study among marriage and family therapy doctoral students. *Journal of Marriage and Family Therapy, 21*, 251–263.

Covey, S. R. (1989). *The seven habits of highly effective people*. New York: Simon & Schuster.

Craig, G. (1996). *Human development*. (7th ed.). New Jersey: Prentice Hall.

Crenshaw, T. L. (1996). *The alchemy of love and lust*. New York: Putnam.

Crewdson, J. (1988). *By silence betrayed*. Boston: Little Brown.

Cunningham, J. & Antill, J. (1995). Current trends in non-marital cohabitation: In search of the POSSLQ. In J. Wood & S. Duck (Eds.), *Under-studied relationships*. Thousand Oaks, CA: Sage.

Dhillon, P. (1989). Leadership styles: Relationship to ordinal position and sex. *Journal of the Indian Academy of Applied Psychology, 15*, 43–50.

Diamond, M., & Sigmondson, H. K. (1997). Sex reassignment at birth. *Archives of Pediatrics and Adolescent Medicine, 151*, 298–304.

Doherty, W. (1997). *The intentional family*. New York: Addison-Wesley.

Dolega, Z. (1981). School adaptation of children from three-sibling families. *Polish Psychological Bulletin, 12*(4), 225–231.

DSM IV (1994). Washington: APA Press.

Duhl, F. J. (1981). The use of the chronological chart in general systems family therapy. *Journal of Marital and Family Therapy, 7*, 361–373.

Durana, C. (1993). The use of bonding and emotional experiences in the PAIRS training. Journal of Family Psychotherapy (accepted for publication).

Durana, C. (1994). The use of bonding and emotional expressiveness in the PAIRS training: A psychoeducational approach for couples. *Journal of Family Psychotherapy, 5*(2), 65–81.

Durana, C. (1996). A longitudinal evaluation of the effectiveness of the PAIRS psychoeducational program for couples. *Family Therapy, 23*, 11–36.

Duvall, E. (1977). *Marriage and family development* (5th ed.). Philadelphia: Lippincott.

Edwards, D. J. A. (1981). The role of touch in interpersonal relations: Implications for psychotherapy. *South African Journal of Psychology, 11*, 29–37.

Egeland, B., Jacobvitz, D., & Papatola, K. (1987). Intergenerational continuity of abuse. In R. J. Gelles & J. Lancaster (Eds.), *Child abuse and neglect: Biosocial dimensions*. New York: Aldine DeGruyter.

Egeland, B., Jacobvitz, D., & Sroufe, L. A. (1988). Breaking the cycle of abuse: Relationship predictions. *Child Development, 59*, 1080–1088.

Eisenman, R., & Sirgo, H. B. (1991). Liberals versus conservatives: Personality, child-rearing attitudes and birth order/sex differences. *Bulletin of the Psychonomic Society, 29*, 240–242.

Ekman, P., & Davidson, R. (1994). *The nature of emotion*. New York: Oxford University Press.

Ellis, A. (1976). Techniques of handling anger in marriage. *Journal of Marriage and Family Counseling, 2*, 305–315.

Engelman, S. R. (1988). Use of the family genogram technique with spinal cord injured patients. *Clinical Rehabilitation, 2*, 7–15.

Epstein, N., Baldwin, L., & Bishop, D. (1983). The McMaster family assessment device. *Journal of Marital and Family Therapy, 9*(2), 171–180.

Erikson, E. H. (1963). *Childhood and society*. New York: W.W. Norton.

Eunpu, D. L. (1995). The impact of infertility and treatment guidelines for couples therapy. *American Journal of Family Therapy, 23*, 115–128.

Eunpu, D. L. (1997). Systemically-based psychotherapeutic techniques in genetic counseling. *Journal of Genetic Counseling, 6*, 1–20.

Falco, K. (1991). *Psychotherapy with lesbian clients*. New York: Brunner/Mazel.

Fanning, P., & O'Neill, J. (1996). *The addicition workbook: A step-by-step guide to quitting alcohol & drugs*. New York: New Harbinger Publications.

Farber, E., & Kaslow, N. (1997). Social psychology: Theory, research and mental health implication. In A. Tasman, J. Kay & J. Lieberman, *Psychiatry* (vol. 1, pp. 382–383). Philadelphia: W. B. Saunders.

Fausto-Sterling, A. (1985). *Myths of gender*. New York: Basic Books.

Feldman, L. B. (1982). Dysfunctional marital conflict: An integrative interpersonal intrapsychic model. *Journal of Marital and Family Therapy, 8*, 417–428.

Fleck, S. (1989). *Psychiatric prevention and the family life cycle*. By the Committee on Preventive Psychiatry, Group for the Advancement of Psychiatry. New York: Brunner/Mazel.

Fleck, S., Quinlan, D., Jalali, B. & Rosenheck, R. (1988). Family assessment. *Social Psychiatry and Psychiatric Epidemiology, 23*, 137–144.

Fonagy, P., Steele, H., & Steele, M. (1991). Maternal representations of attachment during pregnancy predict the organization of infant-mother attachment at one year of age. *Child Development, 61*, 891–905.

Fraiberg, S., Adelson, E., & Shapiro, V. (1975). Ghosts in the nursery: A psychoanalytic approach to the problems of impaired infant-mother relationships. *Journal of the American Academy of Child Psychiatry, 14*, 387–421.

Francoeur, R.T. (1991). *Becoming a sexual person* (2nd ed.). New York: Macmillan.

Frank, E., Anderson, C., & Rubinstein, D. (1978). Frequency of sexual dysfunction in "normal" couples. *New England Journal of Medicine, 299*, 111–113.

Friedman, H., Rohrbaugh, M., & Krakauer, S. (1988). The time-line genogram: Highlighting temporal aspects of family relationships. *Family Process, 27*, 293–303.

Friedman, M., & Rosenman, R. (1974). *Type A behavior and your heart*. New York: Alfred A. Knopf.

Frijda, N. (1988). Understanding the ways that emotions operate. *American Psychologist*.

Garfinkel, I., & McLanahan, S. (1986). *Single mothers and their children*. Washington, DC: Urban Institute Press.

Gelles, R. J., & Straus, M. A. (Eds.). (1989). *Intimate violence*. New York: Simon & Schuster.

George, C., Kaplan, N., & Main, M. (1985). *Attachment interview for adults*. Unpublished manuscript.

Giat-Roberto, L. (1986). Bulimia: The transgenerational view. *Journal of Marital and Family Therapy, 12*, 231–240.

Giblin, P., Sprenkle, D. H., & Sheehan, R. (Eds.). (1985). Enrichment outcome: A meta-analysis of premarital, marital and family interventions. *Journal of Marital and Family Therapy, 11,* 257–271.

Goleman, D. (1995). *Emotional intelligence.* New York: Bantam Books.

Goodwin, J. (1989). *Sexual abuse* (2nd ed.). Chicago: Yearbook Medical Publishers.

Gordon, L. (1993). *Passage to intimacy.* New York: Simon & Schuster.

Gottman, J. (1994). *Why marriages succeed or fail.* New York: Simon & Schuster.

Gould, R. (1978). *Transformations.* New York: Simon & Schuster.

Gray, J. (1984). *What you feel you can heal.* CA: Hearst.

Greeley, A. M. (1991). *Faithful attraction: Discovering intimacy, love, and fidelity in American marriage.* New York: Tom Doherty Associates.

Greenberg, L., & Safran, J. (1987). *Emotion in psychotherapy.* New York: Guilford Press.

Greenspan, S. I. (1981). *The clinical interview of the child.* New York: McGraw Hill.

Grossmann, K., & Grossmann, K. (1991). Attachment quality as an organizer of emotional and behavioral responses in a longitudinal perspective. In C. M. Parkes, J. Stevenson-Hinde, & P. Marris (Eds.), *Attachment across the life cycle.* New York: Tavistock/Routledge.

Grossmann, K., Grossman, K. E., Spangler, G., Suess, G., & Unzer, J. (1985). Maternal sensitivity and newborns' orientation responses as related to quality of attachment in northern Germany. In I. Bretherton & E. Waters (Eds.), *Growing points in attachment theory and research.* (*Monographs of the Society for Research in Child Development, 50* [Serial No. 209], 233–256).

Group for the Advancement of Psychiatry (1989). *Psychiatric prevention and the family life cycle.* New York: Brunner/Mazel.

Guerin, P. J., & Pendagast, E. G. (1976). Evaluation of family system and genogram. In P. J. Guerin (Ed.), *Family therapy: Theory and practice* (pp. 450–464). New York: Gardner Press.

Guerney, B. G. (1977). *Relationship enhancement: Skill training programs for therapy, problem formation, and enrichment.* San Francisco: Jossey-Bass.

Gur, R. & Gur, R. (1995). Sex differences in regional cerebral glucose metabolism during a resting state. *Science, 267,* 528–531.

Halevy, J. (1998). Genogram with an attitude. *Journal of Marital and Family Therapy,* 233–242.

Haley, A. (1976). *Roots.* New York: Doubleday.

Halperin, D. (1996). Sex differences in cognitive abilities. In G. Craig (Ed.), *Human development* (10th ed.). New Jersey: Prentice Hall.

Hardy, K. V., & Laszloffy, T. A. (1995). The cultural genogram: Key to training culturally competent family therapists. *Journal of Marital and Family Therapy, 21,* 227–237.

Harlow, H. (1958). The nature of love. *The American Psychologist, 3,* 673–685.

Hartman, A., & Laird, J. (1990). *Family treatment after adoption: Common themes.* New York: Oxford University Press.

Hartman, A., & Laird, J. (1983). *Family centered social work practice.* New York: MacMillan.

Hartman, A. (1993). *Secrecy in adoption.* New York: W. W. Norton.

Hartman, A. (1978). Diagrammatic assessment of family relationships. *Social Casework, 59,* 465–476.

Haugaard, J., & Reppucci, N. D. (1988). *The sexual abuse of children.* New York: Jossey-Bass.

Hazan, C., & Shaver, P. (1987). Romantic love conceptualized as an attachment process. *Journal of Personality and Social Psychology, 52,* 511–524.

Herman, J. (1992). *Trauma and recovery.* New York: Basic Books.

Herstein, R. J., & Murray, C. (1994). *The bell curve: Intelligence and class structure in American life.* New York: The Free Press.

Hindy, C. G., & Schwartz, J.C. (1994). Anxious romantic attachment in adult relationships. In M. B. Sperling & W. H. Berman (Eds.), *Attachment in adults: Clinical and developmental perspectives*. New York: Guilford Press.

Hochschild, A. (1989). *The second shift*. New York: Avon Books.

Hof, L., & Berman, E. M. (1986). The sexual genogram. *Journal of Marital and Family Therapy, 12*, 39–47.

Hof, L., & Berman, E. (1989). The sexual genogram: Assessing family of origin factors in the treatment of sexual dysfunction. In D. Kantor & B. Okun (Eds.), *Intimate environments: Sex, intimacy and gender in families*. New York: Guilford Press.

Hof, L., & Miller, W.R. (1981). *Marriage enrichment: philosophy, process, and program*. Bowie, MD: Robert J. Brady.

Hoopes, M., & Harper, J. (1987). *Birth order roles & sibling patterns in individual & family therapy*. Rockville, MD: Aspen.

Horvath, A. O. & Luborsky, L. (1993). The role of the therapeutic alliance in psychotherapy. *Journal of Consulting and Clinical Psychology, 61*, 561–573.

Hyman, I. (1997). *The case against spanking*. San Francisco: Jossey-Bass.

Izard, C. (1977). *Human emotions*. New York: Plenum Press.

Jackson, A. (1991a). The inner worlds of 10 happily married couples (Doctoral dissertation, University of Pennsylvania, 1991). *Dissertation Abstracts International, 52*, 06A.

Jackson, A. (1991b). Marriage and attachment: An exploration of ten long-term marriages. *Journal of Couples Therapy, 4*, 13–30.

Jellinek, E. M. (1960). *The disease concept of alcoholism*. New Haven: College & University Press.

Johnson, S. M., & Greenberg, L. S. (1994). *The heart of the matter*. New York: Brunner/Mazel.

Johnson, S. M., & Greenberg, L. S. (1995). The emotionally focused approach to problems in adult attachment. In N. S. Jacobson & A. S. Gurman (Eds.), *Clinical handbook of couple therapy*. New York: Guilford Press.

Jones, S. E., & Yarbrough, A. E. (1985). A naturalistic study of the meanings of touch. *Communication Monographs, 52*, 19–56.

Jordan, J., Surrey, J., & Kaplan, A. (1991). Women and empathy: Implications of psychological development and psychotherapy. In Jordan, J. V., Kaplan, A. G., Miller, J. B., & Stiver, I. P. (Eds.), *Women's growth in connection*. New York: Guilford Press.

Jourard, S. M. (1966). An exploratory study of body-accessibility. *British Journal of Social and Clinical Psychology, 5*, 221–231.

Kagen, J., Snidman, N., Arcus, D., & Reznick, J. S. (1997). *Galen's prophecy: Temperament in human nature* (reprint ed.). New York: Basic Books.

Kahn, M., & Lewis, K. (1988). *Siblings in therapy*. New York: W. W. Norton.

Karen, R. (1994). *Becoming attached*. New York: Warner Books.

Kaslow, F. (1995). *Projective genogramming*. Sarasota, FL: Professional Resources Press.

Kaslow, F. W., & Friedman, J. (1977). Utilization of family photos and movies in family therapy. *Journal of Marriage and Family Counseling, 3*, 19–25.

Keeney, B. P. (1983). *Diagnosis and assessment in family therapy*. Rockville, MD: Aspen

Kinnealey, M. (1990). Sensory aspects of bonding. *Intensive Caring Unlimited*.

Kinsey, A. C., Pomeroy, W. B., & Martin, C.E. (1948). *Sexual behavior in the human male*. Philadelphia: W. B. Saunders.

Kirschner, D., & Kirschner, S. (1983). *Comprehensive family therapy*. New York: Brunner/Mazel.

Kohut, H. (1971). *The analysis of the self*. New York: International Universities Press.

Komatinsky, P. (1997, Summer). The inability to accept love. *American Society for the New Identity Process Newsletter*.

Kuehl, B. P. (1995). The solution-oriented genogram: A collaborative approach. *Journal of Marital and Family Therapy, 21,* 239–250.

Kuethe, J. (1964). Pervasive influence of social schemata. *Journal of Abnormal and Social Psychology, 68,* 248–254.

Kvebaek, D. J. (1974). *Sculpture test: A diagnostic aid in family therapy.* Unpublished technical report.

Kwiatkowski, H. Y. (1978). *Family therapy and evaluation through art.* Springfield, IL: Thomas.

L'Abate, L. (1992). *Programmed writing: A self-administered approach for intervention with individuals, couples & families.* Pacific Grove, CA: Brooks/Cole.

L'Abate, L., & Bagarozzi, D. A. (Eds.). (1993). *Sourcebook of marriage and family evaluation.* New York: Brunner/Mazel.

Lamb, M., et al. (1987). A biosocial perspective on paternal behavior and involvement. In J. B. Lancaster et al., *Parenting across the life span* (pp. 111–142). Chicago: Aldine.

Landau-Stanton, J. (1982). Therapy with families in cultural transition. In M. McGoldrick, J. K. Pearce, & J. Giordano (Eds.), *Ethnicity & family therapy.* New York: Guilford Press.

Landau-Stanton, J. (1990). Issues and methods of treatment for families in cultural transition. In M. P. Mirkin (Ed.), *The social and policital contexts of family therapy* (pp. 251–275). Boston: Allyn & Bacon.

Landau-Stanton, J. (1986). Competence, impermanence, and transitional mapping: A model for systems consultation. *Systems Consultation: A New Perspective For Family Therapy.* In L. C. Wynne, S. H. McDaniel, and T. T. Weber (Eds.).

Leach, P. (1977). *Your baby and child.* New York: Alfred A. Knopf.

LeDoux (1989). Indelibility of subcortical emotional memories. *Journal of Cognitive Neuroscience, 1,* 238–243.

Lee, E. (1982). Chinese families. In M. McGoldrick, J. K. Pearce, & J. Giordano (Eds.), *Ethnicity and family therapy.* New York: Guilford Press.

Leiblum, S. R., & Rosen, R. C. (Eds.). (1988). *Sexual desire disorders.* New York: Guilford Press.

Lerner, H. (1985). *The dance of anger.* New York: Harper & Row.

Levine, S., & Rosenblatt, E. (1997). Sexual disorders. In A. Tasman, J. Kay, & J. Lieberman (Eds.), *Psychiatry* (vol. 2). Philadelphia: W. B. Saunders.

Levinson, D. (1978). *The seasons of a man's life.* New York: Alfred A. Knopf.

Lewis, K. G. (1989). The use of color-coded genograms in family therapy. *Journal of Marital and Family Therapy, 15,* 169–176.

Lieblum, S., & Rosen R. (1989). *Principles and practice of sex therapy.* New York: Guilford Press.

Luborsky, L. (1976). Helping alliances in psychotherapy. In J. L. Cleghorn (Ed.), *Successful psychotherapy* (pp. 92–116). New York: Brunner/Mazel.

Mack, J. E., & Ablon, S. L. (1983). *The development and sustaining of self-esteem in childhood.* New York: International Universities Press.

Mack, R. (1989). Spouse abuse: a dyadic approach. In G. R. Weeks (Ed.), *Treating couples: The intersystem model of the Marriage Council of Philadelphia* (pp. 317–341). New York: Brunner/Mazel.

Madanes, C. (1994). *The secret meaning of money.* San Francisco: Jossey-Bass.

Mahler, M. S., Pine, F., & Bergman, A. (1975). *The psychological birth of the human infant.* New York: Basic.

Main, M., Kaplan, N., & Cassidy, J. (1985). Security in infancy, childhood and adulthood: A move to a new level of representation. In I. Bretherton & E. Waters (Eds.), *Growing points in attachment theory and research.* (Monographs of the Society for Research in Child Development, 50 [Serial No. 209], 66–104).

Main, M., & Weston, D. (1982). Avoidance of the attachment figure in infancy: Descriptions and interpretations. In C. M. Parkes & J. Stevenson-Hinde (Eds.), *The place of attachment in human behavior.* New York: Basic.

Markowitz, L. (1997, September/October) The cultural context of intimacy. *Family Therapy Networker*, September/October, 51–58.

McClintock, M., & Herdt, G. (1996). Rethinking puberty: The development of sexual attraction. *Current Directions in Psychological Science*, 5(6), 178–183.

McGoldrick, M., & Garcia-Preto, N. (1989). Ethnicity in women. In M., McGoldrick, C., Anderson, F., Walsh, *Women in families* (pp. 169–200). New York: W. W. Norton.

McGoldrick, M., & Gerson, R. (1985). *Genograms in family assessment*. New York: W. W. Norton.

McGoldrick, M., Pearce, J., & Giordana, J. (1982). *Ethnicity and family therapy*. New York: Guilford Press.

McKay, M., Rogers, P. D., & McKay, J. (1989). *When anger hurts: Quieting the storm within*. Oakland, CA: New Harbinger Publications.

Milkman, H., & Sunderworth, S. (1987). *Craving for intimacy: The consciousness and chemistry of escape*. Lexington, MA: Lexington Books.

Miller, S., Nunnally, E. M., & Wackman, D. B. (1975). *Alive and aware: Improving communication in relationships*. Minneapolis: Interpersonal Communications Program.

Minuchin, S. (1974). *Families and family therapy*. Cambridge, MA: Harvard University Press.

Money, J. L., & Ehrhardt, A. (1972). *Man and woman, boy and girl*. Baltimore: The Johns Hopkins University Press.

Money, J. (1986) *Love maps*. New York: Irvington.

Montague, A. (1986). *Touching* (3rd ed.). New York: Harper & Row.

Moon, S. M., Coleman, V. D., McCollum, E. E., Nelson, T. S., & Jensen-Scott, R. L. (1993). Using the genogram to facilitate career decisions: A case study. *Journal of Family Psychotherapy*, 4, 45–56.

Mosby, K. D. (1978). *An analysis of actual and ideal touching behavior as reported on a modified verson of the body accessibility questionnaire*. Unpublished doctoral dissertation, Virginia Commonwealth University.

Moyers, B. (1993). *Healing and the mind*. New York: Doubleday.

Nathanson, D. (1992). *Shame and pride: Affect, sex, and the birth of the self*. New York: W. W. Norton.

National Genealogical Society, 4527 Seventeenth Street, Arlington, VA. [Pamphlet].

Nelson, E. S., & Harris, M. A. (1995). The relationships between birth order and need affiliation and group orientation. *Individual Psychology: Journal of Adlerian Theory, Research & Practice*, 51, 282–292.

Nichols, M., & Schwartz, R. (1997). *Family therapy concepts and methods*. Boston: Allyn & Bacon.

Ogbu, J. (1978). *Minority education and caste: The American system in cross-cultural perspective*. New York: Academic Press.

Olmedo, E. (1994). Testimony to the Subcommittee on Health and the Environment, U.S. House of Representative Committee on Energy and Commerce. *CSPP Visions* 7(1), 15–17.

Olson, D., Russell, C., & Sprenkle, D. (1983). Circumplex model of marital and family systems: VI. Theoretical update. *Family Process*, 22, 69–83.

Paul, N. L., & Grosser, G. (1965). Operational mourning and its role in conjoint family therapy. *Community Mental Health Journal*, 1, 339–345.

Paul, N. L., & Paul, B. (1975). *A marital puzzle: Transgenerational analysis in marriage counseling*. New York: Gardner Press.

Pearsall, P. (1996). *The pleasure prescription*. Alameda, CA: Hunter House.

Pendagast, E. G., & Sherman, C. O. (1976). A guide to the genogram. *The Family*, 5(1), 3–14.

Pennebaker, J. (1995). *Emotion, disclosure & health*. Washington, DC: American Psychological Association.

Pennebaker, J. W., Kiecolt-Glaser, J. K. & Glaser, R. (1988). Disclosure of trauma and immune function: Health implications for psychotherapy. *Journal of Consulting and Clinical Psychology, 56*, 238–245.

Perlmutter, M. S. (1988). Enchantment of siblings: effects of birth order and trance on family myth. In M. D. Kahn & K. G. Lewis (Eds.), *Siblings in therapy: Life span and clinical issues.* New York: Norton.

Pert, C. P. (1997). *Molecules of emotion. Why you feel the way you feel.* New York: Simon & Schuster.

Pinderhughes, E. (1989). *Understanding race, ethnicity, and power.* New York: The Free Press.

Pittman, F. (1993). *Man enough.* New York: Putnam.

Pleck, E. (1987). *Domestic tyranny.* New York: Oxford University Press.

Polansky, N. (1981). *Damaged parents.* Chicago: University of Chicago Press.

Prescott, J. W. (1975). Body pleasure and the origins of violence. *The Futurist, 9*(2), 64–74.

Prescott, J. W. (1989). Affectional bonding for the prevention of violent behaviors: Neurological, psychological and religious/spiritual determinants. In L. J. Hertzberg et al. (Eds.), *Violent behavior, volume 1: Assessment and Intervention.* New York: PMA Publishing.

Prest, L. A., & Keller, J. F. (1993). Spirituality and family therapy: Spiritual beliefs, myths, and metaphors. *Journal of Marital and Family Therapy,* 137–148.

Promise Keepers. (1994). *Seven promises of a promise keeper.* Colorado: Focus on the Family Publishing.

Rado, S. (1969). *Adaptational psychodynamics: Motivation and control.* New York: Science House.

Raider, M. C. (1992). Assessing the role of religion in family functioning. In L. A. Burton (Ed.), *Religion and the family: When God helps* (pp. 165–183). New York: Haworth.

Rasmussen, K., Hawkins, A., & Schwab, K. (1996). Increasing husbands' involvement in domestic labor: Issues for therapists. *Contemporary Family Therapy, 18*, 209–223.

Restak, R. M. (1979). *The brain.* New York: Warner Books.

Rinck, C. M., Willis, F. N., & Dean, L. M. (1980). Interpersonal touch among residents of homes for the elderly. *Journal of Communication, 30*, 44–47.

Roberts, J. (1991). *AFTA diversity packet.* Unpublished materials.

Roberts, T. W. (1992). Sexual attraction and romantic love. *Journal of Marital and Family Therapy, 5*, 357–364.

Rohrbaugh, M., Rogers, J. C., & McGoldrick, M. (1992). How do experts read family genograms? *Family Systems Medicine, 10*, 79–89.

Romeo, F. (1994). A child's birth order: Educational implications. *Journal of Instructional Psychology, 21*, 155–160.

Rosen, E. (1990). *Families facing death.* Lexington, MA: Lexington Books.

Ross, J. L. (1995). Social class tensions within families. *American Journal of Family Therapy, 23*, 338–350.

Russell, D. (1986). *The secret trauma.* New York: Basic Books.

Saari, C. (1991). *The creation of meaning in clinical social work.* New York: Guilford Press.

Santa Rita, E., & Adejanju, M. G. (1993). The genogram: Plotting the roots of academic success. *Family Therapy, 20*, 17–28.

Satir, V. (1967). *Conjoint family therapy.* Palo Alto, CA: Science & Behavior Books.

Satir, V. (1988). *The new peoplemaking.* Palo Alto, CA: Science & Behavior Books.

Schilson, E., Braun, K., & Hudson, A. (1993). Use of genograms in family medicine: A family physician/family therapist collaboration. *Family Systems Medicine, 11*, 201–208.

Schnarch, D. (1997). *Passionate marriage.* New York: W. W. Norton.

Schorsch, A. (1985). *Images of childhood: An illustrated social history.* Pittstown, NJ: Main Street Press.

Schutz, W. (1967). *Expanding human awareness.* New York: Grove Press.

Schwartz, L. L. (1984). Adoption custody and family therapy. *American Journal of Family Therapy, 12*(4), 51–58.

Schwartz, P. (1994). *Peer marriage.* New York: The Free Press.

Seaburn, D. B. (1990). *The ties that bind: Loyalty and widowhood.* New York: Haworth Press.

Sears, C. J. (1981). The tactilely defensive child. *Academic Therapy, 16*, 563–569.

Sheehy, G. (1984). *Passages.* New York: Bantam.

Sheehy, G. (1995). *The silent passage; Menopause.* New York: Pocket Books.

Sheehy, G. (1996). *New passages: Mapping your life across time.* New York: Ballantine Books.

Sheehy, G. (1998). *Understanding men's passages: Discovering the new map of men's lives.* New York: Random House.

Silverman, A. F., Pressman, M. E., & Bartel, H. W. (1973). Self-esteem and tactile communication. *Journal of Humanistic Psychology, 13*, 73–77.

Silverstein, O., & Rashbaum, B. (1994). *The courage to raise good men.* New York: Viking.

Sonne, J. C. (1980). A family system perspective on custody and adoption. *International Journal of Family Therapy, 2*, 176–192.

Sotile, W. (1992). *Heart illness and intimacy.* Baltimore: Johns Hopkins University Press.

Spence, D. (1982). *Narrative truth and historical truth.* New York: W. W. Norton.

Sproul, M. S., & Gallagher, R. M. (1982). The genogram as an aid to crisis intervention. *Journal of Family Practice, 14*, 959–960.

Stacy, J. (1993). Untangling feminist theory. In D. Richardson & V. Robinson, *Thinking feminist.* New York: Guilford Press.

Stanton, M. D. (1992). The time line and the "why now?" question: A technique and rationale for therapy, training, organizational consultation and research. *Journal of Marital and Family Therapy, 18*, 331–343.

Stern, D. (1985). *The interpersonal world of the infant.* New York: Basic Books.

Sternberg, R. (1986). A triangular theory of love. *Psychological Review, 93*, 119–135.

Stewart, A. E., & Steward, E. A. (1995). Trends in birth-order research. *Individual Psychology: Journal of Adlerian Theory, Research & Practice, 51*, 21–36.

Stosny, S. (1995). *Treating attachment abuse.* New York: Springer.

Straus, M. (1994). *Beating the devil out of them.* Lexington, MA: Lexington Books.

Sulloway, F. J. (1996). *Born to rebel: Birth order, family dynamics, and creative lives.* New York: Pantheon Books.

Suomi, S. J., & Harlow, H. F. (1978). Early experience and social development in rhesus monkeys. In M. Lamb (Ed.), *Social and personality development,* New York: Holt, Rinehart & Winston.

Tavris, C. (1989). *Anger, the misunderstood emotion.* New York: Simon & Schuster.

Taylor, D., et al. *Women: A World Report* (p. 82). New York: Oxford University Press.

Thomas, A., & Chess, S. (1977). *Temperament and development.* New York: Brunner/Mazel.

Thornton, J. (1997). *Chore wars.* New York: Conari Press.

Toman, W. (1992). *Family constellation: Its effects on personality and social behavior* (4th ed.). New York: Springer.

Tomkins, S. S. (1962). *Affect/imagery/consciousness, vol. 1: The positive affects.* New York: Springer.

Tomkins, S. S. (1963). *Affect/imagery/consciousness, vol. 2: The negative affects.* New York: Springer.

Trepper, T., & Barrett, M. (1986). *Treating incest.* New York: Haworth Press.

Turecki, S. (1985). *The difficult child.* New York: Bantam Books.

Wachtel, E. F. (1982). The family psyche over three generations: The genogram revisited. *Journal of Marital and Family Therapy, 5*, 335–343.

Walker, L. (1979). *The battered woman.* New York: Harper & Row.

Walsh, A. (1991). *The science of love: Understanding love and its effects on mind and body*. New York: Prometheus.

Walsh, F. (1982). *Normal family processes*. New York: Guilford Press.

Walters, M., Carter, B., Papp, P., & Silverstein, O. (1988). *The Invisible Web: Gender Patterns in Family Relationships*. New York: Guilford.

Watts-Jones, D. (1997). Toward an African American genogram. *Family Process, Inc., 36*, 375–383.

Weeks, G. R. (1989). *Treating couples: The intersystem model of the Marriage Council of Philadelphia*. New York: Brunner/Mazel.

Weeks, G. R., & Hof, L. (1987). *Integrating sex and marital therapy*. New York: Brunner/Mazel.

Weeks, G. R., & Hof, L. (1994). *The marital relationship therapy casebook: Theory and application of the intersystem model* (pp. 3–34). New York: Brunner/Mazel.

Weeks, G. R., & Hof, L. (1995). *Integrative solutions: Treating common problems in couples therapy*. New York: Brunner/Mazel.

Weeks, G. R., & Treat, S. (1992). *Couples in treatment: Techniques and approaches for effective practice*. New York: Brunner/Mazel.

Weinberg, R. B., & Mauksch, L. B. (1991). Examining family-of-origin influences in life at work. *Journal of Marital and Family Therapy, 17*, 223–241.

West, J. W. (1997). *The Betty Ford Center book of answers*. New York: Simon & Schuster.

Westfall, A. (1989) Extramarital sex: The treatment of the couple. In G. R. Weeks (Ed.), *Treating couples: The intersystem model of the Marriage Council of Philadelphia*. New York: Brunner/Mazel.

Wheat, E. (1980). *Love life for every married couple*. Grand Rapids, MI: Zondervan.

Willi, J. (1997). The significance of romantic love for marriage. *Family Process, 35*, 171–182.

Williams, R. (1989). *The trusting heart: Great news about Type A behavior*. New York: Times Books/Random House.

Winnicott, D. W. (1964). *The child, the family and the outside world*. Great Britain: Penguin Books.

Winnicott, D. W. (1985). *The maturational processes and the facilitating environment*. New York: International University Press.

Wolpe, J., & Wolpe, D. (1988). *Life without fear: Anxiety and its cure*. New York: New Harbinger Publications.

Woolf, V. V. (1983). Family network systems in transgenerational psychotherapy: the theory, advantages and expanded applications of the genogram. *Family Therapy, 10*, 219–237.

Zetzel, E. (1956). Current concepts of transference. *International Journal of Psychoanalysis, 37*, 369–376.

Zilbergeld, B. (1992). *The new male sexuality*. New York: Bantam.

Appendix

☐ Computerized Genogram Packages

Although there are a number of "family tree" software programs available and ways to draw genograms using basic graphic and drawing methods, these methods have not been specifically designed for systems-oriented practitioners. For those who are interested in using the MFG in conjunction with computerized programs, two programs are available. Descriptive material was taken from websites and promotional materials.

From HUMANWARE: Genogram-Maker, Genogram-Maker Plus, AutoGenogram, and Family Pattern Analyzer

HUMANWARE

History. In 1985, Randy Gerson, Ph.D., in collaboration with Monica McGoldrick, published *Genograms in Family Assessment.* In preparation for that book, Dr. Gerson developed computer software for producing genograms according to the conventions outlined in the book. That same year, Dr. Gerson founded HUMANWARE to publish and distribute software for family therapists and other mental health professions. Originally, the software (called MacGenogram) worked only on Macintosh computers. In 1988, the program was transferred to the MSDOS (IBM-compatible) format (called Genogram-Maker), maintaining the easy-to-use Macintosh interface, but broadening widely the number of people who could use the software. In 1990, by popular demand, an enhanced, research-oriented version of the genogram producing software (the Plus version) was introduced that added the capability of creating a genogram database. In 1991, a separate genogram interview module (AutoGenogram) was added to HUMANWARE's growing list of software products. That same year, Dr. Gerson developed an extensive checklist (the Family Pattern Checklist) for assessing multigenerational family patterns to be used in conjunction with the genogram software. Users would answer over 600 questions and send them to HUMANWARE for a computer-generated analysis (the Family Pattern Report). Finally, in 1992, the Checklist was completely computerized, adding the Family Pattern Analyzer as the most recent stand-alone product. HUMANWARE is committed to upgrading and developing software for mental health professionals. Phone 800-634-8508 or 912-743-2548. http://www.behavenet.com/humanware

MacGenogram©: (Macintosh). Genogram-Maker©: (MS-DOS).

Both programs allow you to quickly and easily produce professional-looking, well spaced genograms that include all the conventional symbols outlined in McGoldrick and Gerson's book, *Genograms in Family Assessment.*

These programs are graphic utilities with tools to create standard genogram symbols. The resulting genograms can easily be moved, rearranged, split apart, reconnected, and stretched.

AutoGenogram©: (Macintosh/MS-DOS).

This program asks users a series of questions about their families. From the information gathered in this way, the program then constructs a professional-looking, well-spaced genogram that can be printed or saved as a genogram file that can be read and modified by HUMANWARE's other computerized genogram programs. The program was designed to allow non-computer oriented people to use the computer to produce a genogram. The program is completely customizable so you can have it gather as little or as much information as you want.

Family Pattern Analyzer©: (Macintosh/MS-DOS).

This is a program for analyzing multigenerational family patterns. The Family Pattern Checklist is a computerized interview of over 600 questions designed to pinpoint the major issues and patterns inherited from one's family of origin. Based on this interview, the Family Pattern Analyzer generates a Family Pattern Report, an extensive description of possible family patterns, which can then be printed out with any word processor. The Family Pattern Analyzer is not a psychometric tool. It generates no conclusions, but it does describe hypotheses about family patterns. It takes the statements that a person checks about his or her family and organizes them in a systemic framework. The Family Pattern Analyzer is primarily a clinical and educational tool for the exploration of family patterns.

From WonderWare: Relativity and Ecotivity
(Genograms and Ecomaps)

WonderWare

Mission Statement.   WonderWare, Inc. is dedicated to the use of modern computer and information technologies to assist in a practical transformation that is occurring in the modes of thought and practice within our interpersonal and community realities, based on scientific and spiritual paradigm shifts brought about by the work of important scientists and philosophers in this century—most notably Albert Einstein (author of the Theory of Relativity), Fritjof Capra, Murray Bowen (pioneer of the genogram), Ann Hartman (pioneer of the ecomap) and other physicists and system thinkers in the fields of ecology, sociology, anthropology, family psychology and others. Their works have expanded and enlightened our awareness of the universe, by process-oriented, perspective-taking, multidimensional, systemic and integrative modes of thinking.

Software and services are offered to assist in the experience of self-esteem, integrated self-and-social awareness and wonder. They aid the effectiveness of therapy and counseling, treatment planning, life planning, family history, rehabilitation, conflict resolution, and prevention. Our products and services are used locally and world wide. They can be applied in arenas as diverse as pregnancy planning and psychohistory in international conflict. As our company grows, we will continue to make its resources available for our local and global community in these and similar arenas, in new and innovative ways.

Relativity and Ecotivity

V2.1 for Windows.   A new Windows versions of both Relativity, our genogram software, and Ecotivity, our ecomap software, are now available. Not only do our Windows versions make the creation and updating of complex process diagramming even easier and more convenient for caregivers using Windows, but they powerfully expand the Multiprocess Time Travel features of our earlier versions, welcoming caregivers and families into the heart and soul of the human experience itself; ongoing multidimensional pattern and change, transformation and transcendence, and interactional being and becoming, in either or both the family and/or community life contexts, over time. The enhanced User's Guides fully prepare the user, both conceptually and practically, for the unforgettable experience this software makes possible. Users will appreciate the on-line help, toolbar shortcut buttons, enhanced multi-display print preview and printing capabilities, the ability to use each product on its own or in conjunction with the other, and a unique combination of other features.

WonderWare, Inc.
301-942-3254 (voice/fax)
http://www.clark.net/pub/wware/wware.html
wonderware@ idealink.washington.do.us

Index

Abuse anger and history of, 132–133
  background and extent of, 130–131
  cycle of violence and, 139
  verification of, 142
Acceptors, 98
Adaptational psychodynamics, 119
Addiction
  alcoholism as, 51–53
  consequences of, 43
  forms of denial regarding, 53–54
  questions about, 43–44
  styles of, 43
Adoption
  questions about, 40–41
  theory addressing, 49
Adoptive families, 49
Affairs. *See* Extramarital affairs
Affective attunement, 60
Affective blindness, 119
Affective-cognitive interactions, 105
Affect theory, 120, 121
African Americans
  gender and, 187
  historical background of, 190–191
  religious orientation of, 182
Agape, 105
Aggression
  anger and, 136–137
  child sexual abuse and, 142
Alcohol abuse, 52–53
Alcohol dependence, 53
Alcoholics Anonymous, 51
Alcoholism
  anxiety disorder and, 121
  categories of, 52
  explanation of, 51–52

  treatment of, 51
Alpha alcoholism, 52
Anger
  abuse and, 140–143
  assessment of, 129–130
  corporal punishment and, 140
  effects of, 125
  expression of, 114, 125, 128, 131
  in family, 135–136
  family violence and, 138–140
  meaning and function of, 128–129
  narcissistic vulnerability and, 137–138
  strategies for dealing with, 130–132
  type A personality and, 137
Anger Family Maps, 133–134
Anger Genograms. *See also* Emotions
    Genograms
  construction of, 126–127
  explanation of, 29
  history of abuse and, 132–133
  preparation for, 127
  questions for, 128, 132
  timing for, 127
Anger Time Lines, 134–135
Anguish, 104–105
Anxiety disorder, 121
Anxious ambivalent attachment, 81
Art techniques, 31–33
Asian Americans
  background of, 192–193
  religious orientation of, 181–182
Attachment
  chemical foundation of, 89
  empathic resonance and, 96–97
  explanation of, 96
  questions about, 79–81

romantic love and, 99
scripts and, 79, 97–99
slavery and, 190–191
styles of, 97–98
Attachments Genograms
  explanation of, 29
  function of, 76
  internal models map and, 81–84
  preparation for, 76–77
  self-esteem and, 50
  touch, bonding, temperament, and attachment and, 77–81, 88–99
Attachments Time Line, 84–88
Attachment theory
  bonding and, 91
  explanation of, xiii, 75, 198
  function of, vi, vii, 99
  internal working models and, 62–63
Attacking, 54
Attunement, 96–97
AutoGenogram, 214

Basic Genograms
  addictions on, 43–44, 51–54
  adoption, infertility, and pregnancy loss on, 40–41, 49–50
  birth order on, 40, 47–49
  eating disorder assessment for, 44, 45
  elements of drawing, 13–17
  examples of, 11, 17
  explanation of, 9–10, 37
  family function on, 38–39, 45
  health and illness on, 42–43, 51
  marital patterns, divorce, and extramarital affairs on, 39–40, 46–47
  self-esteem assessment for, 41–42, 50–51
  symbols for developing, 14, 15
Berkeley Adult Attachment Interview, 82
Beta alcoholism, 52
Birth order
  questions about, 40
  theory addressing, 47–49
Blaming, 53
Bonding
  elements of, 87
  importance of, 89–91
  patterns of, 77
  questions about, 77–78
  ~search on, 89–90
    ~al aspect of, 90
      and, 190–191
        ~ms theory, xiv

Caucasians, 193
Child abuse
  anger and history of, 132–133
  background and extent of, 140–141
  cycle of violence and, 139
  explanation of, 133
Child Abuse Prevention and Treatment Act of 1974, 141
Childbirth, 87–88
Child neglect
  anger and history of, 132–133
  background and extent of, 140–141
  cycle of violence and, 139
  explanation of, 133
Children. See also Infants
  background of avoidant, 81–82
  bonding between parents and, 88–90, 98
  corporal punishment and, 140
  developmental assessment of, 69
  family violence and, 139–140
  historical background of conditions for, 88–89
  loss and, 108
  sexual abuse of, 141–143
  sexual development in, 171–173
  temperament types in, 94–95
Cohabitation trends, 152
Color coding, 31
Communication, stress styles of, 117–118
Companionate love, 174–175. See also Romantic love
Computer software
  from HUMANWARE, 213–214
  from WonderWare, 215–216
Conflict, 135
Corporal punishment
  effects of, 140
  explanation of, 133, 134
  physical abuse vs., 141
Culture
  explanation of, 178
  function of, 177, 178
  gender and, 162–163, 167
  sexuality and, 172–173
  touch and, 92
Culture Family Map, 184–185
Culture Genograms
  African Americans and, 190–192
  Asians and, 192–193
  Caucasians and, 193
  collecting information for, 179–180

ethnicity and immigration and, 180–181, 188–190
family rituals and, 183
function of, 177–178
race and, 180–181, 185–187
religious orientation and, 181–183, 193–194
socioeconomic status and, 183–184, 194–195
Culture Time Line, 185

Delta alcoholism, 52
Denial, 53–54
Disorganized attachment, 81
Distancers, 97, 98
Distracting, 54
Distress, 104–105
Divorce patterns
assessment of, 39
of parents, 156
socioeconomic status and, 183
theory addressing, 46–47

Eating disorders, 44–45
Ecomaps, 59
Emotional allergies, 110
Emotional intelligence, 118
Emotions. *See also specific emotions*
affect theory and, 120–121
benefits of addressing, 117
disclosure of, 102–103
expression of, 113–114, 116–117, 121–122
labeling of, 102
laws of, 120
mind, body and, 118–119
Emotions Family Map, 114–115
Emotions Genograms. *See also* Anger Genograms; Romantic Love Genograms
in clinical practice, 116–118
emotional congruence and, 104
explanation of, 29, 101
fear and, 110–111
function of, 101
managing affect while constructing, 113–114
pleasure and, 112–113
preparation for, 102–104, 106–107
questions for, 107–108
sadness, loss, and grief and, 108–110
special issues in construction of, 104–106
Emotions Time Line, 115

Empathic resonance, 96–97
Empathy, 139–140
Enjoyment, 104
Environment, 95
Epithumia, 105
Epsilon alcoholism, 52
Eros, 105
Ethnicity
elements of, 188, 189
questions about, 180–181
race and, 186
Excusing, 53
Extramarital affairs, 39–40

False memory, 21
Family art therapy, 31–32
Family development, vi
Family functioning
assessment of, 38–39
theory addressing, 45
Family-individual interface, 68–69
Family influences
anger and, 126, 134–136
closeness, distance, and dominance and, 159–160
gender and, 146–147, 149–150
sexuality and, 151, 172
Family life cycle, 66–67
Family Maps
Anger, 133–134
assessing family resources and social supports for, 58–59
background on, 59–60
Culture, 184–185
Emotions, 114–115
example of, 11
explanation of, 10, 57
function of, 57–58
Gender, Sexuality, and Romantic Love, 158
internal models, 62–63, 81
therapeutic alliance through, 60–62
use of, 199
Family-of-origin material, 5, 130
Family Pattern Analyzer, 214
Family sculpting method, 32
Family systems, 25–26
Family systems genograms, 29
Family violence, 138–139
Fathers, 169–170
Fear, 104, 110–111
Feeling-letter technique, 122

Feelings, 121
Felt-figure technique, 32
Focused Genograms. *See also* Multilayered
  Focused Genograms (MFG); *specific
  genograms*
  elements of, 17–19, 27–30
  explanation of, 10, 12, 25
  family system assessment and, 25–26
  function of, xiv–xv, 70
  as projective process, 30–33
  sketch method for, 18
  table method for, 18, 19
  types of, 27–28
Focused writing, 131–132

GABA, 121
Gamma alcoholism, 52
Gender
  biological aspects of, 146
  cultural aspects of, 145–146
  developmental aspects related to, 166–168
  differences and similarities between, 162–
    166
  expression of anger and, 126–127, 134
  family beliefs about, 146–147, 149–150
  family patterns of closeness, distance, and
    dominance and, 159–160
  gender development and, 166–168
  general beliefs about, 159
  influences of, 145–146
  parenting and, 168–170
  physical and psychological illness and, 162
  race and, 187
  reproductive events and, 161–162
  sexuality and, 146, 154–155
Gender Family Map, 158
Gender Genograms
  construction of, 147–148
  explanation of, 29
  gender lens for, 150–151
  questions for, 148–150
  sexuality and, 161
  sexual orientation and, 162
  work and money issues and, 160
Gender Time Line, 158
Genogram-Maker, 214
Genograms. *See also specific types of genograms*
  academic programs and, 5
  techniques for, 31–33
  ...s of, 3–4
  ...or, 31
  13–17

function of, 27
limitations of, 5–7
overview of, v–vii, 4–5
projective, 30–33
Gerson, Randy, 213
Grief
  explanation of, 108
  questions about, 109–110
  types of, 109
Guilt, 105

Haley, Alex, 7
Happiness, 104
Hartman, Ann, 215
Heals technique, 132
Health
  assessment of beliefs and attitudes about,
    42–43
  assessment of patterns of, 42
  emotions disclosure and, 102
  talking about traumatic events and, 111
  use of genograms to explore, 51
Homosexuality
  family messages about, 152, 172
  Gender, Sexuality, and Romantic Love
    Time Line and, 158
  gender identity and, 162, 168
  Sexual Genograms and, 155, 162
Hope, 105
Hormones, 119
Hostility, 137
HUMANWARE software, 211–212

Illness
  gender components to, 162
  stress and, 109
  use of genograms to explore, 51
Immigration
  Asians and, 192–193
  background of, 188
  genograms and, 188–189
  patterns of, 189–190
  questions about, 180–181
Incest
  effects of, 143, 152
  explanation of, 133
Infants. *See also* Children
  assessment of behavior in, 95–96
  effect on marital bond of, 87–88
  importance of bonding in, 89
  selective attunement and, 96–97
  stages of development in, 85–86

tactile defensiveness in, 93–94
Infertility, 41, 49
Insecure attachment, 81
Internal Models Family Maps
    explanation of, 62–63
    function of, 81
Internal Models Maps
    construction of, 83–84
    explanation of, 81–83
Internal working models
    construction of, 82
    explanation of, 62–63

Joy, 112

Loss
    explanation of, 108–109
    questions about, 109–110
Love. *See* Romantic love; Romantic Love
    Genograms

MacGenogram, 214
Marriage
    beliefs about gender and, 147
    parental patterns of, 156
    patterns of, 39–40
    theory addressing, 46–47
McGoldrick, Monica, 213
Memory, 21, 29
Mental health, 50
Minimizing, 53
Mirroring, 97
Mood disorders, 121
Moods, 121
Mothers, 169
Multidirected partiality, 62
Multilayered Focused Genograms (MFG)
    See also Focused Genograms
    attachment theory and, vi, xiv
    basic concepts of, vi, xiv, 8–9
    components of, 9–10
    construction of, 10–13
    example of, 16
    explanation of, v, xi, 8
    false memory and, 21–22
    function of, xiii, xv–xvi, 68
    as narrative process, 19–20
    as projective process, 30–33
    strength of, 27
    uses of, 3, 197–199
Museum tour, 122

My World of Feelings exercise, 103–104

Narcissism, 98–99
Narcissistic vulnerability, 137–138
Narrative truth, 20
National Genealogical Society, 180
Neonatal Behavioral Assessment Scale
    (NBAS), 95–96
Neuropeptides, 118
New identity process, 119, 132
Normative transitions, 66

Object relations theory, 91, 98

Pain, 104, 120
Paraphilia, 171–172
Parents/parenting
    bonding and, 88–90, 98
    gender issues in, 168–170
    marriage and divorce, 156
Patriarchy, 163
Peers, 150
Photographs, 32–33
Pleasure
    explanation of, 104, 112, 120
    identifying patterns of, 112
    questions about, 113
Political attitudes, 48
Post-traumatic stress disorder, 110
Pregnancy, 41
Pregnancy loss, 41, 49
Premarital sex, 92
Pride, 105
Projective genograms, 30–33
Promise Keepers, 164
Pursuers, 97–98

Race. *See also* African Americans; Asian
    Americans
    elements of, 185–187
    ethnicity and, 186
    questions about, 180–181
Rationalizing, 53–54
Rejectors, 98
Religious orientation
    elements of, 193–194
    function of, 181–182
    questions about, 182–183
Reproductive events, 161–162
Rituals, 183
Romantic love
    attachment and, 99

elements of, 105, 146, 155–156, 174–175
explanation of, 106–107
gender differences and, 170
questions regarding, 156–157
Romantic Love Family Map, 158
Romantic Love Genograms
elements of, 174–175
importance of, 157
questions for, 156–157
Romantic Love Time Line, 158
Rousseau, Jean Jacques, 141

Sadness
explanation of, 105, 108
questions about, 109–110
Secrets, 21–22
Secure attachment, 81
Self-esteem
assessment of, 41–42
theory addressing, 50–51
Sex
gender roles and, 161
violence and, 92
Sexual abuse
anger and history of, 132–133
child, 141–143
cycle of violence and, 139
effects of, 152
explanation of, 133
gender issues and, 168
perpetrators of, 142–143
Sexual dysfunctions, 173–174
Sexual Genograms
construction of, 151–152
elements of, 171–173
importance of, 154–155
preparation for, 152–153
questions for, 153–154
sexual dysfunction and, 173–174
Sexuality
cultural norms and, 172–173
development of, 171–172
family attitudes and, 172
gender and, 146, 154–155
sex-role learning and, 170
Sexuality Family Map, 158
Sexuality Time Line, 158
Shame, 105
ʰbling dynamics, 47
ʳ violence, 139
ⁿt families, 46–47
ⁿsitions, 66
ʰus
194–195

questions about, 184
Somatosensory affective deprivation (SAD)
syndrome, 90
Spirituality, 194
Stonewalling, 53
Storge, 105
Stress, 102, 109
Symbols, 7
Systems theory, 28, 198

Tactile defensiveness, 93–94
Temperament
questions about, 78
types of, 94–95
Terror, 104
Therapeutic alliances
differential, 51
explanation of, 59
Family Maps and, 60–62
styles of, 61–62
Therapeutic styles, 61–62
Time Lines
Anger, 134–135
Attachments, 84–88
in clinical practice, 70–71
Culture, 185
Emotions, 115
example of, 11
explanation of, 10, 65
family-individual interface and, 68–69
family life cycle and, 66–68
Sexuality, 151–152
use and function of, 65–66
Touch
cross-cultural studies of, 92
patterns of, 77
questions about, 77–78
role of, 91–93
tactile defensiveness and, 93–94
types of, 93
Trauma, 111
Type A personality, 137

V2.1 for Windows, 213–214
Videos, 32–33
Violence
anger and family, 138–140, 142
cycle of, 139
gender issues and, 168
nurturing style and, 92

WonderWare software, 213–214